Broken Wings

DRC PUBLISHING

3 Parliament Street
St. John's, Newfoundland and Labrador
A1A 2Y6
Telephone: (709) 726-0960
E-mail: info@drcpublishingnl.com

Library and Archives Canada Cataloguing in Publication

Smith, Clarissa, 1947-
    Broken wings / Clarissa Smith.

ISBN 978-1-926689-00-5

    **1. Smith, Clarissa, 1947-. 2. Basse-C te-Nord (Qu bec : Region)--Biography.
I. Title.**

FC2945.B364Z49 2009   971.4'17804092   C2009-901498-X

Published 2009
Printed in Canada
Second Printing 2009

We acknowledge the financial assistance of the Government of Newfoundland and Labrador, Department of Tourism, Culture and Recreation

To my mother, May Laura (Etheridge) Smith,
whose spirit still runs beside me long into the night.

Her voice will be on the wind until I no longer exist.

TABLE OF CONTENTS

⌂ IN DEDICATION

⌂ To my oldest brother Parmenas who, like me, still blames himself for things beyond his control.

⌂ To my precious brother Ronald whom I've been linked with since the day of our births, and who suffered tremendously at the hands of our father. Once free from his bondage, Ronald set the course of his destiny to ease his troubled heart.

⌂ To gentle Brian, who will always remain alive in my heart. He was just 23 when he died. Like our mother, Brian died before he had a chance to live.

⌂ To Raymond, who battled hardships and fell time and time again, but rose above it all to enjoy the simple sound of the ever shifting winds.

⌂ To Clyde, Geraldine, Elliot, Riley and James, all the reasons why I take this painful journey once more, so that they can see our mother through my eyes.

⌂ To Uncle Willie who gave me hope when there was no light at the end of the darkest night. He truly is my hero.

⌂ To Aunt Violet who fed us her bread and fish and kept us from starving to death.

⌂ **PROLOGUE**

Standing here on the marshland looking down in the empty cellar hole where our tiny house once stood, I'm filled with longing, with sorrow, with yearning for a way of life that was and is no longer. I think about my mother, my father, both gone now. I think about my siblings, all of them like rungs on a ladder, the legacy my mother left me upon her dying bed. Racked with pain and misery, her voice haunts me still, as she struggled with some inner god to give her strength to guide me one last time before she left this world for good. The torment in her eyes, the naked misery on her face, her broken spirit, will never leave me. Only she and I knew the extent of her suffering. Sometimes, I doubt if God even cared. I hear her voice, still.

Guard dem youngsters wit yer life, my maid, guard dem youngsters wit yer life! Gawd go wit youse now. Don t ever fergit me!

To forget my mother would be that I no longer exist. She is the reason for me being here, the reason why I keep coming back to this painful place. She's the reason why I can't let go, yet I know I must break this bond of suffering that holds me in its grip still, frozen in time, after all those years. It's been a long struggle, dealing with the loss of her – and them, especially them. The long cold winter nights following her death, the empty cupboard and the empty woodbin, hunger and desperation has taken its toll on all of us. Even though we have survived, those of us who remember are all emotionally handicapped still, individually broken, like ships caught in a tempest with no safe port to go to.

Being the oldest daughter, it was my responsibility to carry on in her place, to protect them, to feed them, to comfort them, to clothe them. Half woman, half child, as she lay there upon her dying bed, gasping for breath, her eyes besieging mine, I promised, I promised her to protect them against all odds. I made that promise while my father sat dozing upright in the chair nearby, with haloed wreaths of cigar smoke circling around his head. I made that futile promise to my dying mother, even though I knew without a miracle from God, I couldn't keep it.

Nothing remains of the house any more, nothing to show that it had ever existed except for a slight indentation in the ground, like my mother's sunken grave. Yet, the house stands before me still, with lime-washed shingles, and two small windows in the peak facing the village in one direction and the marshland in the other. It stood apart from the other eight houses hemmed in a semi-circle along the banks below Labbs Hill. Here on the marshland, above high-water mark it sat, unsheltered by the strong gusty winds funneling down through Western Gulch and Komatik Path.

Woodpiles, scrawny sticks of young birch, juniper and fir, leaned inward like Indian tepees near the sawhorse and chopping block, drying in the late autumn wind. A small wooden bridge spanned the muddy water run-off rushing pass the entrance to the porch. My mother stands in the doorway, in her wedge heel shoes and her crisp white apron, her thick brown hair tied back with yellow ribbon, shaking crumbs from the tablecloth. Loud and clear, I hear her shrill voice, *Stop yer dallying bout urry up an git dem beds made, my maid, I don t hab aw day!* She knew then as I know now that none of us has all day. So, I must stop my dallying about just as she commanded, and say what I must say before I too am nothing more than a voice on the wind and a mere indentation in the ground.

The youngsters play near the chopping block, laughing, shouting, and crying. I see them in the stream, chasing after tiny boats, pieces of scrap wood with flourbag sails, carried along by the rushing water en route to the landwash. I see them sloshing through the black mud filling their red rubber boots, I see them, little children chasing simple dreams, not knowing or caring where their destiny lies. The boggy smell of the marshland, the clam bar, the eerie sound of the wind, and Norse Brook Falls - roaring, gushing water spilling down the gorge to the rocks below, it's as if time had stood still. The footpath, the stream, the wooden bridge, my mother, stand so vividly inside my mind, all gone now, except the agonizing memories, their voices and hers all mingled together warm me and chill me, voices, pictures inside my tormented mind. With the familiar sights and sounds comes a longing, stabbing at my heart for things that used to be and can never be again. I can no longer hide in that safe place inside my mind, when I was a little girl sitting on the snowbank on a clear crisp afternoon waiting for my daddy to come home. I can no longer carry the burden of her death nor deny that perhaps it would have been better if we had died with her, then none of us wouldn't have gone through so much pain and misery just to have this privilege to live upon God's great earth. I'm an adult now, with children of my own, yet I'm still an angry battered child, trying desperately to reason why we were forgotten and abandoned like rats on a sinking ship.

My mother, May Laura Etheridge, was born in Bradore Bay on October 14, 1921. At an early age, she went to live with her grandmother, Pheobe Spingle, in St. Paul's River. She married my father when she was 21. Over the span of seventeen years my mother had several miscarriages and delivered twelve babies, two of whom died in infancy. Bryde Alfreda died shortly after she was born; Rodney died of whooping cough when he was two months old. My mother died of breast cancer on October 9, 1961, five days before her fortieth birthday.

My father, Robert James Smith, was born at L'Anse au Clair on April 30, 1919. When he was a young boy, his family moved to Long Point, known also as Lourdes Du Blanc Sablon. He was 23 when he married my mother. He earned a living hunting, trapping and fishing most of their married life. He died at age 81 on October 19, 2000.

In 1927, when my mother was six and my father was eight, a longstanding dispute regarding the boundary of the Labrador Peninsula between Newfoundland and Quebec was settled. The ruling by a committee of the British Privy Council was in favour of Newfoundland, and the result was that Blanc Sablon became the border separating the Quebec part of Labrador from the Newfoundland part of Labrador. My parents lived above Blanc Sablon, in Bradore Bay, so my family home was not in Labrador, but on the Lower North Shore of Quebec. My family are Protestants of English descent. Like everyone else in Bradore Bay and most other villages around, including Blanc Sablon, they speak English.

Like the majority of people living along the coast, we had a summer home and a winter home. We lived on Basin Island in summer because it was closer to the fishing grounds. In winter, we moved to the shore of Bradore Bay, three miles from the island, to what we called the bottom of the bay. We went to school there, and my father spent many months inland over the hills trapping and hunting with the Indians in fall and winter. I was born on Basin Island on August 19, 1947, delivered, so my mother told me, by midwife Aunt Kate Joncas.

CHAPTER 1

⌂ **RITUALS**
Monday - Washday, 1957

Ever so quietly, my mother enters the kitchen. The door squeaks, it always squeaks. Daid promised to oil it for her, he never did. She curses him then. Scuffling across the kitchen floor she plucks her parka down off the hook. Then, she pulls on her sealskin boots before opening the front door of the stove to remove the ash pan. It scrapes along the iron grate. The porch door slams shut behind her as she hurries outside to dump the ashes over the bank. It slams shut again as she rushes inside to escape the freezing cold.

Hurrying-ly, she jams old catalogue pages beneath the splits. The quiet hissing of the brimstone flaring follows the sharp plick of the match as it strikes against the iron damper (stove cover). A short while later, the splits sizzle and crack and flames spits up the stovepipe. She turns the drafter key and fills the tank at the end of the stove before arranging two galvanized tubs on chairs near the fire. While the heat circulates the room, she removes her parka and hangs it back on the hook again.

A splash of water from the kettle spout hits the bottom of the enamel basin she's holding. After she has her morning wash, she loops a long white bib apron over her head and ties it around her bulging waist.

Habitually, she yanks a pair of white laundered bloomers down over her thick dark hair, looping it over her forehead and behind her ears by the elastic waistband. While the water is heating on the stove, she shapes the bread dough into buns and places them into greased pans sitting side by side on the painted countertop. She drapes the white embroidered breadcloth over the pans and tucks it snugly around the edges. Picking the damper up off the stove with the silver-handled lifter, she scrapes bits of leftover dough and flour from the breadpan into the fire. She pokes at the fire and adds more wood before she puts the damper back down. As she crosses the floor to the water barrel that stands half-full in the corner, she stops near the stairs and hollers at the top of her windpipe, *Clarissy, is youse hup yet?*

The droned out hollow sound of the long-handled dipper touching the side of the barrel as it slaps the icy water dies inside the iron rim. A suckling splash follows, then a hollow rumbling sound like a tuning fork fading away as she swirls the water swiftly around and around in the aluminum pan. Savagely, she attacks the already hardening dough with her bare knuckles and fingernails until the pan is scraped clean. In the same hurried rush she yanks open the porch door and throws the milky substance out at the graying dawn. The sound of her wedding ring clicks rapidly against the pan as she wipes it dry. Before the water hits the ground, the pan is hung on the six-inch nail behind the pantry door, and with the most definite sigh, I hear her say, *Dere now, dats done!*

Hurrying-ly, she throws rolled oats into the dipper, adds water from the kettle, and sets it back on the side damper to cook. Simultaneously, her hand reaches for the kettle to pour boiling water on loose tea in the teapot and set it on the back damper to steep. Slicing the remaining bun of bread, she piles it on a plate in the centre of the square wooden table and arranges the tumblers and bowls before she sits down to devour bread and molasses and unsweetened tea. So much to do before the youngsters get up. In her mind she's thinking that already the day is half gone. In a whirlwind, she rushes to the stove to poke at the fire again.

Clarissy, she shouts. *Git hup, I sez!*

The sound of her knuckles scrapes up and down, up and down on the ribbed glass washboard. She pants and puffs while bending over the tub, struggling with the heavy fleeced long johns, lying like gray seal pelts partly submerged beneath the scummy soap water. Her hands are chafed raw from scrubbing; still she viciously attacks the long johns, venting her frustration on the stubborn stains. Just to be sure she doesn't give the kinfolk anything to talk about later when they're flapping in the wind, she plops them in the heavy galvanized lye tub on the stove. Her rounded belly protruding outward is forever in her way. Frustrated, unable to do anything about her predicament, she curses God for giving her more piss-assed boys.

Perhaps it's at that moment she questions her fate, and in a desperate need to vent out her frustrations on someone, anyone other than God, once again she's at the bottom of the stairs. Her loud piercing voice splits the rafters as she screeches at the top of her windpipe.

Ain t youse hup yet, youse jeesas ardead! Over an our ago I tole youse t git yer carcass outta dat bed - my backs nar broke in half frum bendin over dem tubs, dem youngsters be up t once, be all day befer I gits dat wash on t line agin. Git t hell hup befer I goes up dere with da stick!

I dread Monday mornings. It was the same ritual every Monday, month in and month out, year in and year out, except when it was storming or raining, then the Monday ritual changed to the next fine day. I let her know my displeasure by the sharp thud of my feet connecting with the wooden planked floor above her head. I know only too well that it wouldn't do for me to ignore her this time, even though I know I should have been down there helping her long before she screeched up the stairs, back when I first heard her filling the tubs. Yuk! To think those filthy things were heaped up on the floor next to the tubs waiting – with rings of yellow stains all down the front, brown smears on the back flaps, with those little knobs still stuck on.

Undo dem buttons, scrub dem t proper way!
Whose gonna touch da likes of dat? I say. *Not me, dats fer gawddamn shur!*
Smack!
Mum has a cure for everything.

In the loft, the boys stir in their sleep. All five of them sprawl sideways across the bed, breathing deeply like overheated pups on a hot summer afternoon. The scorching heat from the stovepipe in the center of the room forces them to kick the heavy quilts away. A strong pungent smell wafts past my nose.

I knows now dey cant git hup and piss in dat pail in the dark like I doos, I say. *All dey is is a bunch of piss-assed carly cats. Dey jest likes ta waller in der own stink! Why do I hab ta scrub ta likes o dat! Dat!*
Youse will git anudder back ander, my maid, if youse dont stop dat whinin!
The memory lingers, and in my defiant way so do I, on the upper steps, not wanting to go down yet! I squat there, ever so quietly, watching my mother standing near the stove with the long-handled fork in her right hand, stabbing at the first lot of long johns already steaming away in the lye pot. Like speared flatfish on a prong, she lifts them high, lowers them, and then lifts them again. I can tell they are not done to her liking by the way she plops them back down into the pot with a definite splash that sends tiny lye water beads bouncing across the red hot dampers.

Dere youse is, youse jeesas ard ead! Mum says when she spots me.

Like two old women, worn and bent, Mum on one side and I on the other, we lug the heavy tub outside. On the narrow bridge spanning the brook in front of our house, we lift it above the railing and dump the dirty wash water in the black murk below.

Afterwards, while I shovel rolled oats into my mouth and gulp down molasses drenched bread, Mum refills the tubs from the five-gallon boilers and the water tank attached to the end of the stove. She refills the boilers again from the iron drum in the corner of the porch. She spears the long johns from the lye pot to the rinse tub, soogees them up and down until they are cooled enough to her touch then spears them over to the other tub close by. When she's ready, she twists them over and over to remove the excess water and plops the still dripping long johns in the aluminum pan at my feet.

Dere now, she says, *take dem jeesas tings out and pin dem on t'line!*

Those rituals are embedded in my memory like the roar of Norse Brook Falls and the sounds of shifting tides as they rise and fall beneath the looking glass ice.

CHAPTER 2

△ **THE DANCING STARS**

It's another Monday morning and out on the clothesline the long johns stiffen quickly in the bitter cold. They jerk up and down as I reel the line further along on its pulley. Hanging upside down by the leg bands, the long johns remind me of paper doll cutouts I keep hidden in a cigar box beneath my bed.

It was a lovely teak box that I coveted from the first time I laid eyes upon it. Daid came home one day and stayed long enough to smoke the cigars he brought with him, then he gave the box to me before he left again. A box no thicker than birch skin, with a picture of a crown in the centre. Every time I opened the box, the sweet aroma of tobacco filled my nostrils.

In this box, I kept my embroidering threads, sewing needles, a darning needle and my very own thimble. The paper doll cutouts came from a magazine that Mum brought back from a hospital visit. Even though I had no time now and was too big to play with dolls any longer, I still kept it just because the cutouts wore such pretty dresses, pretty dresses from MacLean's magazine.

Mum screeches at me from the side window facing Ladder Hill.

Make sure youse put plenty of pins in dem, my maid. Youse don't want dem blowin all over creation agin.

One thing for certain, my mother was never going to let me forget that dreadful day when the intangible wind came straight down from the sky and snatched those sheets clean off the line. And it was on that day I finally understood what Aunt Carrie meant when she said my mother's wash was like the driven snow.

I remember watching the sheets go straight up into the sky; I thought they'd never come down. Suddenly, there was a lull in the wind and, caught up in the silent musical display, I stood and watched in fascination as the sheets floated lazily through the air like leaves falling onto the frozen bay. I came out of my trance-like state when my mother's sharp voice hurled curses at my back.

Grab dem sheets! I told youse, youse jeesas ard ead, ta put more pins in dem! NO! Come back ere. Come back ere before youse gits yere ownself lost!

Just as I lunged forward to grab the sheets, a gust of wind came out of nowhere and snatched them clean out of my hands and they disappeared amidst the swirling snow. She found them in the spring, wrapped around the rudder of Uncle Ernest's boat that was hauled up on the slip near Big Head Bluff on the other side of the bay.

With the towels secured to the line, I hurry inside to warm my hands near the stove. Mum sallies around the kitchen, trying to do everything at once. She stuffs rolled oats into Clyde's mouth and fills a nurse bottle for the baby all at the same time. Baby Geddy, short for Geraldine, trashes wildly about, banging her legs and arms against the rungs of the cot. Her screaming blocks out the singing of the kettle on the stove.

Angrily, Mum shakes the bottle, tests the milk with her own lips before propping the bottle up on a rolled up napkin, then aims it for Geddy's hungry mouth. Geddy reminds me of a tiny robin stretching its neck to reach the worm being dropped in its beak.

Dere now, you little frigger, says Mum. *I suppose now ya will shaddup fer a spell. Gawd wudden give me another bye. Naw, he hadda give me another jeesas ardead. One of youse is worse dan ten byes!*

Byes, I said. *Aw dey ever doos is piss demselves to death.*

Watch yer mout, my maid!

In the loft, three beds were placed under the slant of the roof.

Parmenas and Ronald, the two oldest boys, slept in the wrought iron bed with the huge feather mattress. One morning, my mother, in a rare mood, complimented me for getting the middle so puffy and smooth. Little did she know that I pounded the mattress so much with my fists that the seam gave way and feathers shot from the opening like smoke around the dampers when the stove backfired. I sewed the seam together with the red embroidery thread from the little teak box beneath my bed.

Every time I stood on the edge of the bedsprings I'd strike my head on the slanted roof, and before I could get the other end turned over I'd lose my grip.

Gawddamn, I said, then I stretched my arms out as far as I could and grabbed both ends at the same time. Somersaulting in the middle of the bed, I landed on the floor between the wall and the springs. Pinned there like a rag doll folded in half, it took quite a spell before I could wiggle out from under the low hanging spring.

Wot in Gawds name is youse doin hup dere, my maid? Mum bellows up the stairs.

Nuddin Mum, jest pullin t bed out so I can reach dat pail. Dat Pims got im shoved in dere far enuff.

Brian and Raymond slept in the middle bed, and Clyde was transferred from the cot to the little four-by-four foot blue poster bed when Geddy came along. Grandpa Smith made the bed for Parmenas when he was born. It was not much bigger than a fish box, perhaps it was a fish box. It had square wooden legs and a blue painted headboard that was nailed on with six-inch nails. Whenever another baby arrived, it was passed down to the next youngest. *Wots shes habin dis time, I wunder, anudder piss-assed bye, I spose.*

Stop yer dreamin, my maid," my mother says. *"Grab t andle of dat tub. I gotta git dis wash done befer dem anti-christers gits hup. I dont hab aw day.*

I often wondered why my mother thought she didn't have all day.

Even when the village was blanketed with snow and she had to shovel the snow from the upstairs window with the dustpan, we still had all day, all week for that matter. But even when the October winds threatened to rip the house right off its shored up foundation with its savage breath, the days never ended.

The dirty wash water mingles with the dark water below. I watched it rush over the rocks enroute to the landwash. A little red rubber ball stuck in the dead roots jutting out from the side of the mud bank catches my eye. Quickly, I jump down in the brook to fetch it just as my mother screeched.

Clarissy, I wish youse wud stop yer dallyin bout and elp me git dat wash done and dem tubs put away. Dem youngsters be up t once.

When the boys came down for breakfast, Mum clouts the first one closest to her. Dodging her swinging fists, they all quickly scurry back up the steps to change into clean long johns that are already laid out on the trunk near their bed.

While the boys are up there snarling at one another, Mum shovels rolled oats into the blue-rimmed tin bowls on the table. At the same time, she's yelling at them to wash up before either one of them shows their snotty noses at the table.

A flour bag tablecloth with yellow embroidered teacups stitched in each corner is spread upon the square wooden table. Everything in our house is sewn by my mother's hands. No one stitched like her. I tried to be like her, but I could never grasp the basic steps of embroidering. She wouldn't have got so frustrated if I had. She'd get so angry with me the veins in her neck would pop up like bubbles in the guts of dead ducks.

I kint learn youse nuddin, my maid! Yer ead is too tick, she'd say.

Tisn t my fault dat yere fingers moves so quick, I'd reply.

While I clear the breakfast dishes, she scrubs behind the youngsters' ears, swipes the facecloth across their mouths, then sends them scurrying out the door as the first chime of the school bell sweeps down across the bay.

Once the last one is off and running in the direction of the schoolhouse, she sends me upstairs to change the sheets on the beds. While I make the beds and dust the loft, she finishes the washing herself. Then I help her dump the last of the dirty wash water over the rail. She wipes the tubs and hangs them on the six-inch nails driven in the porch wall. Vigorously, I tackle the stairs, one at a time, digging out the corners with an old duck wing, and sweeping the dirt down over each step as I go. All morning long we dust, sweep and scrub. By noon, I'm that tired and hungry I can hardly stand.

By the time the school bell rings – thank God! – I could eat the handle off the big iron pot simmering on the back damper. The pot is chock full to the rim with bologna hash. My hands shake so badly I can hardly hold them together while Mum rushes ahead with Grace.

Gawd bless dis grub now we take. Do us good, fer jeesas sake. Amen!
Now, urry hup and get dat down yer gullets! I don t hab all day.

After dinner, she sends the youngsters back to school.

Once more, I wash the dishes and sweep the floor.

Then she sends me to the clothesline to get the dried napkins and fold them while she goes to the bedroom to wash the dirt and grime of her skin. She always washed the dirt and grime from her skin after a hard day's work, but I wondered why she was doing it so early in the afternoon. The day was only half done.

I'm aware of her movements in the other room. I hear the opening and closing of her wardrobe door and the pulling out of the shoe box from under her bed. All is quiet until she knocks the felt off the roof with her singing. Her singing wasn't so bad, at least I don't think it was. It meant she was happy when she sang. Especially when she rattled out the words of her favorite hymn as she undressed and pulled her dress and petticoat over her head.

Rock of Ages cleft fer me-e-eee
Let me hide myself in dee-e-ee.
Let t water and t blood-d-ddd,
From de wounded side which flood-d-ddd,
Be of sin t double cure
Save from wrath and make me pure.

Outside on the porch, Sparky howls. Sparky always howled when she sang. His piteous howling ceases only when her voice trails away.

The door opens. Like a whirlwind, Mum re-enters the kitchen, wearing one of her bright yellow dresses with a starched white collar. Her thick black hair is tied back at the nape of her neck with an inch-wide ribbon to match. She's wearing long beige stockings and her high wedge heel shoes. My mother is small, just 4 feet 11 inches and weighs less than 100 pounds when she's not pregnant. She always wears brightly colored dresses that she makes herself, mostly in her favorite colors of yellow and red. Hurrying now, she flips open the mirrored compact she's holding and smears bright red lipstick all over the upper rim of her lips, leaving her mouth with a lopsided look.

Dont look at me like dat, my maid! she says. *I m not goin far.*

Then she astounded me by saying, *Youse kin come wit me if youse like. I m jest goin over to Aunt Mildreds place. Shes been after me fer a long spell now, to take a look at Nellies weddin dress. I knows youse is jest itchin t git yer feet inside dat fancy kitchen of hers.* She snaps the cover shut on her compact.

Youse shur Great Aunt wuddent mind? Youse knows how she hates youngsters, specially we.

Too bad about er, I say! If she dont like dat, I jest wont elp her pin hup dat dress. Dats all the odds bout hit. Now, urry up my maid, and dress dem youngsters. We dont hab all day. Dat bread will be ready t bake by the time we gits back.

Mum quickly throws another junk of wood in the stove and shuts off all the vents. She yanks the bonnet down over Geddy's ears while I pin Clyde between my knees to pull on his red rubbers.

Mum, I tinks es rubbers is gittin too small fer im.

Never mind dat now, my maid. Urry up befer I goes off without youse.

She was out the doorway and past the woodpile before I had Clyde's arms through his sweater sleeves. Hurrying, I yanked the cap down over his ears and bolted out the doorway behind her with him on my hip.

Make sure youse latch dat door shut so dem dogs don t git in t house whilst we re gone, she flings over her shoulder as she hurried along.

She was already past Aunt Carrie's place by the time I caught up with her.

Mum, can I lug Clyde on my back? I asked.

Oh alright I spose. Jest don t run with im. E might fall off.

Clyde was much heavier than I'd thought. I bent far over. While supporting him with one hand under his backside, I held his chubby little hands around my neck in front of me. When Mum wasn't looking I ran a few short steps with him, ignoring her previous warning.

Youse likes dat, don t youse, poogy-woogy, I said to him.

His short little giggles gave me away.

If youse gits one of my back anders, youse won t run wit dat youngster, ya jeesas ardead, Mum scolded.

Oh, the shame of getting caught. I bent my face even closer to the ground so she wouldn't notice the smirk. The groove in the path is up to the calf of my legs. As I hurry to catch up to my mother, I noticed a pile of broken twigs in the centre of the path, all placed together like a nest. A handful of tiny rocks are on top of the twigs. In the middle is a perfectly rounded white rock.

Would youse look at dat, poogy, dat rocks jest wot I needs. I bet dat Pim put dat dere. I ll fix e fer robbin my marble t odder day. I m takin dat rock to go wit my odder ones. Youse knows I only got four left now.

Before moving us back to the house in the bay, Daid poured three sets of lead marbles from a mold that he used to make weights for his nets. He made fifteen marbles from lead he melted in a can over a fire on the shore. While we all stood around watching, he poured the hot lead in the mold, folded it together, and then drove it under the water to cool it off. Seconds later, he pried open the mold and produced the first lovely lead marble.

Playing marbles was a favorite pastime for all of us. When we moved to the bay, I kept mine hidden in the teak box beneath my bed. I'd practice as often as I could on a quilt on the floor beside my bed, until I was able to catch all five of them on the back of my hand. Then I'd flick them in the air and catch them in my palm. It was such a good feeling to see the shocked look on all their faces when I won the game.

I always won, until one of my perfect marbles went missing and then I couldn't practice any more. Naturally, I blamed Parmenas for the loss of my marble. If it wasn't him, then it had to be Ronald. They were always getting a lashing for stealing something or another.

Deys gonna git a beatin t nite, jest youse wait and see, eh poog, jest you wait and see if dey don t, I said to Clyde, mentally marking the spot so I could pick the white rock up when we came back along the path.

Clyde gave me his two coppers worth by google-gagging as I ran with him, this time to catch up to Mum again. I was right behind her when she stepped inside Great Aunt's porch.

As I suspected, the porch was spotlessly clean. It had soft yellow painted walls, and brin bags lined the floor in the walkway leading towards the kitchen like a welcome mat. But the scowl on Great Aunt's face spoke volumes. It wasn't a welcoming sight. She seemed more than just a little put out by the likes of us trekking across her clean floors.

This short, thin woman with her hair coiled tightly upon her head, standing there in her long black dress and white lace collar, with her bony hands sitting on her hips, she was someone to be feared.

Wipe dem boots hoff now. I jest scrubbed dem floors hup. Youse too, May! she commands, before Mum could even plunk her shoe on the raised landing in the kitchen.

Mum wipes, I wipe, Mum wipes, I wipe, finally she stops and so do I.

Once more I'm reminded of what the kinfolk meant when they say that Mum and Great Aunt are so alike. They're both short and skinny and they both preach that cleanliness is next to godliness.

Mum commands me to sit on the bottom step with the youngsters while she and Great Aunt hurry upstairs. I hold them between my knees so they can't wander about and leave finger marks on the spotless furniture. I know it's the only chance I'll ever get to feast my eyes on such fine things. There's beauty in every carved leg and polished knob.

Dust free bluish-layered sunlight filters through the bareness between the frilly lace curtains onto a spot directly in front of the stove. There's no hard-caked grease and soot around the handle fasteners on the three gallon kettle. It's as shiny as the nickel rim around the well-polished stove.

The kettle teeters slightly on the back damper as the steam rises lazily upward through the spout. I wonder if she used sand to clean the kettle. I'd never get ours that shiny clean, I thought.

On the floor was the most beautiful square. Red, pink and orange roses ran along the outer border, tumbling over one another, attached to trailing vines, while soft brown and rust colour wind-swirled leaves lay curled in the middle. There are no ugly black carpet tacks in Great Aunt's flooring to stub a toe on; unlike ours, which joins together smack down the middle, where dirt lodges humped up like maggot hills. A peaceful feeling settles down around me as I covet the things in Great Aunt's house.

When Mum and Great Aunt finally came downstairs, I jump guiltily to my feet. I'm thinking that Great Aunt will read the sin of covetous on my face. I lower my head and whisper to the youngsters to keep quiet.

Great Aunt moves across the kitchen and sits at the table with the huge carved legs. Our table seems so plain now; so poor looking with the aluminum molding screwed onto the edge and the foursquare four-inch wooden legs, unpainted and yellowed by wood smoke over the years. It is the same table Brian shoved me over when I was three, and the sharp edges split me wide open and I nearly bled to death. When I opened my eyes, my mother was throwing handfuls of flour between my legs to stop the bleeding.

The orange in the settee in Great Aunt's house blends to perfection with the roses in the square on the floor. Golden head tacks run head to head all along the headrest, the sides, the footboard, and just above the carved lion's feet. My! I wish Daid would bring home a settee like that. I'd beat the youngsters to keep them from jumping their boots all over it.

I'm so lost in the beauty of Great Aunt's house that I hardly noticed my mother fidgeting on the edge of the settee while she talks back and forth with Great Aunt. Only when she bolts upright does she get my attention. My heart smashes against my chest in fright when I see the river of blood run down her legs, covering her thick beige stockings and wedge heel shoes before spilling onto that beautiful linoleum square.

I jump to my feet, bewildered, not knowing what to do. Great Aunt jumps to her feet as well. At the same time she screams at my mother, *Now, look wat youse done wit my square,* as if my mother had committed the most god awful sin.

Quickly, Great Aunt runs to the porch, grabs a handful of brin bags and throws them in the puddle around her feet. Mum just stands there, holding the tail of her dress between her legs, staring at me. My fears heighten when I see her white face.

Come on Mum, lets go ome! I scream hysterically.

Yes, go ome wit Clarissy and take dem ard tickets wit youse. Go ome! Great Aunt shouts with contempt.

My mother moves towards the doorway. I snatch the baby up off the settee, grab Clyde by the hand, and hurry out behind her.

Glancing back, I see my mother's blood on Great Aunt's hands.

Ahead of me, Mum wobbles awkwardly down the path holding the tail of her dress between her legs. I can't take my eyes of the trail she leaves behind her. But when a splatter of red covers the shiny white rock in the make believe nest in the centre of the path, I look away.

I half expected, half hoped, that Great Aunt would rush past me and help Mum before she stumbled across the little bridge in front of our doorway. Instead, it's me who rushes forward to unlatch the door. While Mum shuffles towards her bedroom, I put the youngsters in the playpen. Before latching the porch door behind us I listen intently, but hear only the echo of Great Aunt's voice on the wind.

Go ome, May. Go ome where youse belongs.

Something cold runs through my heart.

It's quiet behind the bedroom door. I try hard to keep the youngsters silent. I don't know why, but I know it's vital that I do. I catch the little red ball as Clyde bounces it across the floor and try to shush him into silence as I prepare a bottle for Geddy. So quietly, I stoke the fire, adding more junks of wood. I'm listening for her voice. I know she'll call me.

Time turns into eternity while I wait and listen.

Finally her bedroom door opens.

Clarissy, come yere, she says, handing me a bundle carefully wrapped in Eaton's catalogue pages. *Burn dis, quick.*

Making my mind blank, I do as she instructs, not daring to ask what it might be. I'm so afraid now. Minutes pass like hours before she calls again.

Dump dis pail in t landwash, far away from t dogs.

The afternoon passes oh so slowly and still no one comes.

I help my mother put pillows underneath her, and elevate her legs to stop the flow of blood. She's so weak now she can hardly lift her head up off the pillows. I keep pacing from the stove to the window, praying and hoping someone will come and save her, yet no one does.

I watched the sun hang over Western Gulch on its descent down the side of Queen's Hill. I knew once it sank below the hill, the darkness would come. I knew death would come to my mother then.

As I stood staring out across the bay, it suddenly came to me that it was all up to me whether my mother lived or died. It enters my mind while I stare out across the bay watching the mail boat, a white speck on the water crossing over to the other side of the bay. Or is that Daid?

I remember now my mother cursing Daid for not being home.

Yer fadder, wheres e at, ya spose? Probably gone hup t Belles Amour with t doctor and t nuns agin. Now dat es got dat longliner, e never comes ome no more.

The sound of her voice pounds loudly inside my head. And now I'm standing beside her bed, looking down on her closed eyelids, *Mum, Mum, I gotta find Daid*, I say. *Youse knows I gotta find Daid.*

Weakly she answers, *Yes, my maid, find yer fadder. No. Fetch Nrst, e knows wot t do.*

As her words trickled away, I flew out the doorway and down across the marsh on wings I never knew I had. I don't stop running until I am face to face with Uncle Ernest. I'm only half aware of Aunt Gert standing alongside of him with an empty kettle in her hand. Uncle Ernest is near the stove, poking the fire. His face goes deadly white when he sees me.

Come quick, Uncle Nrst. Mum s bleedin t death.

Sweet Jesus, he cries, running past me before I can catch my breath.

Aunt Gert runs after him, shouting insanely, *Nrst, come back here. Let dat slut die.*

As strong as the wind that swept past me and scooped Mum's sheets up off the bay, Uncle Nrst flew, not looking back or heeding the contempt in Aunt Gert's voice. He ran with all his might over the marsh and towards our house.

Wots youse gawking at? Aunt Gert glared in my direction. *Git outta dis house before I scaw yer face off.*

I was used to Aunt Gert and her evil ways, but Great Aunt? Why didn't Great Aunt help my mother? I couldn't stop wondering about it all the way back to our house. A little while later, I stood at our kitchen window and watched Uncle Ernest running along the footpath on his way to Bradore Plains. I watched him dash up one hill and down the other until he was a mere speck in the late afternoon sunlight. I visualized every twist and turn he made in the footpath I knew so well.

The two littlest ones fell asleep in the playpen. Before the rest of them arrived back from school, I lugged Clyde upstairs to bed and put a blanket over the baby in the playpen. While I waited I added more wood to the fire and baked the bread. I estimated that it would take Uncle Ernest about an hour before he reached the Postmaster's house and Uncle Weston would then send a wireless message to Daid, I suspected.

When Parmenas came home, he gave the others bread and molasses and sent them outside to play. I didn't have to tell him anything. He knew. But I couldn't tell him about the blood, I couldn't.

Daid will come t once, I say. *Daid will come.*

I picture the longliner, with long white spars, steaming in through the gut under dormant sails. I could actually see it rolling back and forth, stem dipping under the swell as I willed it through the gut in Jack's Cove. I judged Jack's Cove to be two miles away, perhaps further.

When the bread was baked, I took it out of the oven and removed it from the pans. I put the loaves on a cloth on the countertop. When all the others came back inside I tell them to be quiet and not to expect any supper until Daid got home.

Pim, gib Geddy t bottle, I command, as Geddy begins fussing in the playpen.

Why kint youse gib er t bottle yer ownself?

Youse knows I habs t watch out fer Daid. E s comin from Jacks Cove, I snap.

Why aint e comin in the bay?

Cause the tide s out, stunface!

I never leave the window, my eyes are fixed below the purplish hue where the sun went down, where the footpath leads to the village by way of Jack's Cove. I shield my eyes from the glare as light fills the room from the kerosene oil lamp as Parmenas sets it down on the kitchen table. I watch the evening star, bright and shinier than any of the rest now appearing in the sky. It sits on top of the ledge where the sun disappeared.

I make a silent wish and speak to God in my mind, all at the same time.

Gawd, I knows youse sees me ere beside t winder, watchin out fer Daid. I knows youse p tect Uncle t day. I knows Daid s comin t git Mum, aint e Gawd? Please Gawd, don t let Mum die befer e gits here. Give me a sign like youse did fer dat man with dat burnin bush dats in my catechism book. Please Gawd, dont let my mudder die, not my mudder, Gawd!

Time crawls so slowly; the evening star steadily rises above where I think the path is. Suddenly, it begins to dance, tiny pinpoints of lights like baby stars seem to tumble downwards over the ridge, zig-zagging this way and that as they tumble.

In awe, I watch this miraculous sight until it finally dawns on me, *Dere comin! Oh my Gawd! Tis Daid! E s comin.*

I run to my mother's room.

Mum. Mum. Daids comin! Daids comin! I shout. *Mum! Mum! Can youse hear me?*

Only when her hand rises slowly from the quilts do I know she's still alive.

Parmenas, Ronald and the rest rush to the window to see for themselves.

I se sees em, Ronnie! Deres lanterns a hole slew huff dem, cried Pim.

Giddily, they danced around the floor, swinging the little ones by the arms. We hardly notice the cold night air as we rush outside to stand on the bank and wait. We could hear them shouting among themselves as they approached the falls, making their way along the landwash on the other side of the brook. A short while later the lights appeared near the schoolhouse, half a mile away. We were making such a racket and so still was the night that kinfolk in the houses along the bank came outside to see what all the commotion was about. We could see Daid and the others in the lamplight shining from their windows as they passed on their way to our house.

Suddenly, I heard my father's voice above the roar of the falls.

Moments later, I could see the outline of figures in the darkness. Daid and the doctor were coming towards us carrying something between them, a stretcher. Six nuns, all dressed in white and black, followed closely behind them. We moved to one side to let them pass. Daid led the doctor into the room. About ten minutes later, they carried her out. As they lifted the stretcher, Uncle Ernest burst through the doorway.

Mum motioned for me to come close. I knew what she was trying to tell me.

I will, Mum, I promise.

Then they carry her out into the darkness.

Right and gladly so, I spread the white cloth on the table and sat a plate on it. I ran to get a can of duck from the pantry shelf and opened it. I put out a jar of bakeapple jam, sliced fresh bread, and piled it beside Uncle Ernest's plate.

While he wolfed down the food, I kept refilling his mug with tea. I was bursting inside with such joy. I was overwhelmed with this special feeling I had for Uncle Ernest, and for God for saving my mother's life.

After Uncle Ernest finished eating, Parmenas and Ronald went with him to his place down on Israel's Point. I fed the youngsters, washed them, and got them ready for bed. Before sending them upstairs, we knelt beside the rocking chair to pray. With eyes closed and hands folded, we recited our prayers, asking God to bless Uncle Ernest and to keep us all safe.

Much later, while the youngsters slept and the house was quiet, I tidied the kitchen. Before going to bed, I shaved the splits with Daid's pocketknife and piled them on the oven door to start the morning fire with. I hung the vamps on the line above the stove. While waiting for the flankers to die down in the stove, I knelt beside the rocking chair to give my own special thanks to God and asked Him to bless everyone, except Great Aunt. I knew I'd never forgive her for leaving my mother to die. On my knees, with my head resting on my arms, I mulled over the strange happenings of the day.

As the quiet of night fell down around me, I heard a soft rolling sound. I suspected it was a shrew. My eyes dart in the direction of the sound, waiting for the tiny animal to scurry across the floor. But what I see is my long missing marble. It rolls across the floor and stops in front of me near the rocking chair.

Where d dat come frum, ya spose! I knows I dug out t legs on dat stove when I scrubbed t floor dis marnin, I say to myself. Suddenly, this day is all too much for me. Clutching the marble in my fist I put my face down upon my hands and wept.

CHAPTER 3

⌂ LESSONS

It was late November before my mother returned home again. All during those long weeks she was in the hospital, we stayed alone. No one in the village came to see how we were, just like no one came to save my mother's life that day. It was taken for granted that I, being the oldest girl, would be responsible for minding the youngsters. I never questioned the reasons why; I just did what was expected of me.

Bread was our main substance. Although there was dried caplin, salt cod, pickled herring and a barrel of pickled beef down in the cellar hole, I was too afraid to venture down there in the dark. My biggest fear was that one of the youngsters would close the hatch and I'd be trapped with the rats and weasels that would eat the eyes right out of my head. So, since it was up to me, and it was, bread would be our main substance until either Parmenas or Ronald went down in the cellar hole, or my mother returned home. As time went on and she didn't return, I had no choice but go down in that cellar hole, holding the broom handle for protection against the rats.

Habitually, Mum made bread three times a week. Each batch consisted of eight to ten loaves. In lean times, when there was very little else to eat, as long as there was bread, we didn't starve. I would learn a very harsh lesson when I got up one morning to a bare panty shelf. I cursed, ranted, and raved, just like my mother would have, and cursed some more when Parmenas demanded to know what all the fussing was about.

Being the oldest, he soon solved my dilemma. He mixed flour, salt, and water together, forming a thick paste that he slapped on the hot dampers to brown. While the youngsters stood around, he told them about the time Daid took him into the country and they were caught inside for a whole week without grub. The wind and wolves howled all night long, he said, the snow piled high around the lean-to. When the last of the grub was gone, he was so hungry he thought he would die from the pain in his stomach. As he lay shivering on fir boughs, Daid mixed the flour and salt with melted snow, he said, and slapped it on the stove dampers to cook, just like he was doing now. Pim said proudly, *Wees dint starb t deat den and wees wont starb now, by t lard jumpin, not if I habs hinnyting to doos wit dat.*

They all sat around the table, listening to Pim and happily dunking the stove cakes in their tea. They were sated by the time he had finished telling them the story, ending with, *By d time I come down over Komatik Patt I wuz way aw ead of Daid and way aw ead of Spot and Rover too, I was sum glad to see t ouse.*

It was obvious to me now why my brother always made himself scarce each time Daid announced he was going inland to hunt.

Late afternoon, before the darkness fell, I did what I'd seen my mother do so many times. I took the huge aluminum pan down off the nail, filled it half full of flour from the barrel in the pantry and, carrying it by the handles, placed it on the oven door to warm. I was so eager. I could hardly wait to mix my first batch of bread. I sweetened some water in an enamel bowl and tested it with my little finger to be sure it was lukewarm. I sprinkled the yeast on top of the water and sat it on the tank cover to rise. While the yeast was rising, I threw a handful of salt into the breadpan, then scooped the flour up in the middle before adding water. With my baby finger, I tested the water before adding it to the flour. It took quite a while to knead the dough. When I was certain it was kneaded enough, I turned it over and punched in the sign of the cross like I'd always seen my mother do, *In t name of t Fodder, t Son and t Holy Ghost, Amen!*

I was clear bursting at the seams I was so proud of my accomplishment. I could hardly wait to tell my mother. I knew she'd be proud too. She'd probably tell all the kinfolk what a fine job I did while she was away. I knew it would rise; Mum's dough always rose after she blessed it with the sign of the cross.

I could tell just how good the bread was going to be by the way the dough cracked each time I stretched it over and kneaded it under with my fists, until it looked like a doll with a chalk face. So carefully I wrapped the dough with a clean white bread cloth and placed it near the stove to rise. After washing my hands, I wrapped the dough in flannel blankets, threw a parka on top of it, checked the fire and went straight to bed.

Sometime after daybreak, when Geddy began to fuss, I jumped out of bed and hurried out to the kitchen to light the fire. While the fire got under way, I washed my hands and face, then greased the pans and placed them in the oven to warm. Before pulling a pair of my mother's laundered bloomers down over my hair and donning her long white apron, I prepared a nurse bottle for Geddy to keep her quiet. I didn't want anything spoiling the moment when I felt the elastic dough, squeezed it through my fingers, and heard it crack like the splits on the fire as I shaped it into balls to fit into the pans.

My spirits were so uplifted that I couldn't imagine anything going wrong. That is, until I moved the kettle from the tank cover to the front damper and there sat the enamel bowl, the forgotten yeast lying on top of the cold water like slub. I ran to the breadpan, yanked off the cloth, and stared stupidly down at the un-risen dough, looking much like an unmade feather bed, kind of sunken in the middle. It's then I cursed out loud, *Ow kin youse be so gawdamn stupit, my maid? I could kick youse in the ass. I knows now youse habs t look like dat, youse stupit dough*!

In a fit of madness I sloshed the cold yeast liquid all over the bread dough and squeezed it savagely through my fingers. I kneaded it over and over again, willing it to do the job it was supposed to have done in the first place. It would rise now, surely gawd! Quickly, I covered that sickly looking clump of dough and hid it from my sight.

By late afternoon I was thoroughly disgusted with myself. The dough was still as flat as an old man's ass. But, still, being the jesus hardhead like my mother always said I was, I put it in the pans and baked it anyway.

Time slipped by so quickly and when it came time to take the bread out of the oven, it was harder and blacker than coal. Oh, what was I to do? I knew I couldn't throw it to the dogs or wash it down the brook. It was against everything my mother had ever taught me, so I left it there, sitting in the pans, on top of the tank cover. Every so often, I'd stare at it, willing it to do something other than just sit there, but nothing happened. Again and again, I cursed myself for such stupidity. How could I have forgotten to add the yeast?

I was still ranting and raving when Ronald, tired and hungry, came back from the woods. One glance at the burnt black bread sitting on the tank cover was enough to drive him over the edge. I knew by the crazed look in his eyes he was going to do something awful. He sprang towards the stove and snatched a blackened loaf from the tank cover. Dodging my swinging fists, he dashed outside.

Don t youse give dem dogs dat bread, I screeched.

Straight to the chopping block he went and grabbing the axe, he chopped the blackened outer crust off that molten loaf like rind on a stick.

After the initial shock of it all, I laughed out loud. We both laughed as he chopped the yellow inner core into cubes; we laughed like pure savages gone right out of our skulls. I went back inside and poured the tea and we dunked the pieces of bread in it. Between us all, including the baby, we ate every last crumb.

I could almost feel the pain of my mother smacking one of her backhanders up the side of my head, if she had seen the awful mess I made out of her manna from heaven, as she called bread. But then again, we did exactly as Mum had always preached. Waste not, want not!

When Mum finally came home, and I thought she never would, she took charge of the household. Like Monday's rituals, Christmas began with my mother baking all Christmas Eve. She'd make venison as well as bakeapple and redberry pies, as many as twenty-four of each. She sent me down into the cellar dugout to store the pies on the shelf. She always made extra pies in case some of the kinfolk dropped by. In fear, I climbed down the shaky ladder into the pitch-blackness below, into that mud-caked grave. Rats, weasels and mice chew their way through everything. My fears doubled with the thought of stepping into one of the steel traps Daid has set in the corners.

Cabbages, turnips and onions hang from the wooden beams. Sacks of potatoes, flour, and sugar stand upright in rows on the lumber planks. Beef/pork barrels and redberry kegs stand under the shelves where the pies are stacked. The apple barrel is stored near the Carnation milk; the apples' lovely scent is attacked by the strong stench of dried salt fish. Before I reach inside the apple barrel, I kick it to scare the rats away. They're never there, only in my imagination, so Mum says. I know the difference though. Many times I danced in fright when some furry thing ran across the toes of my rubber boots.

I steal the soft green tissue paper wrapped around each apple. I stuff the fragrant paper inside my slacks so I could sniff the soft apple scent later when I was alone in my room.

Wots takin youse so long down dere, my maid? my mother yelled. *I won t git dem h apples baked dis day if youse don t urry hup now, my maid.*

Two years ago, on Christmas Eve, Santa came to the schoolhouse staggering like a rabid dog, not knowing in which direction he was going. I knew something was amiss with the vision I had conjured up inside my head when he didn't swoop down from the sky like he was supposed to, but instead fell off the komatik and crawled across the bay on his elbows. It was nothing like the image of him flying through the sky with eight tiny reindeer on a beautiful sleigh filled with toys on a starry night as depicted on the cover of *"Twas The Night Before Christmas.*

Pieces of fuzz hung from the sides of his face like a ragged white coat pelt ripped to shreds by the dogs. Daid and Mr. Teacher Sir dragged him up over the bank and through the schoolhouse doorway. He was laughing all the while as they tried to prop him up in a chair near the teacher's desk. There they stood, one on either side of him, keeping him seated in the chair while he tried to read out the names written in bold letters on each present.

Parmenas...Smit. Naomi...obbler....Eldon...Partridge....Ho-oh!...Is youse good little young uns?...Murry Chriss mus!...Ho-oh...Lit me see now, wat one of ye fellars is next? Oh yaw...Clarissy...Claris-sy... Smit!

When those bloodshot eyes found me on the opposite side of the room, he rose unsteadily to his feet. As he staggered in my direction, I dove under the desk. Everyone was laughing and someone was screaming. It was me! My grip on the iron legs of the desk was such that even the Devil himself couldn't pry me loose. My screams bent the rafters in the roof. My tongue was sucked down my throat with fright. Thanks to God Almighty Aunt Carrie was there to save me.

Let er be, I say, she said, *youse wanna turn er blood t wadder, fer cripes sakes, dat will appen if youse dont let dat maid be, now git aw way from er, git!*

Just as Aunt Carrie predicted, I had the hag (nightmares), for a long time afterwards. In my know-how of right and wrong, Santa Claus died that year and I prayed to Jesus he'd never come back.

Last year at Christmas, for the second year in a row, my friend Naomi Wobbler was given a porcelain doll from the Red Cross Box. I was heartbroken, and it was with pure disgust I accepted the black Indian doll with the slick straight black hair held back with a brown felt band. When Daid came back from the country with the Indians in February month, I shoved it into their eager waiting hands. Naomi thoroughly believed that the reason she got the doll with the blonde curly hair and I didn't was because I didn't believe in Santa Claus anymore. It was true I didn't believe, but oh how I coveted that porcelain doll. From the first time I saw her pink smiling face sticking out of the corner of the Red Cross box, I coveted her with all my soul.

In January, winter came down from the mountains. Heavy snowfalls and gale force winds funneled down through Western Gulch and Komatik Path, burying the village for days. During a pending storm, like squirrels storing berries in dead tree stumps for winter, we stacked the wood bins, filled the water barrels, and chopped enough splits for a whole week. The huskies long mournful howls swept the entire land. One by one they commenced, until all of them were howling continuously, grouped together on snow banks surrounding the houses. The dogs' howling ceased only when the fury of the storm was upon us. The huskies dig down under the snowdrifts and stay there until the storm blows over.

When Easter came, we fasted on Good Friday morning. We weren't allowed to starve ourselves for forty days and nights like Jesus Christ. But during Lent we hardly sinned at all. Youngsters weren't allowed to play Old Maid and marbles and the men in the village stopped playing poker, piss-jacket, and drinking dry the moonshine keg. The Catholics gave up eating red meat during Lent.

After Easter came the long spring thaw. The bay broke up in May and the pack ice drifted out to sea. As soon as school ended, Daid moved us back to our summer cottage on Basin Island. In the wee hours of each morning, the put-put of Daid's motorboat could be heard leaving the wharf to go to the fishing ground. Sometimes he returned early with the gunnels of the boat barely above the water. While he pronged the cod from the boat and up onto the stagehead, we'd drag ourselves out of bed and down to the stage to help him. All day long, we'd gut, head, split and wash every quintal of fish before spreading it on the salt bulk. The backbreaking chores continued all summer long. Day and night, we smelt of decaying fish.

AUGUST, 1956

Elliot Ward, as my mother named him, came screaming into the world. The rain pelted hard against the felt on the roof. Thunder clapped loudly in between great flashes of wild lightning. I hear his cat-like howling; it's a familiar sound, one I've heard so often before. I scramble from my bed and out to the kitchen where Aunt Violet stands near the drop-leaf table, rubbing the baby down with a wet flannelette cloth. I rush forward to look upon my new little baby brother; I could hardly wait for Aunt Violet to put him in my arms.

A week before Elliot's birth, my brother Ronald had nearly drowned. Daid came back from the fishing grounds with fish that was ready for the salt bulk by noon. When Daid wasn't looking, Parmenas, Ronald and I climbed down over the stagehead and got into the flat that was tied to the stern of the boat. Pim claimed the paddles as always, and Ronald leaned over the stern looking for lumpfish while I stood pouting in the stem of the canoe. I could tell by Pim's bossy way that he wasn't going to let me row. When he refused to give me one of the paddles, that's when I decided to go ashore. I plucked on the painter to pull the flat back to the wharf. I plucked so hard that Parmenas lost the paddles and Ronald went headlong overboard.

Determined to climb up on the wharf, I didn't know anything was amiss until Mum came streeling down the slope screeching her head off and trying to get Daid's attention. I was halfway up the ladder when I heard her shout, *Bob, quick! Ronnies drownin! Ronnies drownin!*

I jerked around and there lay Ronald face up on a paddle, kicking wildly and chomping at the wind. Daid came flying through the air and landed in the bottom of the flat, causing a swell. Suddenly, Ronald disappeared. Daid jumped in the water with his hip rubbers on. Down, down he went as the bluish black water swallowed him up. Swirls of bubbles rose up to the surface, followed by his pipe and tobacco pouch, which drifted lazily on the soft rippling water. It all happened like in a dream.

The next thing I know Mum was there beside us, frantically searching the water. With feet tucked under the seat of the boat, balancing on her belly, she ducked over the stern, with only her backside sticking up. Moments passed before she broke water, holding Daid by his hair. Daid broke the surface with Ronald held high. Mum brushed the wet hair out of her eyes and plucked Ronald from Daid. Ronald was as blue as the bluing she uses in her wash. She screeches at the top of her windpipe, shaking him for all he's worth. Daid, coughing and sputtering, clinging to the stern of the flat, shouts, *Roll im May! Roll im!*

She flings Ronald across the seat of the boat like a sack of potatoes. Back and forth, back and forth, she rolls him. Still screeching hysterically, she cries out, *E s gone, Bob, e s gone!*

Keep rollin im! he shouts.

One minute, Ronald is being thrown about, the next he spouts water like a whale. Only when he whimpers does Mum stop rolling him. Hysteria rises when she spies me. With one swipe of her hand she knocks me flat. *Tis yer fault e nar drownded, youse jeesas ard ead!* she screams at me.

Daid grabs me and drags me aboard the motorboat out of her grasp. He howls in pain when I land on his bare feet.

Youse aw gonna git t belt dis day, bejesus, he bellows. '*Ow often doos I habs ta tell youse not t play in t flat! Git hup t house and wait dere.*

Suddenly I was up on the stagehead and running. Faster than the wind I ran, faster than Parmenas, who already had a headstart. I didn't stop at the house. I ran right through the cabbage patch, on up over the ridge, never stopping until I was safe on the other side of Miscopic Rock. I crawled in a small crevice between two split rocks in the side of the ridge and hid. There was no one and nothing but the breakers on the distant shore and empty swallow nests in the side of the bank that heard me sobbing out loud. *Gawd*, I cried. *Youse knows I dint mean to drown bruddy, youse knows. Youse knows.*

Summer was finally over and autumn was approaching fast. We moved back to the bay and it was time to return to school. My memories of schooldays are unforgettable. They begin with the loud ringing of the heavy iron hand-bell that summons us all to the schoolhouse before the last echo died away. The long rounded stove stands in the centre of the open classroom, its rusty pipe, tall and straight, reaches up through the rafters and roof. A heavy layer of frost coats the upper walls of the school when the temperature plummeted below zero. The nail heads, rounded and bulged by the frost, snap and pop in the heat circulating around the room.

The wind, howling outside on snowy days, sifts fine powdered drifts under the door, piling it there like windswept sand dunes.

A combination of chalk dust and wood smoke assaults the nostrils upon entering the door. In late afternoon, when the sun's rays splay across the hardwood floor, particles of chalk dust hang suspended in the smoky haze. Everyone, including the Master, kept their parkas on during the winter months. Mittens, frozen to the shape of hands and with ice balls clinging to them, are piled beneath the stove to dry.

Mr. Teacher Sir leads the class of sixteen from Primary to Grade Seven in the Lord's Prayer. This is a daily morning ritual, followed by "*God save the King,*" only now it was "*God save the Queen.* The patriotic figure centered above the blackboard unscathed by wood smoke still. The beautiful face of the new queen looked down upon us while we sang "*The Maple Leaf Forever.*

Sometimes, a new book arrived at the school. The printed matter was always a welcome sight. Every year, used books were passed down to us from siblings and others gone on before. Always, there were pages missing and rips and scribbles all over. Some smelt of pee, some had tea or molasses stains, and brown smudges.

Last autumn, a new reader, geography book, and speller were sent from some school board far away in Quebec City. The pages were as white as fresh fallen snow. The books had the most heavenly scent, a combination of pencil shavings, dried tobacco leaves, and newly planed wood. I wished with all my might the Master would give me the reader, and he did! But not before he warned me I would get ten lashings with the cat o' nine tails if I brought it back at the end of the season soiled or damaged in any way. I rushed home after school and promptly got a brown paper bag and covered the book.

Schooldays were filled with spelling bees and sums. We memorized the twelve multiplication tables found on the back of our scribblers. If we were caught cheating during tests we were quickly sent to the dunce corner. All of us, at some time or another, were sent to the dunce corner with the huge dictionary weighing heavily on top of our heads. God help us if it should fall to the floor. If it was my turn and I made it there without mishap, I'd carve a little slice of the devil on the side of the old warped bookcase. I used the tin stub end of my chewed down pencil, where the eraser used to be.

On days when we weren't in school, the boys were back to catching trout in Big Head Brook with safety pins and flour bag line. We climb Ladder Hill and pick kegs of redberries for the winter ahead. Daid goes to the foothills to cut wood. He stacks it near the path to haul back home when the snows arrives. Sometimes we went with him and carried the wood home on our backs. Mum makes quilts on her sewing machine or knits new vamps and mittens late into the night. There's a new hooked rug taking shape on the laths. When the unpredictable October winds sweep down from the mountains, we're prepared for winter.

It was late in winter when I noticed how often Daid went away from home. Perhaps I noticed it only because I was older now. For weeks and weeks he'd stay away. Sometimes, he was inland trapping beaver or hunting caribou with the Indians. Other times, perhaps, he just forgot to come home.

On nights when the winds whistled fiercely in the eaves and dogs howled spasmodically all night long, Mum stood in the upstairs window looking out on the dark of night, waiting, watching, and fretting over Daid.

Sometimes, when he returned like she expected him to, she'd run to the stove, pile the wood on the fire, and have his tea brewing blacker than coal. At the same time, she'd be commanding me to get his big mug with the gold rim and wild flowers down from the cupboard and place it near his plate. It would be there, ready and waiting, long before his boat steamed into the mouth of the bay, or the dog team pulled up to the door. So happy she was then, and we were too, because Daid had come home at last.

My father wasn't a big man. He was about 5 feet 7 inches tall with bright blue eyes and a loud laugh and he usually wore a tam in summer and a fur hat in winter. Whenever he returned home from fur trapping, Ronald and I would watch him skin the foxes and help him stretch the pelts down over the molds. Pim made himself scarce, as scarce as he could, by bending his head to the homework he brought home from school and memorizing it out loud while sitting at the kitchen table, mere feet away. The smell was too much for him to stomach. Ronald and I would hold the legs of the foxes apart while Daid peeled the pelts off the carcasses.

It was such a peaceful settling thing, to watch Daid nail the pelts to the board with tiny carpet tacks, while the sweet smelling aroma of his Aurora pipe tobacco smoke drifted lazily above his head in the lamplight. The house seemed to settle down around us then. The kettle sizzled soothingly as the fire died down in the stove. The brown and white crackie curled up and slept beneath the oven door.

Daid seldom whistled or sang and he said very little while he worked, but his presence always calmed my spirit. I felt so proud, so privileged, to share those special moments with him. I'm sure Ronald did too. Whenever Daid left to go behind the ridge where the Indians lived, a part of me went with him.

CHAPTER 4

⌂ **YER STRETCHIN DEM NOW, MY MAID!**

The dawn breaks as I stand on the butter box at the back of the house pinning the first lot of clothes out on the line. Husky dogs meander around low clumps of juniper bushes rooting up old buried bones. Every so often they stop and sniff at the morning air. They stand stock still like pelicans, with one raised paw tucked inward, tails straight out, and noses pointed in the direction of Komatik Path.

I can tell there's something moving around up there by the dogs' agitated movements. I hope it's not a mountain cat or a wolf. I'm so afraid of wolves and mountain cats. Sometimes, on a still moonlight night, we can see them slinking across the marshland. I'm afraid of what could be up there on Komatik Path. Mom is always warning the youngsters not to go up there alone. I'm scared now; my eyes are fastened on the woods closest to our house.

Suddenly, Spark leaps forward with teeth bared. I leap off the butter box and beater around the house to the porch door. While I'm frantically clawing at the latch on the door, Bren, our female dog, saunters across the half-frozen marsh.

Wot did youse hab ta scare me like dat fer, youse stupit dawg! I say, as all the other dogs run to greet her with tails wagging, their meandering forgotten.

Mum is still bent over the washboard scrubbing viciously as I inch my way upstairs.

I habs ta use dat pail real bad! I say, when she glares in my direction. *Hurry up and be smart bout it. I dont hab aw day!*

Afterwards, back outside on the butter box, warm and snug in clean bloomers hidden beneath my plaid dress and parka, I stand subdued and continue hanging out clothes. The air warms slightly as the morning sun skims slowly across the mountaintops towards Lac Carie. The smell of juniper emanates from the freshly dug ground in the air around me. The soft poke of the wind sweeping gently down the gully sends shivering waves over the half frozen pond at the back of the house. Gulls fly high in the sky. The lazily drifting clouds above me are forgotten by the sight of the one lone eagle soaring above Ladder Hill. The sound of someone chopping wood in the distance lends to the peacefulness of the morning.

A burst of soot pellets shoots upward from the stovepipe and falls silently down around me. The soot lands on my face, my eyelids, my hands, and the white wash. I squelch the urge to run inside to tell my mother to stop poking at the fire. I still feel the sting from the last backhander she gave me when I so boldly accused her of doing just that.

Tis all yer fault, youse jeesas ard ead, fer stayin out dere so long! she said.

I reave the line out as fast as I could. The knot brings up to the end of the other pulley attached to the pole. Perhaps the wind will swoosh the soot away.

Clarissy, git t lead outta yer ass! Is youse gonna stay out dere aw day? Come ere and git dem towels! Dem youngsters be hup t once! I dont hab aw day!

I m cummin, Mum! I m cummin! I shout, jamming the pin in the pulley so t doesn't reel back again.

Gawd! Wot makes youse so slow, my maid? Youse dont take after me, dats far gawddamn shur! Must be dat lazy Gert down on t point!

Uncle Ernest, my mother's brother, and his wife, Aunt Gert, and their family live on Israel's Point, about a quarter of a mile from our house. Their house sits on wooden posts on a grassy knoll, a tiny mound of land jutting out into Big Head Brook. The grey weather-beaten house has never seen a lick of lime in all its days. The house is usually the last one in the village to have smoke curls leap up from the stovepipe in the mornings. I can tell who is up by the smoke rising up from the stovepipes. Of course, no one gets up earlier than my mother and me.

Mr. Wobbler's smoke rises steadily upwards through the filtering dawn as it breaks over the bay. Then Great Aunt, Mr. Thomas, Aunt Carrie, and Mr. Jones. The schoolhouse is last.

In no time at all the roof tops come to life, smoke rising straight up to the heavens, a clue a storm is approaching. And before the day is done, all the villagers stack wood in the porch, enough for a week, chop and shave splts, and fill the water barrels, like squirrels storing nuts for winter. The huskies begin their excessive howling, stopping only when the cold rain falls, or the first snowflake flies. Perhaps the wind will blow at Mum's command and perhaps the clothes will dry and perhaps I wont have to lug it up over the stairs and hang it over the trawl-line clothesline.

Uncle Nrst chops wood down near the woodpile. I hear him cursing before I actually see him. His lips move faster than the tide riplets in Muskrat Brook. Like my mother, it appears he's already poisoned with the day before it begins. Just then, the object of his vexation sallies to the woodpile, waving a finger in his face. At the sight of her, he dances around the chopping block, clicking his heels together and swinging the axe over his head. Aunt Gert barely escapes Uncle Nrst's madness as the axe sails through the air and sticks in the shingles beside the doorframe. She manages to run safely into the house, and a short while later she's at the upstairs window. Her fist rams through the window and the broken pane falls to the ground. She sees me now, stuck like a bluebottle fly on the clothesline at the back of the house. In a crooning voice I hear her say, '*Urry up, Nrst bye, an git dat fire goin! Freeda s gotta git dat wash hout! Wees been ard at it aw marnin, youse knows!*

It's been quite a spell since I've seen my cousin Alfreda, perhaps a week or more. I haven't seen her since the day Aunt Gert chased me with the prong. I've been too scared to go anywhere near Uncle Nrst's place ever since that happened. I get shivers just thinking about what could have happened if I hadn't been quicker than her. It was Mum who sent me there in the first place. Earlier, I had felt so proud when she singled me, instead of Parmenas or Ronald, to go to Long Point to the merchant's shop.

Go down dere and ask dat ting on t point if Freeda can go wit youse, she said. *Youse knows ow riled up she gits when I cums near er. Youse ask er! She ll let Freeda go if youse asks er! Go on down dere, my maid, see wot she sez! Go on, now. Go on!*

Mum didn't tell me it was a good chance I wouldn't come back. She didn't tell me how crazed Aunt Gert really was. And neither did she tell me it was fourteen miles, round trip, from the bottom of the bay where we lived to Long Point.

God only knows what Mum was thinking, but Daid (Hitler, as she always called him) was never around when she needed him. That particular week she was desperate for molasses and coal-oil. She was was never one to put off for tomorrow what had be done on that particular day, so come hell or high water she would get her molasses and coal-oil, even if it meant sacrificing my life to do so. She promised me nothing, only told me it was something I had to do.

I was excited about going to Long Point, and when I saw Alfreda making her way to the brook behind their house before dark, I beater down the path to intersect her.

Kin youse go wit me, Freeda? I say. *Kin youse go wit me?*

Stay ere! she commands. *I m gonna tell mummie and see wot she sez!*

Draping the water hoop around my shoulders, I walked to the brook and filled the two galvanized buckets while waiting for Alfreda to come back. It wasn't long before she returned, running towards me in a half skipping fashion, her eyes bulging with excitement.

I kin go wit youse, I kin! I kin!

Naw, my maid! I bet youse is tarmentin me!

Onest t Gawd, I m not! Cross my art and ope to die, she squealed, making the sign of the cross on her chest. I squealed then too.

As we jumped around in circles like two dogs with the rabies, neither of us saw my mother leave the upstairs window where she'd been watching me.

Huh, I knows yer not stretchin dem now, my maid! she said a little later, when I arrived home to tell her the good news about Alfreda.

Naw, onest t Gawd. Freeda said dat Aunt Gert said she kin go wit me!

Ow do youse knows dat Freeda is tellin the truth?

Cus she crossed er eart and hoped t die. Youse knows Freeda wud nebber cross er heart. She knows dat Gawd up dere in the sky wud strike er dead!

Wot! You means dat ting dint go hoff er head? Wots hup er sleeve, ya spcse? my mother asked, while sitting in the rocking chair with her arms crossed over her bulging belly and her foot doing a tap as she pushed the rocker into motion.

I was so excited I didn't close my eyes all night. I was scared to death too. I'd never been farther than Big Head Bluff, just on the other side of Muskrat Brook, barely a mile away. Anywhere we traveled it was always by boat, like when Daid moved us to Basin Island or, on the rare occasion when the sea was calm and it was Sunday, he'd take us for a steam to Greenly Island.

Mum always sent Parmenas and Ronald up to Big Head Brook to catch trout whenever she felt the need. She'd give them safety pins for hooks, and salt pork for bait, anything to get them out of her face. But me, being a girl, it was my place to stay home and help her with the endless chores. It seemed I was doomed to stay in the house scrubbing shitty napkins or freezing to death at the clothesline hanging out the wash until then. Who was foolish enough to stay home making beds and washing shitty napkins? *Not me. Not Freeda eider, dats fer gawddamn shur*!

When dawn broke over the marsh I was up and ready. Mom had darned the holes in my red striped sweater the night before. It wouldn't do for strangers to see me with threadbare elbows. I could hardly contain my excitement as she forced me to sit down at the table and eat a hearty breakfast of rolled oats and molasses drenched bread.

Youse bedder eat yer guts full, my maid, youse gotta a long ways t go t day! she said.

While I shoveled rolled oats into my mouth, Mum spread lard on four slices of bread and heaped spoonfuls of redberry jam and sugar on top. She put the bread into a cotton sugar bag knotted together with twine and slung the bag over my neck like a noose.

Keep to the main pat now! she fussed, as she shoved two one-gallon cans into my fists. *Be quick now, no dallying bout, ya hear. Be back befer dark.*

With the bag flapping in all directions, I sped across the partly frozen marsh towards Uncle Nrst's place at the crack of dawn. I felt so protected, knowing my mother was watching me from the safety of the upstairs window. If she had second thoughts of her foolish notion to send me on such a long journey that I knew nothing about she hid it well. Within minutes, I was on Uncle Nrst's bridge. Hesitantly, I looked back at my mother, like a dog to its master, looking for guidance. With an agitated wave of her hand she motioned for me to enter. I lifted the latch and walked in, leaving the door wide open. I prayed Alfreda was ready. I couldn't wait to be on my way. I knew if Aunt Gert suddenly changed her mind about letting Alfreda go with me, I could never go to Long Point all by myself.

Alfreda was standing near the stove clutching her sweater coat when I entered. Her bulging eyes sat almost on her cheekbones. They rolled around and around in her head like marbles. Her mass of tangled curls bounced around her face as she jumped from foot to foot. Oh, she can hardly wait to be gone like me, I thought, until she screamed, *Run, Clarissy, run!*

At the same time Alfreda screamed, Aunt Gert popped out from behind the inside door with an iron fire poker raised above her head and a fish prong pointed towards my face.

Git outta dis ouse! she shouted. *Freeda s not goin nowhere with da likes of youse. If dat May wants lasses she can git dat erself. Freeda s got nuff work to do roun here.*

The poker cracked against the door. As I cleared the steps the dogs, curled up and asleep under the bridge, got such a fright they leaped in the air on all fours and ran down to the landwash, yelping their heads off.

I felt the heat from the poker as it flew past my head. I ran so fast, I'm sure I was way ahead of the wind, yet the gap was closing between us. Then, suddenly, like a crack of a whip, a string of curse words longer than Komatik Path itself cut the morning air.

Youse touch Clarissy, ya measly son of a bitch, and I ll murder youse befer dis day is done, as shur as jeesas made little green h apples I will! shouted my mother.

The sound of my mother's voice drove Aunt Gert clean out of her feverish crazy mind. With bulging eyes and froth foaming around her mouth she came after me with speed I never knew she had. Her uncombed hair stuck off from the side of her head like dog hairs caught on a willow branch. She was a frightful sight!

Around and around the pond we went. I kept looking towards the house to see if Mum was coming to help me but she wasn't. She was still up there, wringing her fists at Aunt Gert from the safety of the upstairs window.

Just as Aunt Gert lunged forward to stab me with the prong, she got caught up in the tongue of one of her cutoff rubbers and fell flat on the marsh. While she teetered back and forth on her rounded belly, I kept on running. For the sake of my life, I kept on running.

Clarissy! Clarissy! Ober yere! Ober yere!

I could hardly believe what I was seeing. There was Alfreda on the other side of Muskrat Brook, high and dry upon the knoll, waving me on with her sweater coat. I bolted like a jackrabbit towards Alfreda, running this way and that across the swamp, gathering speed. My rubber boots hardly touched the six-foot log spanning Muskrat Brook as I crossed over to the other side.

Alfreda was still running. I didn't catch up with her until she was way beyond Big Head Bluff. Out of sight of the madness behind us, we surged onward. Before we went around Googin's Hill, I glanced back over my shoulder. Mum was still in the upstairs window, wringing her fists in the air, while Aunt Gert danced in spite near the pond, waving the prong in her direction. The morning air was thick with their curses, blacker than stovepipe soot.

Ducks and geese that had been swimming peacefully in the ponds rose in the air and flew away as we hurried along. With their loud honking and quacking filling the air, we quickly forgot the commotion behind us. It was a different world beyond the bluff, quiet and peaceful, but we were too hyped up to enjoy the serenity of it all.

The long winding footpath maneuvered along the ridges, across the marshes and up over the hills, weaving its way through the lowlands towards Bradore Plains. Perhaps an hour went by before we reached the flat land. On past the Postmaster's house, we continued on through the footpath up over Bradore Hill. With the ocean to the right of us, the marshlands to the left, and the sun climbing higher in the sky we continued steadily onward. Perhaps it was mid-morning by the time we came to the crest of another hill that sloped down to the landwash. We were so tired we lay down on a layer of huge flat rocks stacked like stove cakes, and ate the bread Mum had given me.

It was such a beautiful place that we lingered there longer than we should have. Directly below was a valley of grassy meadows and sand dunes, stretching down to a white sandy pebble beach that curved in and around the shoreline like the lip of a gold-rimmed bowl. Grassy fields and blackberry bushes crept upwards and touched the gray mossy flat land beyond.

Some distance from shore, eight porpoises schooled near the breakers, rolling over and over like slinky toys flipping downstairs. Huge funnel shaped waves rolled swiftly to shore, spilling mountains of foam upon the sands. On the other side of the beach, identical stacks of layered rocks rose up from the sea. Behind the ledges was Long Point Harbour.

Lah Freeda lah. Deres dat statue mum sed to hab an eye hout fer, I shouted, pointing to where it stood like a miniature carousel high upon a cliff.

Where? she squealed. *I don t see nar statue!*

Dats cause youse is lookin in t wrong direction, my maid. Over dere, lah, I say, yanking her around.

I sees it, I sees it! she squealed. *But urry up, my maid, wees gotta git to dat shop and back before dark!*

Aw, wait another little wee spell, Freeda. I m not done yet!

Come on, slowpoke, yer jest wanna watch dem jumpers sum more, dats all. You knows wees habent got nar minute t dally about!

Wot is youse talkin about, my maid! The sun isn t up ober our heads yet Daid sez tis nar dinnertime when dat sun is hup dere. We got hours yet

Naw, we don t, my maid! Now, come on! she says, stomping her feet.

Oh, aw rite. I m comin, I say.

Throwing a crust of burnt bread over my shoulder, I bolt down the hill ahead of Alfreda, shouting, *I ll be down to t botten befer youse.* Just as quickly, Alfreda leaped down the hill behind me, but I beat her by an arm's length.

Dats no fair, she screamed. *Youse robbed!*

Dint.

Did too!

Whose da slowpoke now, eh!

Aw, shaddup, my maid, before I goes ome and lit youse walk t rest of t ways aw by yere ownself.

Naw, youse won t, youse carly-cat, cause, cause I'll tell Mum.

Whose scared of Aunt May? Not me, dats fer gawddamn shur! she said, as she turned and stomped off in the direction of home.

I knew if I made Alfreda spitey enough, she'd walk back home and leave me there all by myself.

Aw, cum on, my maid, I said, *I m only tarmentin youse!*

The argument was soon forgotten when three hairy heads popped up from the grass nearby. Horses!

Arses! screamed Alfreda

Wait fer me, Freeda, wait fer me-e-e-e. I screeched.

Arses hates red! She yelled back over her shoulder. *Member dat story Misser Teacher Sir tole we in school t udder day?*

Wot story, I don t memb r nar story?

Yer so stun, my maid, t one where t arse chased dat man over t fence cause he waved es red handkerchief at im.

Alfreda's slacks were red all over and my sweater was choking to death with bright red and white stripes. It finally came to me what Alfreda was trying to put through my thick skull.

Wots wees gonna doos, Freeda? I say. *Wots wees gonna doos?*

Back on the ledge, where the forgotten cans were still sitting, we lay side by side on our stomachs, peeking up every now and again to make sure the horses were still down there in the grass and not sneaking up the hill after us.

Time passed. The horses kept on feeding and ignoring us completely. Yet they were still standing near the path leading to Long Point Harbour.

Now, wees in some fix, my maid, youse knows wees kint go back wit nar gallon of lasses or coal-oil, so wots wees gonna doos!

One thing I knew for sure was that if the horses bolted up the hill towards us, Alfreda would leap to her feet and run with all her might towards Bradore and I'd be right behind her.

Mebbe wees can crupp along t landwash, whispered Alfreda.

Naw, we kint do dat, wot if deys comes in t water affer we, and drowns we t deat?

While we were arguing back and forth, a float plane flew over our heads and landed in Trout Pond. *Dats hit,* I squealed.

Dats wot? screeched Alfreda, jumping up in full view of the horses.

Wees can go on t udder side-da Trout Pond, tis n dat far away. If wees crupp down real low behind t ledge, dey won t see we at all. Ere, grab dem cans, Freeda, urry hup, quick!

Once more we were off and running, dashing this way and that, bent almost to the ground so as not to be seen by the horses. We neither knew nor cared how wide the lake was, nor did we notice the other lake in the distance, the real Trout Pond, so desperate we were to put distance between us and the horses grazing idly in Lanse au Din.

Only God and Uncle Willie knew it was four miles around Trout Pond. I knew I couldn't go back home without the molasses and coal-oil. I was as scared of my mother as I was of the horses. I knew I'd get a switching and Freeda would not.

We kept on running, stopping only long enough to drink from the brook to soothe our parched throats. Kneeling down on all fours, we lapped up the water with our tongues before surging onward. Running always in a crouching position, we ran across swamps with little fear of anything but the horses in the valley behind us.

We crossed brown bakeapple marshes, waist high bushes, and knee deep streams. We got stuck in the mud and went over our rubbers dozens of times but still surged onward. There's no doubt in my mind that we went straight to purgatory and back before we reached that statue on the hill. I never ever told my mother we went the long way around. She wouldn't have believed me even if I had. She would have said, *Yere stretchin dem now, my maid.*

Worse still, I would've been crucified if she knew I kissed Saint Anne's feet, *Yer close nuff to dem Roman Catholics now,* she'd have said.

I remember how small we felt beneath that saintly presence, that cream colored face with the heavenly smile, and those outstretched hands. Standing so tall, draped in blue and white, with bare feet, looking down at the two of us, she seemed so real, *Mebbe if we kiss er feet she will bless we,* whispered Alfreda, and we did!

For the first time since we left the ledge, we stopped to rest. Panting heavily, we lay at the base of St Anne's feet, looking upon that peaceful face and the cotton ball clouds behind her, not wanting to go one step farther. It must have been instinct that pressed us onward, or perhaps it was the declining sun alerting us of the darkness ahead, and the long trek back home. Moving down over the hill, single file, on a well-worn path, Alfreda remarked, *Deres more dan we dats been frighted by dem arses, my maid.*

By the time we reached the general shop the sun's rays were slanting across the village. An Orange Crush sign hung above the shop entrance. We stood there staring up at it, stalling for time before opening the door and going in. A woman with iron-rimmed eyeglasses came forward and stared down at us. Perhaps she was wondering who in the name of good St. Anne those ragamuffins were. Too shy to look up, we kept our heads bowed. We were unaware of our state, with mud caked to our heads and smeared over our faces, boughs and twigs caught in our hair, and redberry juice dried in the corners of our mouths. It was Mum who told me how shameful we looked that day, *Youse shamed me t deat, my maid, goin t Lucy-Annes lookin like dat. Youse wus clean nuff befer youse left yere. I knows now youse had t git yerself in dat state.*

The woman finally spoke to us, *Whose ye fellars? And where did ye come frum?*

I m Mays girl, Ma am, I half whispered, but she heard me.

May? May? Not May Smith from Bradore?

Yes Ma am, I said, my eyes still glued to the floor.

Wot in t name of good Saint Anne is ye fellars doin all the ways down yere?

Alfreda nudged me, *Give er dat ledder, stunface.*

I had completely forgotten the letter my mother had stuck in the pocket of my slacks. I quickly pulled it out and shoved it in the woman's outstretched hand.

Mum sez fer me t give youse dis.

The woman's eyes seemed to cover the whole page as she read the scribbled note, all the while saying, *Tch, tch, tch-tch. Deres sumting t madder wit Mays ead, sendin ye young uns aw t way down yere. Wot time did ye fellars leave Bradore?*

Daylight, Ma am.

Alfreda nudged me again. *Ask er wot time it tis!*

Wot time tis, Ma am?

Her head bobbed up and down, and her eyes grew behind her glasses as she strained to see the time on the watch dangling from a braided string around her neck.

Tis pass tree o clock, she said. *Jimmie, vite! Put some melasse in dat odder can, eh, sacrament, poor young uns, deys got sum ways ta go yet.*

Quickly, she screwed the cover on the oilcan, and handed the can to Alfreda. Then she reached in her apron pocket and pulled out a stick of Doublemint gum and shoved it in my direction.

Yere, she said. *Slit dat in haff, vite, befer da woofs gits youse.*

Alfreda screamed. The can hit the wooden plank floor with a loud thud as she bolted straight up into the air and through the open doorway. Clean off the bridge she leaped and sped down the path, like a goose taking flight. With hands flapping wildly at her sides she screeched, *Wees gonna git et by d woofs, wees gonna git et by d woofs!*

In stunned silence, we watched her as she flew.

The woman, suddenly realizing that I was still there, looked down at me and hissed, *Allez! Allez! Vite!*

I grabbed the cans up off the floor, and like Alfreda I too leaped clean off the bridge and sped down the path after her.

Freeda! Freeda! Wait fer me! Wait fer me-e-e-e!

Wees gonna git eat by d woofs, wes gonna git het by d woofs! she screeched, and kept on running.

Eventually, I caught up with her.

Take one of dem cans, Freeda, I panted. *If we git coal-oil mixed up wit dat lasses, Mum will kill we first before dem woofs gits we!*

Tears ran down Alfreda's face and into her mouth. Both of us were wailing now, wailing from fright, from fatigue, from both, and, unbeknown to us, the worst was yet to come. We had little choice but push onward through the village and along the gravel road that would take us back to Lance au Din, where we had first seen the horses. As we continued onward, we kept on wailing. There was no one else on that path but us. One thing for certain was that we had to get to the other side of Lance au Din before dark. We were too exhausted to walk around the pond again. We had to walk back along the shore and take the path we should have taken in the first place. We had to stay in the path if we were to make it back home at all.

Tisnt bad nuff wees aw mos got attacked by dem arses, now wees gonna be et by t woofs, Alfreda sobbed.

Dont bawl, Freeda, I coaxed, sobbing right along with her, *Yere, take my and. Gawd wont lit nuddin urt we. Lits say our pray rs. Our Fodder, who art in eaven allowed be dye name, dye will be done on eart as it is in heaven...wots t rest, Freeda?*

I dunno, my maid, lets ask e to keep we safe til we gits ome.

The sun was sinking low as we approached the ledge on the opposite side of Lance Au Din. We strained to see what was in the valley. Not seeing horses or wolves, we walked painstakingly onward.

Dere, see, Freeda, I tole youse Gawd wudden lit nudden appen to we, e will protect us like e did wit Saint Francis. Ya knows dey woofs nebber attacks befer dark. Youse knows dat, my maid.

T wasnt Saint Francis Gawd protected. Youse got dat all mixed hup. Twcs Saint Daniel in the den. Tot youse knows yer catechism, my maid! See I told youse, youse dint learn it good.

Dont matter none who e twas. Gawd protected e jest tsame, dint e?

By the time we reached the ledge on the opposite side of the valley, darkness draped down around us like a coffin veil. We kept walking steadily towards home, seeing nothing but the long dark shadows that crept over the land. We never stopped, not even long enough to pull up the sopping vamps that kept riding out in the toes of our rubber boots. It didn't matter much, our feet were raw and bleeding anyway. We just kept on walking, never looking back. We were still a long way from home. By the time we reached Bradore Plains, a purplish hue lay on the horizon where the sun went down behind Basin Island.

Lamplight shone from the windows of the houses scattered here and there along the path. The loneliness of it all crept through the marrow of our bones. Yet, just like head dogs in the traces, we kept on going in the direction of home. As we limped slowly along, the hills got darker still.

Not one word we spoke, but clung to each other like bluebottle flies stuck to a molasses jug. All around us were the strangest nightly sounds. Bats and nighthawks filled the dark windless sky. Our fear was so great we were unable to speak, but we still kept plodding along.

It must have been extremely late by the time we reached the bluff. The hills loomed black and menacing against the night sky, the apple slice moon that hung so precariously above Queens Hill was hardly enough to light our way. As the night grew darker, we often strayed from the path. Frantically, we'd cower close to the ground and felt around with our rubber boots until we found the deep grooves in the path. Our fingers were numb and pained from gripping the cans so tightly. Too afraid to change sides, we held on tight to each other, afraid of losing one another in the dark. The nearer we got to the river, the louder it roared. Common sense told us that if we followed the sound it would take us to the bridge. Then, suddenly, there it was, looming out of the darkness like a ghost. But something even whiter was moving over it, almost floating towards us. *Googins Ghost. Oh my Gawd,* whispered Frieda.

He was hovering over the bridge just the way Mr. Teacher Sir had said he would. Googin, the first Indian ever to stomp the ground on the opposite side of the river near Big Head Bluff, had died many years before, he said, but his ghost came back to haunt those who tried to cross the bridge unto his land at night.

Wots e comin affer we for, Freeda? We dint do nuddin to e, we dint.

Whimpering like snared rabbits we sank to the ground, trying to bury ourselves in an invisible hole. There was no escape, the ghost and the bridge were merely yards away from us. Old Googin couldn't help but see us. But just as our blood was about to turn to water, out of the darkness came this terrible screech.

Clarissy? Clarissy? Is dat youse? Answer me! Gawddamn! It was my mother. Screeching hysterically in the still night air, we leaped to our feet and streeled towards her, nearly knocking her off her legs. Like drowning children we clung to her, trying to tell her everything at once.

Tank jeesas youse is safe, she cried. *I was jest comin t look fer youse. Weer in gawds name wuz youse hat all dat while? Woofs? Arses? Wots youse talkin bout, my maids? Nebber mind dat now. I hab t signal Nrst from t knoll. Stay yere.*

Stay there? Oh, she had the craze all right! That definitely was not the thing to say to the pair of us who had just been to that Catholic place and back.

Mum flashed the light on and off, and another light appeared in the distance near Uncle Ernest's house. After much coaxing, Mum finally persuaded us to take her back to the spot where we had dropped the cans.

Wak hup aw head hoff me, my maids, she said. *I kint lug dem eavy cans wit youse two draggin on me skirts, now kin I!*

Still bawling, Alfreda and I walked on ahead of her, holding hands again. The flashlight that Mum was holding while trying to carry the cans kept throwing light in every direction but ahead of us. We were too tired and hungry to notice or stop bawling.

Uncle Ernest met us near Muskrat Brook. Anxiously, he scurried towards us. When he was certain Alfreda was safe, he snatched her up and carried her across the log on his back. While I crawled shakily across the log on hands and knees, Mum kept yelling at me to move faster. Alfreda and Uncle Ernest disappeared in the darkness before I could sob, *See ya tamarra, Freeda, see ya tamarra.*

CHAPTER 5

⌂ **MUM DIDN'T HAVE ALL DAY**

With spring came gentle flowing winds. Soft and alluring, they swooped down through the hollow in Komatik Path. Ice candles hanging from the roof, some four feet long, begin to drip, tunneling holes in the snow below the windowsills. The heat from the sun bared the hilltops and turned the ice along the bay a dirty gray. Ballicatters disappear, blue jays, robins and chickadees find their way back into nature's swing of things. Mum flings open the upstairs windows to air the loft. *T stink in dis bloody place es nuff t knock me down off dem stairs,* she hollers.

Like a sudden whirlwind she strips the patchwork quilts from the beds and runs downstairs to pile them in heaps by the tubs ready and waiting near the stove. Pots of brook water filled to the brim sit on all the damper holes while the roaring fire heats it to the boiling point. While the first heavy quilt is soaking in the tub, she goes to the pantry to get the washboard and Rinso soap powder. I watch her grabble the corners of the quilt with both hands and scrub it up and down on the washboard. All the while she curses God for giving her more piss-ass boys!

When the quilt is scrubbed to her liking she screams at me to help her lug it to the rinse tub nearby. She raises it up and plunks it down in the cold water to rinse the soap away, then I help her squeeze out the excess water. Afterwards, I lug the quilt outside to the clothesline. The line sags to the ground beneath the soggy weight. While I struggle with the quilts she sews new pillow covers made from Robin Hood flourbags on her hand driven sewing machine, all the while cursing Daid for not saving the feathers from the many ducks he killed last spring.

Like so many countless times before, I listen to her prattle on nonstop. *Tings done by haffs is nebber done rite,* she laments. *Nebber, nebber put off fer t marra wot can be done t day. Heights of laziness I calls dat.* I watch her nimble fingers fold the material under and pull it from behind the foot of the machine as she turns the knob with lightning speed, making perfectly straight stitches.

Wots yer gawkin at, my maid? Grab dat pail and empt it, I doan hab all day.

Ritually, every spring, Mum goes on a cleaning rampage. She rants and raves and angrily swipes at the many cobwebs hanging from the rafters like kingfisher nests. While she swipes at the cobwebs with the washrag, I dig the wood chips and shavings out of the woodbin then sweep the porch floor. With a bucket of scalding hot water and a piece of old seine net and lye soap, I scrub the wooden planks. My hands soon shrivel up like dried prunes and blister. Before I'm through, they're raw and bleeding. A little hard work never kills anyone, Mum says, so it wouldn't do for me to snivel.

I was only half finished when she sallied through the open doorway and flung the dirty water out on the wind. Before it lands, she has the bucket wiped clean. Side-stepping my freshly scrubbed areas, she hangs the bucket on a six-inch nail above the woodbin again. *Urry up, my maid, we don t hab all day.*

Mum always sang when she made headway with the chores, but on this particular spring day I noticed her singing spirit had faded away. I listened intently for the familiar sound of the *"Rock of Ages* but the hymn never happened. She changed without me knowing somehow.

It was around Easter time, when my mother confided in me, *Luk, Clarissy,* she said, *dere s sumting growin under my arm, I wonder wot dat is, ya spose?*

Unprepared for this sudden show of comradeship, I shrugged my shoulders, *I dunno Mum, p raps dat be gone t marrar.* I tell her in the quiet that follows, *I hope dats not sumting we kin catch, youse knows we gits eberting dat comes yere, chicken pox, mumps, scarlet fever, measles and pink-eye Dat dirt, I nebber wants dat agin, t last time I got dat I pulled strings of pus outta my eyes tree feet long,* I say in a high pitched voice, with arms outstretched. *We gits eberting cept rickets, and biles, BILES! I hope dats not wot youse habs.*

Aw shaddup, my maid, you shur kin prattle yer ead hoff win youse gits started, Mum says in disgust. My prattling about boils ceases. I'm back in my rightful place again.

JULY 1958

Mum went to the hospital to have the lump removed. I knew it was a serious operation, she told me so, and she was gone so long I was afraid she would never come back.

For a short while Daid went fishing every morning. Parmenas and Ronald fished with him, but I wasn't alone with the youngsters any more as Mum had hired a serving girl. She wasn't much older than me, but I didn't like it that she was staying with us. I didn't want her there playing her silly grown up games. *Dats not t way Mum pins t clothes on t line,* I screamed at her. She knocks me flat with her fist and when I'm back on my feet again I revel in sweet revenge when a junk of wood catches her in the ankle. When I see the blood squirt, I ran and hid behind Miscopic Rock. I didn't want the likes of her to see me cry. I'd rather choke to death on a wishbone than have her tell the island crowd what a sissy I was.

After supper, all the courting couples came to our house. All the courting among the younger crowd went on in my mother's house while she was away. Cass was there among them. Good-looking Cass was my third cousin and I had a crush on him. I wanted him to notice me but he didn't. Even though I had nar tit like the rest, the moss growing under my arms should have counted somehow.

I despised Cass that summer. I don't know why I did, I just did. Maybe It was because he paid more attention to the serving girl who was three years older than me.

I wished my mother would come back and get the serving girl out of my confined space. Just because I forgot about Clyde one day and the tide nearly washed him out to sea, Mum didn't have to go off her head thinking I couldn't be trusted with the youngsters alone. The serving girl's mother, some aunt from Middle Bay, had told her about Clyde. No one had seen him, not Ronald, not Eldon or any of the rest. All afternoon I searched for him. *Yer spose t be mindin im yer ownself,* Parmenas shouted when I tried to blame him. I ran from pond to pond looking for him. Sometimes the youngsters sailed their boats in the ponds nearby. I knew if he fell in the swamp I'd never find him ever again. I searched for him everywhere, Beetle Pond, under the stage heads, behind Miscopic Rock, over to Uncle Alfred's place on the other side of the island until I realized that I hadn't checked Uncle Ernest's stage. I found him at last near the landwash, fast asleep, the tide lapping around his little feet, his red rubbers floating off with the rising tide. I hugged him first then I slapped him. *Doan leabe dat door no more, youse bad, bad boy. Sissy aw mos lit youse git drownded*, I said, as I ran back to the house dragging him by the hand. He was only little, I took my eyes of him for only a minute, just a wee minute, I tried to convince myself as I made a vow never to let him out of my sight again. I wouldn't have then, it was just that I was trying so desperately to finish the embroidered pillowcase that was a present for Mum when she got back from the hospital. I wanted so much for her to be proud of me. It didn't matter so much afterwards because I gave myself and her such a fright.

When Mum finally came home, I howled and cried and carried on like some overgrown sissy. When I was through spilling my guts, Mum sent the serving girl home. I was sorry afterwards, because Mum was so weak that I had to carry the workload alone.

I shied away the first time Mum showed me her long ugly scar. A pain shot through my own empty chest. The shiny pink scar like knotted hemp twine reached from her neck bone down to the bottom of her ribcage, then criss-crossed like an embroidered stitch from the centre of her chest to her side. A vacant spot over shallow bones. Perhaps the breast will grow back, I thought. Mum knew the difference. She stuffed flannel in the empty cup of her brassiere.

As each day went by she got a little stronger. I'm not sure when I began to notice the difference. She confides in me, telling me everything. I wish she'd stop. There are things I have no desire to listen to. *I m gonna die*, she states, right out of a wind-still morning. *Tis cancer, youse knows, dey don t hab nar cure fer dat yet. I ll be long gone befer dat happens.*

Aw Mum, I wish youse d stop tellin me youse es gonna die, youse knows youse es not gonna die! I state, half cross with her.

Lissen t me, youse jesas hardhead, if I sez I m gonna die, I m gonna die, now hurry hup and git dem beds made, I doan hab aw day!

CHAPTER 6

⌂ STREAKS OF RED

In the cold, bright, wind-still morning the snow crunches loudly beneath my feet. Tiny frost flakes, clinging to the cold air, reflect the sunlight, like trinkets casting beacons of pinpoint light here and there, spewing across the frozen landscape like a magical fairy wand. The blue in the sky runs deep against the sleeping ridge of snow covered mountains, as bay ice unfolds like a train on a wedding dress as far as the eye can see. Seldom subdued except by the hand of Old Man Winter, Norse Brook Falls is silent. Bay ice cracks like gunshots as the tide rises beneath it unseen. Huskies meander silently around the houses, and smoke rises straight up from the stovepipes of our tiny village snuggled beneath the foothills. Both are telltale signs of a distant storm brewing.

The only other audible sound is that of my sealskin boots making contact with the crusty snow as I jump around to warm my numb feet. A peaceful soothing feeling descends down around me as I stand on the snowbank beside our house, absorbing all the familiar sights and sounds. Suddenly that peace is broken by dogs barking, commencing one by one all through the village.

Somewhere in the distance, there's a dog team approaching. Across the flatness of the bay I see them moving, not one team, not two, but many, coming down over the ridge in the distance like ants down over a hill, only faster. The air all around me is filled with the sounds of barking dogs, the faster they move and the closer they get to the village. Eight teams speed across the frozen landscape, some with seven dogs, some eight, some with all black dogs, some with all white, and some with a mixture of brown and white dogs. It's a vision, a rare and spectacular sight. Huskies running neck to neck, men shouting, women laughing, runners rumbling over the bay ice like low thunder. All headed in my direction. I bolt towards the porch and latch the door behind me, foolishly thinking the dogs will come straight through the door after me. My mother stands near the window with a flat iron in her hand, stamping the print of the hot iron on the windowpane to melt the ice so she can see the teams approaching. When the men bring the teams to a halt out on the same snowbank I had just vacated, she rushes outside to greet the visitors.

The first team to come to a halt on the snowbank is from Long Point. I recognize the man in the white cassock and the make of his komatik nose, curled like the tails on his white dogs. Most men from Long Point have komatiks with turned up noses. Their komatiks and seat boxes are painted green or red with red or white diamonds. Sealskin harnesses are decorated with red and green boot strings or ribbons. They match the bows on the rackets that are tied on the back of the wooden boxes lashed to the sleds.

The barking huskies quiet down while the loud voices of the men and women travel clear across the bay. I recognize my mother's friend from Long Point, and a man from Lance au Clair. They had all came to pick my mother up to take her with them to the time in Middle Bay.

During winter, to break up the long winter months, villagers all along the coast gather in a designated area to celebrate. People come from all directions, from Lance au Clair to St. Augustine, for the racket contests, gun sport, pie baking and dog sled races. The word spreads up and down the coast through Chesley Thomas, the lighthouse keeper on Greenly Island, who broadcasts the news by radio. The night of the time the air is filled with the sound of accordion, fiddle, and guitar music, and there's singing and square dancing in the local schoolhouse. This year, the chosen village is Middle Bay. Now I know why the dogs are all decked out.

There's so much excitement in the air. Some of the men were already taking swigs from their moonshine crocks. Some stayed outside untangling the dogs in their traces, while the women go inside to wait for my mother to get ready. Until then, I had no idea my mother was going up along to the time.

A short while later, they left. I watched the dog teams climb Western Gulch. Standing outside on the snowbank, I picture the square dancing going on in the schoolhouse I had never seen. There was no mention of the distance to Middle Bay. It didn't seem to matter at the time. I just knew that once my mother disappeared up over the gulch, she wouldn't be back for a couple of days.

Before leaving, she gave me strict orders to pile the wood in the bin and have the boys fill the water barrel when they got back from the woods. And not to forget to make the splits to start the morning fire just in case bad weather sat in. And, she said, *Keep dem youngsters inside so dey dont get frostbite, and make sure dat fire is out befer youse goes t bed. Dont use my Aladdin lamp, dem youngsters might break t shade. And I ll only be gone a day or two, I ll be ome t once.*

If luck was in Mum's favor, she'd be home again before Daid arrived back from the country. She hadn't been anywhere since she returned from the hospital after her cancer operation. She was extremely weak still but after much coaxing she agreed to go along with her friends. She looked back and waved at me before the teams went behind the ridge at the base of Western Gulch. I watched until they disappeared over the crest of Queen's Hill.

I pictured the women in frilly dresses, high wedge heel shoes with crinolines underneath and accordion pleated scarves knotted tightly around their necks with gold bands. I didn't see women dancing around the floor in sealskin boots, nor did I envision men dancing in their white cossacks. I visualized them all dressed to kill and swinging around and around. I once heard Mum say how different dances in Middle Bay were from ours. I heard others say that the Lance au Clair crowd swing too fast. Oh, how I longed to see them swing. I longed to hear the many accordions rattling out tunes like "*I se t bye*" and "*Chase me Charlie*" and see the men stomping their feet upon the wooden plank floors. I could hardly wait for my mother to come back and tell me all about the time in Middle Bay.

It was late Saturday afternoon when the storm struck. The wind howled its way all through the night and on into the beginning of the week. Ronald and Brian filled the water barrel. Even the smaller ones did their share. They all helped lug the wood to the bin and pile the splits beneath the stove to dry. Saturday night, I scrubbed the youngsters down in the galvanized tub near the fire, dressed them in clean long johns, put vamps on their feet, and sent them to bed. While the wind howled outside and the fire died down in the stove, I shaved the splits and put them on the oven door. Ritually, I hung their parkas, pinned the mittens and vamps together with clothes pins and slung them over the line above the stove. I swept the floor, fastened the latch on the door, and blew out the light before going to bed. But not before I wound up the Big Ben clock on the shelf above the radio next to my mother's room. Always, when my mother was away, I slept downstairs in her bed with the younger ones and with the baby in the crib nearby. The last chore of the night was to get the youngsters up to pee. It was always a difficult time. Some fussed and cried, while others slumped against my legs as they peed and often missed the pail. By the time I was settled down for the night, I was too tired to notice that the spot where I usually slept was already wet. The nail heads cracked and popped with the frost as if someone was pounding the house with rocks. It seemed I was barely asleep before I was up again, to the sounds of the wailing baby wanting to be changed and fed.

All day Sunday, while the storm raged, we stayed inside, passing the time away, playing lead marbles or a game of Old Maid. Keeping the fire burning was my responsibility. Keeping the noise down was impossible as the youngsters, cooped up inside our wee house, had very little space to vent their pent-up energy except on one another. The day dragged on, the night went by slowly, and by Monday the storm had lessened somewhat.

Yet it was still storming too much for Mr. Teacher Sir to make it to the schoolhouse from Bradore Plains. Caught inside for the third day, with hardly anything to do, there was nothing but chaos in our house. By nightfall I was ready to tear out my hair or the childrens' hair if my mother didn't come back from upalong soon.

There were no boarding houses or hotels in Middle Bay, just as there were no boarding houses or hotels in any of the villages along the coast. People opened their home to visitors as if they were prodigal sons returning, so glad they were of the company. It wasn't just when something was going on, but anytime. It was always a cause for celebration whenever a team of dogs came across the ice, or a boat steamed into the bay. During the games, everyone was so hyped the celebrations went on all day and all night until the final shot was fired or the last pie eaten. No one slept, not even the children. Everyone in the village, young and old alike, took part in the square dances, with men swigging from moonshine kegs out behind houses and snow banks. People hunkered down wherever they could. Some fell asleep where they sat, while others danced and spewed yarns all night long. When the celebrations were finally over and the last dog team left the village, it was a quietly accepted sadness to watch them go. That's the way it was.

It was around noon when I saw the first team coming down over the Gulch while the others followed single file behind. The air was so still, I could hear the men cursing and shouting, mingled with the sound of chain drags slowing the teams down. The tired dogs, with froth-frozen jowls and dangling tongues almost licking the ice, hung low in the traces as they crossed the bay.

Some veered off towards Mister Wobbler's place, while others headed in the opposite direction towards Bradore Plains. Relieved that my mother was finally coming home, I ran to the stove, threw a handful of loose tea in the pot and filled it to the brim with scalding hot water, then set it on the back damper to steep. Quickly, I sat the table. Excitement replaced the frustration I had felt all weekend long while the storm brewed. I was mere minutes away from hearing all about the time in Middle Bay. If I wasn't so petrified of the dogs, I would have ran down over the bank to greet everyone. Instead, I ran inside with the youngsters and stood safely near the window while the teams came to a halt on the snowbank.

The men looked as tired as the dogs in the traces. As soon as they had their mug-up, they pulled on their cossacks, uprighted the komatiks and left. My mother ran outside and waved goodbye as they headed out across the bay. I was disappointed because I hadn't got to hear a single word about the time in Middle Bay.

When the school bell rang, I headed up across the bay towards Madame Wobbler's place. I knew most of her sons and daughters had gone to the time and I knew for sure they'd all be talking about it for days to come. Since my mother had said very little, I was more than determined to find out about it one way or the other. I knew Mum wouldn't talk about it until someone came to the house later on that night. I couldn't wait that long.

Mrs. Wobbler seldom had anything nice to say about anyone, least of all my mother. And just by the way her face lit up when I walked through the door I should have known that something was up. I was barely inside the door before she began to tell me all about the time my mother had in Middle Bay. Until that day, I never really knew just how evil spirited she was.

Nar decent woman shud act like dat, she said, *Whoring after the men like a dawg in heat. Jest wait til Bob finds out, e will tame er down. Youse can stop glaring at me now, and git on home and tell er dats wot I sez.*

She stood back on to the stove, holding the tail of her dress in both hands, warming her ass like she always did. I resented the way she spoke about my mother but, being brought up to respect my elders, I said nothing. I just turned and walked out the doorway without even seeing or speaking with Matilda. Down deep inside, I knew my mother was in grave trouble. I knew when my father got wind of the gossip that Madame Wobbler was spreading there would be no telling what he would do. I was thinking all of this as I ran along the bay towards home. Normally, I would have told my mother everything. This time, I didn't say one single word.

It was early the next afternoon when I saw my father's dog team coming slowly across the bay. I wished with all my might that it wasn't him, but I recognized the dogs. He ran beside the caribou-laden komatik, commanding the tired dogs to go faster. As I watched him from the schoolhouse window, I silently prayed for a miracle to stop him from going over to Madame Wobbler's place that night.

When the gun was blued and the hunting gear stored in its rightful place and the deer hung, Daid's kill was always shared with others in the village. It was the thing to do. Hunting and trapping was his way of life. After supper, Daid cleaned the partridges and put them in the bowl for soup the next day. Then, while all the youngsters stood around him, he blew air in the partridge crops with a pipe stem, tied them with flour bag twine, and hung them up above the stove to dry. *When dem crops is full like dat, youse knows deres some pretty awful weather ahead yet,* he says to Mum. They seemed so contented, yet I sensed the dread ahead.

Mum filled the washbasin with warm water to scrub the youngsters while I did the dishes. After Daid left, Ronald, Brian, Raymond and Clyde went outside to randy down the hill. Parmenas was already back to school in Lanse au Clair. One of Uncle Willie's sons took him there by dog team.

Mum began to sing, switching from her favorite hymn to the one the youngsters learned most recently in school:

Do no sinful action
Speak nar angry word
Ye belong to Jesus
Children of the Lord
Christ is kind and gentle
Christ is pure and true
And his little children
Must be holy too
Deres a wicked spirit
Watching roun you still
And e tries ta tempt youse
Wit his charm and will
But ye must not hear im
Though tis hard fer you
To resist the evil
And t good ta do
For ye promise truly

In yer infant days
To renounce im only
And forsake is ways
Ye are new-born Christians
Ye must learn ta fight
With ta bad within you
And ta do t right
Christ is yer own Master
E is proud and true
An es little children
Must be Holy too-o-o-oo

After the dishes were washed and put away, I swept the floor and hung the dustpan on the nail behind the stove. I was only half listening to my mother singing as I strained my ears for sounds of running feet over the crusty snow.

I knew it was only a matter of minutes before he returned.

I knew he'd be running when he came.

Suddenly, Mum stopped her singing. *Yer awful quiet, my maid,* she said. *Wots eatin at yer guts? I noticed you been like dat all evening.*

Nothing, I said. *I m okay. I m just tired, dats all.*

Satisfied with my reply, Mum went back to her singing.

I heard the youngsters outside, hollering and laughing as they randy down the slope and across the bay. I know Alfreda and Naomi are among them. I know they're waiting for me to come outside to randy down the hill with them. It's such a beautiful night, with a full moon riding high in the sky. The wind is still.

Mum tells me to go outside once the dishes are dried and floor swept but I can't. Instead, I sit and wait, why I'm not sure, except I knew I had to stay inside the house. Voices fade in and out like the echo of tide riplets beneath thin ice. The Big Ben clock on the shelf ticks loudly in my ears like a dripping icicle in dead calm. I could feel the evil. It surrounded me like a thick black sheet. A mixture of shame and fear of the terrible truth scraped along my innards like a fine-toothed comb. Did I do wrong by not telling my mother about Madame Wobbler's intent? Should I have said, *I knows bout dat man from Long Point?* But that would have sent me sprawling in the corner with one of my mother's backhanders. She and I were on good terms these days and I wanted it to stay that way.

Amid the loud hooting laughter outside and my mother's singing, I mistook the sound of running feet for dogs chewing frozen blubber from the meal tub. Mum had the bone meal in the pot on the stove cooking, ready and waiting when Daid came across the bay. And before he hung the traces in the porch he chopped frozen blubber junks and threw it down from the scaffold into the tub. He sloshed the hot bone meal over the blubber and kept the dogs at bay with his feet while stirring the meal around with a stick. The dogs were fed before the sun went down.

Mum went to the room to put the sleeping baby in the crib. She entered the kitchen again, reaching for the washbasin to go outside and empty it out on the night.

The hand of fear clutches me around the throat when I hear the door bang sharply against the porch wall. Before she could say, *Wat in Gawd's name is dem youngsters doin out dere in dat porch?* the door breaks free from its hinges. An evil wind follows him in, smacking against my face where I'm crouching on the bottom step of the stairs near the kitchen door. There's no escape, there's nowhere to hide. Mum stands white-faced in the centre of the floor. Daid lunges at her. He grabs her by the hair and drags her to the floor. He trounces her time and time again with his brutal fists. The baby screams, frightened by all the loud shouting. Geddy and Elliott hide under the table and I hide with them, cowering beside them, protecting them and myself from the flying debris.

Mum screams at him to stop. He shouts and curses her. Their voices, his loud, hers high-pitched, penetrate to the rafters above. Unaware of the name calling, I see only my mother's busted lips, the cuts above her eyebrow, clean to the bone. Something falls from her mouth into the blood around her. I see the blood on the tail of her dress.

A scene from another time flashes cuttingly across my tortured mind. I see the whip come down across the bitch's back. I see his knarly hand clinging to the dog's tail while the whip comes down, time and time again. Trapped, the dog struggles in vain to free herself from his savagery. Her painful howls fill the morning air. Her unborn pups fall from her to the ground in front of me. Tremors slide over her injured body, over their injured bodies. I feel the pain traveling every inch of my being as the forgotten episode comes savagely to the surface of my fogged over mind.

But now I see the trapped and anguished look on my mother's face as he raises the wooden chair above his head. Time has no beginning and no end while it hangs suspended in mid-air. Something snarls. The Devil enters my soul and rips my insides out.

His glazed eyes clash with mine. With feet planted firmly in the limited space between us, unyielding I stand, my fists clenched tightly against my sides, loud hissing sounds escape from my mouth. I didn't fully understand that I wrestled with the Master of Death, only that I stood in my rightful place.

Gawddamn youse, I hiss.

His eyes, once laughingly blue like chips of sea ice, were now smoldering embers like I imagined the fires of Hell would be. His eyes and mine were deadlocked in a raging emotional battle, both unrelenting.

My mother cries piteously. The youngsters whimper. The dogs howl and the chair comes down. The kitchen explodes around us, splintered wood scatters in all directions, and his eyes of fire and brimstone break free from mine. The evil wind smacks hard against my face as it follows him out. Standing in the centre of the kitchen floor, with clenched fists still, I stare at the doorway, perhaps expecting him to come back. Then, writhing in the aftermath of evil and emotional shock, my legs crumble beneath me and I fall to the floor beside my battered mother. Shame, guilt and torment streak through me like the blade of his hunting dagger as Mum crawls towards the bedroom door. *I knew I had broken the fifth commandment. Worse still, I knew I was capable of a far greater sin. Why hadn t he killed me instead?*

Streaks of red, like paintbrush strokes, trail across the floor leading toward the bedroom door.

Git away frum me, sobs my mother as I reached to help her, *I doan want youse ta see me like dis.*

Like wounded animals, my mother bleeding from the outside and the inside, and I, from the inside, crawl to our respective corners. My mother's sobs filled the bedroom while I crawled back under the table with the youngsters. They cling to my neck, I cling to them, all three of us howling like wounded dogs. I was out of control, unable to soothe them or me. Our wailing traveled upwards through the rafters and the roof and on into the nightly wind. The others were still outside. I don't know why they hadn't heard the commotion within; perhaps it was fear that kept them away. A cold vapour tumbles across the kitchen floor as heat escapes from the open doorway where the splintered door hangs by one hinge.

When Brian, Raymond and Clyde finally came inside, the disarray of the kitchen was enough to send them scurrying upstairs to bed, afraid of what might happen if he came back. Holding the second youngest on my hip, I follow the rest upstairs. None of them were washed and dressed for bed. Beside the little blue poster bed, I knelt with them, Ronald had not yet arrived home from Uncle Nrst's place and I doubt if he even knew what had happened that night.

With eyes closed, hands folded in front of me, sobbing still, I lead them into prayer, *Now I lay me down to sleep*, I begin.

I deliberately skip the Lord's Prayer and go on to the last prayer Mum had taught us, the prayer we always said before going to bed.

> *Gawd bless Mummie*
> *Gawd bless Pim and Ronnie*
> *But Sissy, youse fergits Daiddy*
> *Gawd bless Brian and Raymond*
> *Gawd bless Clyde and Geddy*
> *But Sissy*
>
> *GAWD BLESS ELLY AND ROLLY*
> *KEEP WE ALL SAFE DIS NITE*
> *AND FOREVER AND EVER AND EVER*
> *AMEN. GAWDDAMN*

Then I tucked them beneath the quilts and went downstairs to rock the baby to sleep. He was still sobbing. Groping in the darkness for him, I picked him up and carried him from the crib to the rocking chair. I didn't sing as I normally would have, instead I just shushed him into silence while holding him closely to my chest. I could hear my mother's muffled sobbing coming from under the heavy quilts on her bed. Later, when I put Riley back in his crib, her face was turned to the wall.

Like a well trained dog whipped to heel, I picked up the broken teapot and the dented washbasin and placed them back on the stand. I shoved the splintered pieces of wood in the fire then swept the floor once more.

Driven by a desire to put things back together again, I filled the scrub bucket with hot water. With an old rag, and a cake of Sunlight soap, I scrubbed the kitchen floor, washing away blood and making the floor spotlessly clean. I put the kitchen back in order, but nothing could wash what had happened from my mind. I knew it was locked inside my soul forever.

Sometime during the night, Daid harnessed the dogs and left. A dark cloud hung over our lives. Something died inside of me; something else took its place. Perhaps it was on this day that I became my mother's keeper. Gone in the blink of an eye was my childhood; perhaps it was gone way before then. Perhaps God should have never allowed me to see the face of the Devil. But I had, and there was no turning back. In the days that followed, the cuts above my mother's eyebrows healed, the bruises disappeared. And slowly it seemed she became her old self again. She sent me back to school. The days passed slowly while I dreaded the day when he'd return home. I wished with all my might that he would stay away for good. But he didn't.

Between the time when my father nearly beat her to death, and February month, my mother had another miscarriage. The boys drove the tired and hungry dogs out to Bradore Plains to get our cousin Pernell to come and get her. No one in the village would take her to Long Point hospital because there was a storm brewing. Pern, as most called him, had the fastest team for miles around. The year before, while sealing, he had come across two Labrador dogs astray on the ice. He brought the starving dogs home and later one gave birth to eight pups. They proved to be even faster than the huskies trained in the harness. So, when the boys went out to fetch him he came without hesitation and was gone back across the ice with my mother in the coach box long before they arrived back home again.

It was Easter time when Daid returned home again and life went on as if nothing had happened. She was back to pouring his tea in his oversized mug, ladling the bologna hash in his plate, and sometime in the night I would hear a familiar grunting from the room below. I asked God that there be no more babies.

CHAPTER 7

⌂ THE CHANGING WIND

Daid's meagre catch of fish, one lone bulk, sits laughingly upon the knoll, battened down with tarpaulin and heavy boulders to protect it from the wind, rain, and the sun. Other fishermen, ecstatic by the over glutted codtraps and calmer seas, steamed back and forth to the stageheads several times a day with the gunwales barely above the water. Late into the night they gut and split fish by the light of coal-oil lanterns. Meanwhile, Daid cruised around in his longliner, carrying the doctor and the nuns from Long Point to other villages up the coast apiece. Once he got the longliner, and I have no idea where he got the money to buy it, fishing was the last thing on his mind, so Mum says, and that caused her to fret even more, *Be bedder fer im if e got es lazy ass out dere on dem fishin banks like t rest instead of fartin roun wit dem outsiders like hes Joey Smallwood or sumbody. Fat lot es gonna git outta dat now. Dere be nar copper agin dis fall t buy t grub with. Gawd only knows wots gonna appen to t lot of youse when I m dead and gone.*

Still weakened from her ordeal with cancer, Mum had spent most of the previous fall and winter in the hospital rebuilding her strength. Every time she left I worried she wouldn't come back.

We children hardly survived the freezing cold with so little firewood to burn. Daid never bothered to cut any in the fall like he was supposed to. The empty spot on the ground where the woodpile was supposed to be was enough to upset any daily routine. It was a constant reminder of the long cold winter still to come.

I was used to Mum's way of doing things. Her daily chores were always plotted out ahead of time. I tried to do things her way. But, without firewood in the bin and splits drying on the oven door each night, and pots of water heating on the stove to do the early morning wash, the day was lost long before I ever got started. While the rest were in school, most of my days were spent in the foothills cutting down small birch. I took the youngest three with me. I'd dress them up and take them with me to the foothills. I dressed them with extra sweaters beneath their parkas, two pairs of mittens on their hands, double wool vamps over their rubber boots, and scarves tied around their faces to ward off frostbite. The baby would be wrapped in quilts with only his eyes sticking out. I pulled him along in the coach box on Parmenas's komatik. Sometimes I hitched the two remaining dogs up to the water barrel komatik and went as far as Ladder Hill, a short distance from the house, where I could see birch sticking up through the snow. The wood I chopped down with the axe was barely enough to keep the fire going.

Every day, Parmenas and Ronald would chop more wood before the darkness came. On weekends, they'd go to Jack's Cove and bring back a partial load in the chocks. Sometimes, Eldon and John, Uncle Ernest's sons, went with them. They'd harness their five dogs, and together with the two dogs Daid had left home, sometimes they managed to cut and haul back a full load.

All of us, children still, battled the elements alone. No one in the village ever came to lend a helping hand. It was a never-ending struggle for Parmenas and Ronald trying to cut enough wood to keep the fire going so we wouldn't all freeze to death.

It seems we spent most of our waking hours outside either sawing wood or pulling water from Norse Brook Falls across the bay ice on the komatik. Sometimes we'd fight over whose turn it was to fill the water barrel. Most of the time it was me fighting with Parmenas. I figured since he was the oldest it was his place to make sure the water barrel was full and the splits chopped each night before dark. Sometimes my anger was such I cursed my father to the bowels of Hell and back again for not cutting the wood in the fall like he was supposed to.

Most evenings we went to bed early, burrowing down under the many quilts on our beds to keep warm. Seldom was there any coal-oil for the lamps. In late winter, we ran out of flour and potatoes. We no longer had bread and hash to eat. Sparingly, I spooned the remainder of our sugar on the porridge in the mornings. As each hopeless day went by, I searched in vain for signs of Daid's dog team coming across the bay. Days before either he or Mum came home again, we were down to a bare pantry shelf. When the potato boat arrived in the fall from Nova Scotia or Prince Edward Island or St. John's, there was no shipment of supplies for us.

Last summer, after Mum's long stay in hospital, Daid brought her back to Basin Island. He dumped her there and left again. Not that he was ever home much anyway. He came by for a few hours at a time, like a black cloud moving across a summer sky, then vanished around the point in his long liner, going off to God knows where.

He arrived home one day, in early September, and packed everything in his fishing boat that had lay idle on the mooring all summer long, and moved us back to the house in the bay.

Mum aired out the house. She took the cotton bag blinds down from the windows and opened them wide and let the wind and light flow through the house. She hung her lace curtains while I made the beds. Moving was always a special time. It was like having something new, it was something different, it was a strange feeling sleeping beneath the roof in the loft again. And for a few short days, when his six pipes hung in the rack near the stove, it felt good knowing Daid was home for a while.

The next time he went to Long Point, Daid came back home with two pigs, one he gave to Uncle Ernest, the other he kept in a makeshift stall in the cold pantry. When he left again, Parmenas and Ronald had to take care of the pig and each time they cleaned the stall, they shoveled the contents down in the brook near the house. In late October when he came back again, he butchered it. We would have backstrap bacon if very little else to eat.

I never saw Daid butcher the pig, and I was glad I didn't. But Uncle Ernest murdered his. I can still see the pig hanging upside down on the nail behind the storehouse with its hind legs tied together. I can still hear the horrible squeals in my ears. I can still see Uncle Ernest beating the pig to death with the hammer. I can still see the blood upon the ground while all of us stood around witnessing this terrible act of cruelty.

After Daid butchered his pig, and pulled his boat up high and dry on Fishing Point, he went inland fur-trapping with the Indians. When the first snows came he arrived back home. Within a few days, he harnessed the dogs and went back to the country to hunt caribou. He came back again before Christmas with two stags lashed to the komatik.

And on that particular day, like every other time he arrived back from the country, we would forget the hardships we endured while he was gone. It was a ritual with him, to slice up the caribou heart and liver, and fry it on the stove with the few onions still in his komatik box from his trip in the country.

After supper, Daid would blow air into the partridge crops. It was a gift, a special moment, when all the youngsters gathered around him, watching him stretch that skin down over the stem of one of his pipes and blow up the crops like a balloon. He'd tie flourbag string around them and hang them above the stove to dry. Sometimes there was one for each one of us. It was a good time then, the partridge crops hanging above the stove, with the stink enough to knock us of our legs, yet I'm sure we never noticed it. I was happy to see his six pipes sitting in the rack again and his sealskin boots and rackets hanging on the nail in the porch. His times at home were so few. When Christmas was over, he'd be gone again. Perhaps it was only me who watched his dog team moving further and further across the bay. Perhaps it was only me who longed for him to come back.

It was Easter time when I noticed my mother's belly taking on that oddly round shape again. I suspected she was in the family way, yet she couldn't possible be having another baby with only one breast, I thought. She couldn't, unless it was growing back!

Mum's moods were like the changing wind. I never knew from one day to the next from what direction she was blowing. I stayed awake at night, fretting and worrying about the changes going on around us.

On Sunday evenings, all summer long, young couples still hung out at our place. They came to our house to court. Mum didn't seem to have any control over the matter anymore. She was never one to drive anyone from her door. None of them were much older than Parmenas, Ronald or me, maybe three or four years in the difference. Some more, some less, especially the girls. I will never know her reasoning for not stopping them from carrying on so in our house. She didn't seem to care anymore about anything. Perhaps when all the young people came to the house it helped her to forget, or perhaps help her remember how life could have been if she'd had a chance. A whole year had gone by since her operation, and being in the family way again didn't help her illness much, although she hadn't been back to the hospital since Easter month. As hard as I tried to sympathize with her, I couldn't. I began to resent the upset in our house. I refused to help her anymore. I rebelled every time the courting couples came to our house. I didn't want them there, sprawled all over our beds, and I told her so. Perhaps it was the fear of Daid coming home and finding them there, but the few times he had come back they stayed away.

Aw, git t bed, my maid, and stop goin on wit yer fullishness, Mum says, turning her back on me.

How kin I when dere s udder people in dere? I shout at her.

Mum tried to shoo me into silence as my raised voice fell upon her deaf ears. Seething, I leave the kitchen and enter the addition attached to the house, out in the dark where the other room is. I crawl in the already overcrowded bed beside my younger brothers and sister. In the limited space, I lay on the edge of the springs fully clothed, with feet dangling over the edge, hoping somebody in the top bunk would get the hint and scrabble from it. Ignored and frustrated, I laid there in the dark, listening to the smooching sounds and low whispers coming from my own bed nearby. Our summer home was not much bigger than a lean-to, a small cabin, a place of shelter, with cramped quarters to sleep at night.

The smell of stale pee emanates from the enamel pot under the bed. I bend over to push it farther underneath so I don't smell that repugnant smell no more. Then, like a sudden windstorm, it happened. Satan was doing a full square dance set inside my head. While I wrestled with my subconscious uncontrollable evil spirit, laughter bubbles over my lips. I can't help but reach under the bed once more. If only they weren't lying In my bunk. I wish they were in Parmenas or Ronald's. I shudder. I can't dump that piss over their heads. If I do, she'll make me strip them beds, and scrub every single pillowcase and every single quilt, them walls, them floors, everything. My back will be broke in half before I'm finished. But that's tomorrow. What's the difference anyway? I'll still have to scrub them like I always do. It will probably be two whole days before I get that awful smell out, that sickly smell like dogs in heat.

What s dat maid laughing at, youse spose?

Swoosh!

It makes fer a fine t marr.

On Sunday night, the rain came pelting down, slapping hard against the felt on the roof and the windowpanes. Thunder such as I never heard before clapped together causing me to tremble beneath the covers. When I first heard those strange sounds, I thought it was the dogs under the house ripping each others throats out, or bitches eating each other's pups. I just hoped she wouldn't make me crawl up under the shored up foundation to save another litter. I knew there was still another bitch that hadn't dropped hers yet.

In the stillness, that pause that comes between the flashes and the aftermath of thunderclaps, was when I heard it again. So intently I listened then and on the ebb of the next fading clap I heard the angry shouts, a woman crying, then loud rapping upon the windowpane. *Is Agnes in dat Protestant hoors ouse?* screamed an unfamiliar voice. I jumped from my bed and ran to the kitchen. I stared at the blackness behind the bare windowpane, with rain streaking down like tears. I knew the woman was out there, but I couldn't see her. I expected my mother to do something, anything, not just sit there pretending nothing was going on. She continued her darning by the light of the Aladdin lamp. Perhaps she too was afraid. Uncertain, I stand there, wanting to let the woman in out of the rain, not wanting to for fear of what might happen.

Agnes solves my dilemma. She bolts from the bunk - not mine this time, thank God - like a scared rabbit, darting this way and that way, before finding her way through the open doorway between the kitchen and the porch. Her thick-lipped lover follows in hot pursuit, no doubt to slink away, to hide in the tall grasses beside the house until they were gone, the backless coward! I didn't have to worry about them courting in my bed anymore. Mum took care of that on the night I threw the piss-pot over their heads. From that moment on, I slept on the folding cot in her room, so they wouldn't have to deal with that humiliation any more. Agnes and her mother had a terrible row out there in the rain. My mother just kept on darning by the Aladdin lamp. When their voices faded upon the night, a deep shame washed over me. Those scared and angry words spoken by the woman kept running through my mind. Newcomers to the island, they too will hate Mum now, I thought.

The next morning, after a sleepless night, Mum and I had our own private row, the sounds of it reaching clear across the Basin and back. Even after she smacked me across the face, I didn't back down until I said it all. I even threatened to tell Daid (if he ever came home again) about all the things that were going on. I never did, I knew I never would, but I needed to say something, anything, to make her listen to me.

I m takin all the sass I m gonna take frum youse, my maid, she shouts. *As soon as Willie comes over ere in es flat agin yer goin back to the mainland wit im. P raps im and Violet can tame youse down a notch or two, cause I shur kint.*

True to her word, right after my twelfth birthday, Mum sends me to the mainland. Uncle Willie rowed over to the island in his flat one calm Sunday afternoon. All the fishing boats lay idle on their moorings, hardly moving. I could see the upper ridges of the Basin upside down in the water, the boats, long and silvery. Flat calm, that's what the fishermen called it. I heard the paddles rubbing in the bullocks, a dull clumping sound like someone beating on a half filled oil drum each time they sliced through the water. I knew it had to be Uncle Willie. My heart leaped with gladness. Mum never knew how eagerly I waited for his coming.

I visualize him with pipe clenched in his teeth, legs sprawled, feet braced against the laths, his long sinewy fingers gripping the paddle handles, leaning far over, pushing them out in front of himself, drawing back with all his might, grunting under the strain until the flat slices smoothly through the gut. That's where I pictured him to be. I ran down to the water edge, skipping rocks, watching the ripples playing silently on the water until he came into view.

Uncle Willie's visits were precious to me. Sometimes he took us around the island in his motorboat in search of driftwood. Daid never thought of things like that, he said it was our place to comb the landwash for pulp junks to keep the fire burning. Uncle Willie came to visit many times during the summer months, while Daid was like a puff of smoke that vanished on the wind.

Whenever I was able to escape Mum's prattling tongue, I'd run to the other side of the island to comb the beaches alone. In the quiet, I gathered my thoughts while walking along the landwash, watching the breakers roll and listening to the seagulls crying.

Mum always said that I should have been born a boy because I was useless to her as a girl. But who else, I wondered, would scrub the floors and make the beds, who would carry the pail to the landwash and dump it every single morning? Parmenas? Ronald? Fancy that, Parmenas scalding out the shit pail with Gillette's Lye, or Ronald, with his runny nose, leaning over the breadpan pounding dough, while mum's bloomers keep slipping down over his head. Fancy that. I could laugh all day!

Yer in good spirits t day, my maid, says Uncle Willie, as I walk out to the tops of my rubber boots to catch the painter he throws ashore.

Naw, I m jest tinkin crazy like. Glad t see ya, Uncle Willie.

For two whole weeks I stayed with Uncle Willie and Aunt Violet, who was my father's sister. I did absolutely nothing but follow my many older cousins about and read comic books. I read them all, all the western ones, "*Wild Bill Hickok* and *Billy the Kid,* *Have Gun Will Travel,* and "*Annie Oakley* and many many more. Stacks of them were piled high in one corner of the room. I never ever had so much free time on my hands.

A cowgirl's life didn't seem as complicated as mine. It seemed to be filled with excitement. I wouldn't mind standing around all day with a gun slung low on my hip, like Annie, sporting a rifle, wearing checkered shirts, cowboy hat and throwing a rope over my head. Yeah, I could hogtie Parmenas and Ronald real quick the next time they pelted me with rocks. Hogtied, I liked the sound of that. Perhaps Annie, I feel I know her now, would change spots with me for a spell. She only has one anti-Christ to contend with while I have six, some in shitty napkins still. I search for an address in the back pages, but there was none.

One morning, while I was still on the mainland with Aunt Violet and Uncle Willie, the dogs got hold of my cousin Sissy's cat and killed it. We took it over to Lanse Kinard and buried it. We said the Lord's Prayer and Sissy asked God to take her straight to heaven with Him. Perhaps he did, but I doubt it.

I didn't know why I acted the way I did. So many things were going on inside of me, perhaps I was gone off my rocker just like my mother said I was, or perhaps it was fear of being alone on tomorrow's dawning. I was changing, more so than my mother. I was unsettled, right down to the roots of my tortured soul. I hated housework! I was so sick of minding youngsters too. All I wanted to do was to escape to the other side of Basin Island, beyond Miscopic Rock. I yearned more and more for things I couldn't have. It didn't matter so much before, but when Alfreda came back from St Paul's River on the *Northern Pioneer* the first week in July, wearing shiny black buckled shoes like Naomi, it smarted. If only I could own a pair of ankle socks and, just for once, twist them in every shape like Alfreda and Naomi. I heard the nurse Alfreda had stayed with had a real bathtub. I heard Alfreda had her ears rinsed out. They were stogged full of wax, she said. She had many pretty dresses too. If only I could have pretty barrettes for my thick brown hair instead of those damn yellow ribbons. I was so sick of yellow ribbons.

How did Alfreda get to own such fine things, I wondered. Her mother and father were as poor off as mine.

Selina Wobbler tosses her blond silky wavy hair, scrubbed clean with rainwater. The ringlets hang down and curled tight waves roll back from her forehead, held in place above her ears with glass rose clips. Those girls all have their own accordion pleated neckties, with gold bands tight enough around their necks to choke them. I'd die for a store bought lace hanky, toilet scent and a frilly dress, the kind with the satin trim. My, those snobs, how proud they walk, holding their heads so high in the air, walking on ahead of me, holding hands on a Sunday afternoon. They look back at me as I lag behind, snickering while I retreat farther and farther behind, feeling so out of place, ever conscious of my turned down rubber boots, with grey woolen stockings rolled over the tucks so I don't chafe my calves some more. There were already three brown burned circles around my calves. The boys appear around the bend. They run to catch up with Naomi and Alfreda, who proudly show off their finery, still holding hands. Alfreda so stuck up now, in her frilly crinoline dress, with the pink satin trim, points in my direction. Oh, if only Cass wasn't among them.

Quickly, before he turns, before he sees, before I die of humiliation, wallowing in my impoverished state, I squat down among the tall blades of grass growing beside the path. *Old Squaw*, they chant. I slink away like some wounded dog until I'm out of sight behind the house, then run, like I always do, behind Miscopic Rock.

If only Mum hadn't promised me a birthday cake, if only I hadn't boasted to all of them that she had. Purposely I stayed away all day long so she could surprise me. I promised Alfreda I'd give her a piece of the cake if she would be my friend again, a large piece with thick hard icing, the kind like candy, I promised. The stove was cold when I arrived back home late that afternoon. No sweet chocolate aroma wafted past my nose. Instead, my mother rushed forward to clout me upside of the head, *I thought I tole youse, ya jeesas ard ead, t stay ere and elp me wit dem youngsters. Where in jeesas name wuz youse hat all day?*

Alfreda says, *See, I tole youse, youse jest made dat hup agin.*

I cried myself to sleep that night, for the loss of a cake that was there perhaps only in my imagination, for the loss of Alfreda, and for the want of my mother's affection that I felt I never had.

The next time Mum went to the mainland she brought back two half moon cakes, black chocolate coated, rich with sweetness, '*Ere,* she said, *youse jeesas ard ead, dats fer youse, I spose yer happy now, my maid!*

Mum's cruelty cuts me like a knife. Nothing can take the place of her broken promise, a cake she promised to make with her own two hands. The half moon cakes sit on the ledge above my bed. At night, I hear the mice happily nibbling. I hear the stiff plastic wrap rustling.

I complain to Mum always now.

Why do I hab t lug aw t water, why do I hab t chop aw dat wood hup, why kint youse make dat lazy Pim git off es ass and do sumting fer a change? All he eber doos es catch scuplins every day. I m not doin nuddin no more. I m not, I shout, stomping my feet over and over again.

Smack!

Her backhander sent me sprawling in the corner, *Youse doos wot I sez youse doos, ya jeesas ard ead,* she yells. *I m not takin no more of yer fullishness. Now, pick up dat hoop and git to dat pond. I ll beat ta livin piss outta youse, my maid, if youse sasses me agin as shur as jeesas made little green h pples, I will!*

She yanks the hoop down off the nail and throws it after me as I run outside to escape her madness. Her final stance is to slam the door shut to block me from her mind. Angrily, snatching the hoop up from the ground, I fit it over the rim of the galvanized buckets that came tumbling after it. I step in the center of the hoop then grudgingly stomp my way to Beetle Pond. Still bawling, I filled the water barrel to overflowing. Then I sawed the wood on the sawhorse, and stacked it in the corner of the porch. All the while I'm doing her bidding, I could see Parmenas lying on his stomach on the wharf with a jigger line, catching tommy-cod and sculpins and brushing flies of his head like the lazy dog he is. Suddenly, I no longer like my brother.

CHAPTER 8

⌂ **THE LOOKOUT**
September 12, 1959

Where s youse off ta agin now, my maid! Youse bedder not be goin over da odder side of dat iland. Youse knows dem dogs es runnin loose over dere! Mum's voice runs into nothingness as I sped up over the hill, past Daid's stagehead, across the mud flats, towards Saltwater Pond. Inwardly, I hurt, I cry out loud, venting out my frustrations on the earless wind.

I knows I shudda stayed up yere in t first place! I knows she wuz gonna make me do aw dat work agin. Aw I ever doos is wash dem shitty napkins, split da wood and lug water frum Beetle Pond. Naw, dat Daid, he cudden lit me go wit im. Naw, he habs to take Ronnie all the time. E nebber lits me go hinny weers wit im. Jest cuz I m a stupit girl, I habs ta do all da work. Dat Pim nebber habs ta do nuddin. I m sick and tired of doin eberting. I hope I m dead win I gits up ta marr.

Loneliness breaks over me like the sea over Gun Point Shoals.

Unchecked, the tears run down my face, dropping on my sweater sleeves. In defiance, not heeding my mother's command, I kept on running until I reach the forbidden other side of the Basin to Mister Wobbler's Lookout. From Lookout Hill, I can see every cove and marshland on the back side of the island. Heavy surf pounds the rocky ledges near Gun Point. The water spews high into the air, several seconds pass before the booming sound echoes across the island, carried along by the heightening wind. Far off in the distance I see white spray pounding the cliffs below the ridge of mountains on the mainland. The mail boat with flattened sails is tied securely to Wharf Island wharf. Dark rolling clouds move swiftly across the midday sky. The sea is too heavy for the fishing schooner to come down the coast today.

I hear gunshots coming from the direction of Saltwater Pond. I see no birds on the wing. It's a good sign; we might have teal stew for supper tonight. I see no sign of Daid and Ronnie. If only I could run over to the next ridge, I might see them coming back. But my mother's voice keeps playing over and over inside my head like a broken gramophone record. *Youse bedder not go over dere where dem dogs is at, my maid! How many times doos I have ta tell youse not ta wander off, youse jeesas ard ead!*

Saltwater Pond is directly below the ridge. I see the white lops dance across its surface. Behind the pond, the land slopes downwards, a gentle lazy curve toward the sea, touching the white pebble beach of Seal Cove. Little ponds, dark spots of water, here and there on the reddish marshes. Saltwater Pond is just beyond the hill above Mr. Wobbler's Lookout. I think about Naomi sleepwalking in the dark of night. I think of what might have happened if Mr. Wobbler wasn't there to catch her before she fell headlong into the pond's muddy depths. A chill runs through me.

Everyone on Basin Island is waiting on the arrival of the schooner to sell their cod. Due to stormy weather, she was late. There's ten bulks of dried cod upon the Lookout belonging to Mr. Wobbler's crowd, sitting in uniform rows all along the ridge of the hill. Wrapped in tarpaulin anchored down with rocks, they stand like puncheon barrels against the noonday sky.

Like everyone else, Aunt Carrie, my mother's first cousin, is still on the island and I wish I could go over there to visit her. Her house is at the far side of Basin Island. Mr. Wobbler's dogs, I'm sure, are over there. I can't leave the safety of the ridge. I can't see her, but I know my mother is watching me from the window. Once I go beyond the ridge she won't be able to see me anymore. I hear her voice still inside my head; I hear the command in her angry voice.

The wind and sun upon my face soothes my battered spirit as I sit there on the ledge hugging my knees. My mind wanders in every direction. I think about Aunt Carrie's house in the bay, with the stained glass windows that throw purple light across the kitchen floor when the sun strikes it. I remember the small green wooden crate near her stove where I always sit when I visit her; where I watch her smack bluebottle flies on the windowpanes. They lay dead, belly up, in heaps on the glossy windowsills. While she waits for Uncle Kelson's boat to come in the bay, she serves me brown potatoes and teal gravy from the iron pot in the oven, extra potatoes she cooked just for me. My mother never browns her potatoes, she says it's just a waste. Boiling them is so much quicker.

Aunt Carrie puts the swatter down only long enough to dish up the potatoes, so carefully she arranges them on a pretty rose patterned plate.

She hums all the while, then hands me a fork with real silver tines, *Don t teli yer mudder I gave youse dat,* she whispers, then picks up the swatter again while I wolf down the potatoes like a starving dog.

I long to be down in Seal Cove combing the landwash with her. I wish I could walk quietly beside her and hear the soft pitch of her voice amidst the breakers on the shore, the gulls soaring and the sand larks dancing sideways across the sand. Such contented moments. I wish I could spend them with her gathering driftwood along the shore. I'd rather be doing anything than be over there across the cove, washing shitty napkins and listening to my mother complain all day long.

The long summer was nearly over, and I could hardly wait to be back in the bay in our winter home. If Mr. Wobbler or my mother only knew how many oaths I put on his back for letting his dogs run loose, for restricting me from roaming over the island like I was used to. If he kept his dogs chained on like everyone else I wouldn't have to be stuck up here on this ledge. I'd be over there in the cove visiting Aunt Carrie. It enters my mind that perhaps she too was afraid of the dogs, since I could see no sign of her down along the landwash. Everyone knew about the dogs. The talk all summer was about Mr. Wobbler's dogs running loose all over the island. Gawddamn him and his dogs, I say!

Dark clouds move swiftly across the sky, covering the sun entirely. A mere second later the sun springs out from beyond the clouds again. A sudden flash of red catches my attention. A patch of bright, ripe, redberries, they hang down from the mound half hidden behind blackberry bushes, like red cherries, enticing, so big, so ripe. Teal stew and redberry pie for supper. Mum would be so pleased. I leap from the safety of the ridge to fill the tin cup and the glass jar I'm holding, and then scoop as much as I can in my sweater sleeve before going back to the safety of the ridge.

Suddenly, theres a strangeness on the wind. I sense the danger, like a million sea lice crawling over my skin. I jump up from my kneeling position to run back to the safety of the ridge but its too late. The ridge is now occupied. Five pairs of yellow eyes stare back at me. The dogs' low guttural growls stop me cold. There's nowhere to run. Commonsense tells me not to run, the dogs stand between the ridge and me. Then, four of them surround me, moving in for the attack. The leader stands upon the ridge, blocking my escape.

Panic-stricken, I search the ground for something, anything, to ward them off. There is nothing here in this godforsaken place; nothing stands between me and them but the sudden deadly calm that hangs in the air around me. My heart is pounding loudly in my ears.

Brazenly, the dogs circle me, honing in, they seem to be testing me, their long lapping tongues licking the froth forming around their jowls. he nearest one hugs the ground then leaps towards me from a crouching position. I strike it with my fist. It backs off, and then circles again. The second one lunges, my knuckles make contact once more, hitting them again and again as they close in on me from all directions.

Swinging the sweater frantically over my head, I see the berries spill onto the ground. Huge prancing paws squish them in the dry mud. There's a flash of red again, this time like blood, my blood. Oh Gawd! A vision of an injured dog down among the pack dances inside my head. I see the others snapping jaws make contact with the injured animal. Too weak to fight, I see it being ripped apart as it succumbs to death. I see my soul inside the weakened dog.

Fright suddenly turns to rage. It bellows up inside of me leaving my mouth in a long string of curse words. Each time another dog rushes towards me, I lunge towards it screaming, fighting and pummeling them with my fists, *Youse sons o bitches. I ll fix youse if youse tinks youse is gonna eat me. I ll kill youse first, youse sons o bitches.*

As the heat builds up inside me, five pairs of snapping jaws hone in for the kill. I feel the tug from behind, a hot searing, tearing sensation rivets through me. The impact spins me around on the heels of my rubber boots. I see a large piece of my flesh go down the throat of the dog that savagely tore at my right hip. I'm spinning around and around in circles now, trying to ward them off, but I'm no match against those brutal fangs as they drag me to the ground.

There's a whisper on the silent wind, a voice that echoes inside my head, *Fall on yer face, fall on yer face*! I heed the command. The prickly moss comes up to meet my face, yet I feel no pain as the dogs lifted me up off the ground, ripping the flesh away from my bones. The smell of mud blocks out the stench of dog sweat and warm blood. I tear the moss from the ground in fistfuls.

Perhaps it's only in my mind that Mr. Wobbler struts across the lower ridge heading in the direction of his house. Perhaps I only imagined his favorite dog, Leader, trailing close to his heels, lifting its head to sniff the wird before turning away,

MISTER WOBBLER! MISTER WOBBLER-R-R-R! ELP ME-E-E-EE! ELP ME-E-E-E, I was screeching so loudly, yet man and dog continued on down over the ridge with heads bent low in the wind, leaving me there to die.

The wind blows much fiercer now, sweeping lops rolling outside the gut, behind Mr. Wobbler, rushing against the mail boat tied to Wharf Island, yet all around me the wind seemed still.

In a sudden rush, it comes to me. I'm gonna die. God is punishing me for disobeying my mother. It comes to me as I see the last of Mr. Wobbler's head disappearing down behind the ridge in the footpath leading towards his house.

Fear and regret ripple through me. I'm only vaguely aware of the snarling going on and my flesh being ripped from my body, and that I am clutching the mossy ground. I talk out loud, *Oh Gawd, don t let Mum lose t baby, don t let im die because of me. Youse knows tis not his fault. Youse knows, youse knows, youse knows!* A loud and piteous wailing fills my ears as a fire rips through my body, erupting inside my chest.

Above the ridge appears a soft luminous light. Something is floating in the air, I think it's my mother. I sense her calling me, yet I hear no sound. Wispy tails of shimmering light trail behind her, like smoke from candlelight. Her arms, long and elusive like stretched molasses candy, reach out towards me. I reach towards her. She floats away. *Mum. Mum. Save me. Save me. Mum!*

Up there above the ridge I'm looking for something, I don't know what or who. Down below me I see something struggling on the ground. I see dogs ripping something apart, huge paws braced against the moss. I can actually see the claws on the paws. I can see the fangs, the snapping jaws, and the red moss.

And then I see my mother's face. I feel her screaming, yet I hear no sound. I see her coming towards the dogs in a crouching position. She's crawling towards me but something holds her back, a twisted rope, something is chomping at the wind, it fights to breathe, it's blue – like Ronnie – it's drowning! I see the pain in her face. I see her covering something on the ground. *NO! GAWD. NO!!!*

CLARISSY! CLARISSY! IS YOUSE DEAD? IS YOUSE DEAD?

One of Mr. Wobbler's sons is standing over me, staring down at me with wild and frightened eyes. I stare back, unable to grasp the reality of the moment, until I see between his legs, some distance away, two yellow eyes piercing mine, licking blood from its mouth. I will myself to reach towards his outstretched hand.

He yanks me from the ground. In haste he runs up over the ridge, dragging me behind him. Like a dead seal, he drags me by the flipper towards his father's house. I keep falling down. I think I have no legs.

His other brothers run along beside him, keeping off a distance. Raoul swings an iron over his head, keeping the dogs at bay. I see them running in the same direction. Raoul hit the dogs with the swinging iron, chasing them away. Gabe drags me down over the hill, through the open doorway of the house and drops me at his father's feet.

Mr. Wobbler stands in the centre of the floor, his coat still on. He lets out an awful yell. Hands reach down to pluck me up again. *Don t put er on dat chair. Run down to t store and git dat old one!*

Minutes pass before one of them returns with the broken split-seated chair. Plunking me in it, they pin me against the table, holding me upright. I notice the missing rungs, the missing board from the centre of the seat, the different colors of paint splashes that have dried on it. Mister Wobbler's sons, all three of them, jump around the floor wringing their fists in the air, blaming each other for letting the dogs run loose. Mr. Wobbler paces back and forth in front of me, repeating over and over again,

We gotta git er to t hospital. She s bleedin ta deat! Howse we gonna git er over to the mainland on a day like dis? I tole youse not ta let dem dogs run loose!

Matilda stands near the doorway, trembling, ready to take flight as soon as I keel over.

I'm aware of the large puddle of my blood on the floor around the chair. I'm aware of my naked state. Nothing remains on my body but my tattered short sleeve sweater, with frazzled ends and strings of wool dangling above my navel. My rubber boots, still on my feet, are punctured here and there.

My legs are opened. I tried to close them but I can't! Through the opening in the splintered chair, my flesh lays open from my inner thighs. Large splashes of red drip silently from a coil hanging down. It resembles the guts from a duck. Bones show through my raw and ragged flesh. I remember the large chunk of flesh tossed to the back of the dog's throat.

I know I'm sitting on open wounds. It enters my mind as I watch my blood splatter onto the floor and hear them fighting among themselves that I'm already dead in their eyes. It's just that I haven't fallen yet. I know they're not able to save me. I know who would.

Mr. Wobbler has purplish lips in a chalk white face. He tries in vain to get the attention of his three sons, his words go over their heads, and his hands shake as he rakes them through his graying hair. He stops his pacing only long enough to stare down at me when I faintly began to speak.

Get Daid! Daid will save me! Don t tell Mum. She s gonna lose t baby! Git Daid. Daid will sa-ave me!

Dear Jeesas! Y-ees! Bob knows wot t do. Run Matilda. Run quick. Find er fodder. Tell im t dogs got Clarissy.

Don t tell Mum, I call silently after her vanishing back.

I can see Matilda running with all her might up over the hill. When she's out of sight, Mr. Wobbler paces again. The fighting among the three sons continues. They're certain now that Daid will have all their dogs shot or the Mounted Police will lock them up for letting the dogs run loose. God knows how much they will have to pay, they say.

Mr. Wobbler begins to scold me.

Tis all yer fault for been over yere in the first place. Now dis is some fix. Yer fodder won t git youse to the mainland in dem seas. Youse knows youse gotta go t hospital.

I m not goin t hospital. I m not. Daid will be here t once! Daid will save me! I say inside my mind. Mum's hands, black and blue, flash before me. *Dats dem nurses sticking dem long needles in my arms, dats wot happened!* she said, when I inquired about the bruises.

My eyes are on the latch, on the dirty hemp twine, knotted in the hole of the stick, sitting in the slot, grease oil and dirt caked all around it. I willed my father's hands to lift it from the slot and walk through the doorway. I willed it with all my might.

The tingling begins in my lips and face. I feel numb and cold. I desperately need to see my father's face. I know if he doesn't come I'm gonna die. I know it as sure as I know I'm sitting on this split-seated chair. I hear the wind again amidst the shouting going on around me. With a mighty roar, the wind soars through me. An eternity passes before it drives the door back against the wall. Daid came bursting through it. *See, I told youse dat Daid wud save me,* I say inside my mind.

The illusion becomes reality when I heard him shout, *Sweet Jees-as!*

He rushes forward and scoops me up off the broken chair.

The smell of the wind is on his clothes, then he runs with me towards the settee in the parlor, shouting over his shoulder at Mr.Wobbler, *Git some quilts! Quick!*

Mr.Wobbler doesn't know where to find them. Madame Wobbler didn't tell him where she kept them before she went up the coast, he said. *Find dem quilts!* he yells at Matilda, who came in behind Daid. Matilda runs upstairs.

Daid left me on the settee as he rushed to the downstairs bedroom. He yanks Madame Wobbler's spread off the bed. As quick as a wink, before I could say, *Dont leave me, Daid!* he's back again. He wraps me up, kneels down beside the settee and holds me close to his chest. Rocking back and forth, he reassures me over and over again that I'm going to be okay, as I kept repeating that I don't want any needles. I kept remembering Mum's bruised hands.

A mixture of emotions washes over me. I've never been this close to Daid, neither had I ever been this cold. While he's holding me, rocking me like a baby, something wet falls on my face.

Why es Daid bawlin? Daid, dont bawl. I m so cold. I feel a shudder go through my body and he holds me tighter still. I hear him curse. *Youse gawddamn stupit sons of bitches. Where s yer jeesas sense, letting er sit dere on dat chair all dis while? SHE S GOIN IN SHOCK! I gotta git er t hospital! I m gonna lose er if I dont. DAN! BRING YER BOAT ROUND T STAGE EAD. QUICK!*

Not mine, Bob, take yer own, dats all I have ta fish wit!

Youse measly grey-headed son of a bitch. Deres no time ta git mine from t Basin. I m taking yours. If I dies crossin over to the mainland youse can have mine. I wont need er den, now will I? RAOUL, FETCH DAT HANDBAR!

The ceiling spins around and around and the angry voices fade away.

The long slim boat driven by a four-Acadian horsepower motor nitpicks her way through the thunderous seas, slowly down in the lull, then gathering speed and racing ahead of the next one, fighting to reach the other shore. For those on the island and the mainland watching the boat stand up on end, then dive down beneath the waves, it must have seemed that Daid and Raoul would never make it to Red Rocks. I, in my unconscious state, never knew how close they came to death.

A huge wave hit me in the face, bringing me out of the blackness. My face is pressed against a coil of rope that smells of oakum, of lube, of gasoline. Dried herring scales are on the green planks. The bailer bucket floats in the water beside me. The turbulent sea is barely inches from my head.

Raoul crouches down beside me holding the tarpaulin around us as seawater streams down his face. Above the roar of the waves and the puttering of the motor I hear my father's voice, *If I kin git er thru t gut we ll be aw rite*, he shouts to Raoul.

The boat slowed down. I heard strange voices,

Is dat May?

No, tis Clarissy.

Clarissy? Wot appened wit er?

Dan s dogs gotta hold of er!

Is she hurt real bad?

Real bad, bye. I don t know if we can save er. She lost all er blood.

Here, catch dat painter quick!

Whose dat dere talkin bout? Dat kint be me. I m okay, I say inside my mind.

It's quiet here inside the cover. How did I get here? Cocooned like a butterfly, I see the sun shining through the opening in the roof above me. I can sense the wind. I don't know what I'm doing here but I know I'm in Godfather's car. *Why can t I move? Where s Daid? Where s Daid?* A face appears. It stares down at me through the opening, blocking out the sun. It doesn't speak. Suddenly there are several faces, faces of angels, all dressed in white with crucifixes hanging around their necks. They carry me along on a white bed. Where did I see that bed before?

Where s Daid? Where s Daid?

I have a sense of moving along a long white corridor towards bright lights. I'm draped in white. Six angels with silent faces move around in front of me. Their mouths open and shut, open and shut, like trout on dry land. One comes closer, looks deep into my eyes, while another holds a long miniature bottle with a pointed needle on one end. She flicks it gently with her finger.

Git away frum me! Daid! Daid! Where s Daid?

I feel the plunge go deep inside my heart as she jabs me in the left hip. My screams are loud only in my own ears. A burning fire ripples through every fibre of my being. I trash wildly about. Something pins me down; they come at me from all directions with long pointed fangs.

DAID! D -AID!

When I open my eyes again, he's sitting in a chair beside me; his eyes like two piss holes in the snow, his face dead white. I see the white bandages on his arms. I see bags of blood with tubes attached. An angel in white comes towards me with a pair of scissors in her hands; she begins to cut away the dress I'm wearing.

I must be dead. Why am I wearing dat frilly dress? Dats Naomis dress! Git it hoff! Git it hoff! Git it hoff! No, dont cut it hup. Dont cut it hup.

She continues on with the cutting, soothing me with her soft voice, telling me it's okay. The scissors make contact with my skin and burn down deep inside. I scream and scream and scream.

Much later, I'm told that before they put me on the hand-bar and carried me to the boat, someone put Naomi's new dress with the crinoline on me. Perhaps they thought that I would die, or perhaps they didn't want anyone to see my nakedness. Whatever the reason, I was dressed for death when I arrived at the hospital in Long Point.

I woke up to the sound of a woman screaming. She's there on the table next to me. Angels run to her. She gives birth. Daid is there beside me still. I feel weights on my arms. It feels like two large rocks are pinning me down. The room spins, so does Daid, and so do the angels as they move away. So do the blueberries and redberries, which are rolling everywhere. I sit up with my heaving. The ground turns red. I see the blood, *Git away. Git away. Git away.* Once more, my father's voice fades away.

On the shelf on the far wall stands a statue of Mary, draped in blue.

The shawl covers the cream colored gown she's wearing. The gown reaches down to her pink clustered toes. Her head is bent in prayer, her hands clasped beneath her chin. On another shelf beside her sits her prickly heart, with purpled painted blood dripping down over it. It's the Catholics' fault. How cruel are they to put her heart up there on the wall.

Why didn't they bury it where it belongs? My stomach turns. I look upon her face instead. Where have I seen a statue like that before? I remember now. Alfreda was with me, we kissed her feet, so long ago.

I sense peacefulness in these high white walls, behind this big oak door. Tables with dangling knobs stretch across the beds, two beds, no three, all empty with smooth white cotton spreads, crisp and clean, covering each bed. On each side of the bed where I lie, there are shiny metal stands with plastic tubes hanging from hoops that hold bags of blood upside down. One bag is filled with clear liquid, water perhaps. All tubes trail downwards to my arms. I am attached to it, it to me. I try to sit up.

Sister! Quick! someone shouts.

I turn in the direction of the voice. I see my father standing in a white gown. This time I know he's alive. He isn't dead, as I suspected. We are both alive. I can speak. The roar of the sea has left my ears. I can feel the hot tears run down my face.

The angels are all around me now. I recognize the nuns as they come streeling through the doorway. *Bien, ma petite, you up!* says one, gently stroking my cheek. Her hands are warm and soft, their pink flesh covers mine. I'm aware of the endearment. I sob harder now.

Es Mum and t baby okay? I ask.

Deres nuddin t madder wit yer mudder or Rolly, dere okay, says Daid.

He thinks I'm talking about Rolly. I don't tell him the difference. I'm so weak I can't stop bawling. The nuns check the blood flow, the white liquid, and the mummified bandages all over me. Holding a needle, one nun jabs me again. This time I have no fear. She pats my hands, then leaves me alone. But I'm not alone. Daid is there beside me. I'm safe now.

Days and nights go by while I drift in and out of a nightmarish sleep. Each time the dogs attack me I wake up screaming, but Daid is always there beside me. When the waters inside my mind had calmed, Daid leaves me to go back to Basin Island.

It's a Sunday afternoon. Mum, Aunt Carrie and Aunt Violet come to see me. Aunt Carrie brings me a bright red apple that she takes from her sweater coat. The potato boat must have come and brought supplies, I thought.

I wish I had more, she said tearfully, dabbing at her eyes with her sweater sleeve. *It shud hab happened t me, not youse. I m t one dats always down round the landwash. Gawd musta meant it dat way, I spose.*

I look towards her. I can't take my eyes of the apple she's holding up for me to see. I can't look upon my mother's face, but I can feel her fidgeting near the bed on the opposite side. Suddenly, it's all too much for her. She begins to yell and cry all at the same time.

Youse wudden lissen ta me, youse jesas ardhead. I told youse not to go past dat ridge. How many times do I hab t tell you? Now, look at t state yer in!

Up until then, Aunt Violet hadn't spoke one single word, just gazed at me with sad and frightened eyes. Now tears are streaming down her face. Aunt Violet dabs at her eyes with a white lace hanky that she yanks from her sweater sleeve. Through blurred vision, I see my mother's stomach jerk up and down. I know the baby is still in there, safe and sound. The vision I saw, I was sure it was real. How could I tell her what I had witnessed? Above all else, surely then, she would think that I'm really gone in the head.

Shaddup, May, shaddup! Luk wot youses doin to dat maid agin! Aw youse ever doos is knock dat maid down. Tis all yer fault shes layin dere half dead in dat bed. If youse paid more mind to er instead of working er t deat, she wudden be trampin aw over t island. Now shaddup, before I trows dis gawddamn h apple at youse!

Aunt Carrie didn't know I was crying because my mother and the unborn baby lived. No one understood.

My fault, my mother said angrily. *I ll tell youse whose fault it is. Yers. Dats who. Shes always chasin yer ass about. Dats probably why she went over dere dat day. I tole er not to go near dat gawddamn hole where you lives.*

As they took turns stretching across the bed, wringing their fists up under each other's noses, I sobbed even louder. Aunt Violet sobbed right along with me.

Shush child, dont bawl no more. Youse gonna tear dem stitches out. Shush child, shush! she coos, rubbing my hand. I'm wailing now, out of control again.

The sister enters. She ushers them all from the room, including my mother. She jabs me with another needle to calm me. She turns me on my side and pats me on the shoulder, *You sleep, ma petite, you sleep!*

I don't know what it was I wanted from my mother. I don't know what my mother wants from me. Even though I feel ashamed of her at times, I know I need my mother. I know if one of us must die it must be me, not her, never her! I'm certain I'm alive now for the unborn baby's sake. For all their sakes. Perhaps I've always known, perhaps this is why I'm so disturbed within. The baby and I are connected somehow, he's a part of me, I'm a part of him. I didn't know or understand how this could possibly be. I just know it is.

I hear my mother's voice again. *Youse gotta be t mudder to dem youngsters when I m dead and gone. Dat lazy no good fodder of yers. Aw dats good fer is to t run about. Youse aw gonna starbe t deat when I m gone. Promise me, my maid, youse wont lit im give youse all away. Promise.*

Even Aunt Carrie didn't know the real reason why I trekked over the island. Out there, I unshackle my spirit. I run with the wind in my hair, the sun on my face, and the sound of the breakers in my ears. I escape my mother. I run from them, from everything. For a few short hours I allow myself to forget about her impending death and the future up ahead for me and them. I unshackle my spirit and fly across the marshlands and comb the landwash, looking for treasures that wash up upon the shoreline. Anything, so I don't have to think about the future closing in so fast.

Most days, I tried to block it from my mind, but lying there in that hospital bed it was all I could think about. What will I do when the time comes for her to leave the youngsters and me all by ourselves? What will I do? *Oh Gawd, why doos she hab t die? Why kint youse make her bedder Gawd?*

CHAPTER 9

⌂ THE GUARDIAN ANGEL
October - 1959

I spent almost a month in Notre Dame Hospital, recuperating. About a week after my encounter with the dogs, I was moved to a ward with other patients. There was a woman there from Buckle's Point. She had been badly burnt and would stay in hospital for almost a year. She was someone to talk to, someone to listen to my woes. What I remembered later is her husband sitting by her side, always there.

As my body began to heal, and I was able to pull the stitches out of my wounds, I realized that I hadn't said my prayers and I needed to say my prayers. Even though I couldn't walk or get out of bed, each night after the rosary was heard over the intercom and the lights were turned off, I would try to get up on my knees to pray. Since I wasn't a Catholic, I needed to say my own prayers and I felt that if I didn't get on my knees God might not hear me. After many attempts, I fell out of bed onto the floor. The lady from Buckle's Point screamed for help. The nuns came scurrying to the ward, picked me up, scolded me, and put me back into bed.

The next morning, I began therapy. The untrained nurses aides, girls not much older than sixteen who were working on the ward, would lift me out of bed. Holding me beneath the armpits they tried to make me walk across the floor on useless legs. And each night, I would try again and again to kneel upon my knees after the lights were turned off. Finally I succeeded, and from then on my legs did as I commanded. A week before I was sent home, I was able to walk. It didn't occur to me to ask God to help me walk again. My reasoning for getting down on my knees was so He could protect my mother and my brothers and sister, and the unborn baby. My faith was such that I knew He would answer my prayers once I was on my knees again.

On a cool, crisp, wind-still morning, Mum and I walked along the footpath leading from Big Head Bluff to our home in the bay. Fear was there inside of me, like a grapnel anchoring me down. Since Dr. Marcoux, the new doctor, informed me that I could go home, I should have been glad, but I wasn't. I had no desire to leave the safety of the hospital walls.

If only Alfreda was here holding my hand again, if only I could see her running along Big Head Bluff to meet me. Perhaps then I wouldn't be so afraid, so afraid of the unknown that awaits me behind the hill.

Why Alfreda was sent to St Paul's River to live with the nurse, I'll never know. She was gone by the time I arrived back from Uncle Willie's place. I only wish she'd come back. There's so much I have to tell her now. Perhaps she will be back on the steamer when it runs again in the spring.

Mum walks up ahead of me, quietly walking, deep in thought. I can see the back of her wedge heel shoes, the back of her beige stockings and the hem of her dress. I can see the deep groves in the well-worn path where she walks. I see the blackberry bushes hugging the rim beside the path. I can see our house as we top the rim of Googin's Hill. I can see the youngsters playing near the chopping block.

Yoo-hoo! Yoo-hoo!

After I make several attempts to get their attention, they finally look our way. I see them dashing across the marsh in our direction. I find the inner strength to hurry quicker as I hear them calling out my name.

Sissys home!

Sprinting along behind them is my husky pup. He too seems glad to see me, bolting past them and coming directly at me. For one split second I forget he's mine. I see only the row of long white teeth, the lips drawn back, the lolling tongue. I see only a dreaded enemy. When he pounces in joy, I scream in fright. Mum rushes up beside me and shoos him away, warding the youngsters off at the same time so they don't knock me off my legs. I'm still shivery and weak from my lengthy stay in hospital. Finally, when I'm able to push myself up off my knees again, I walked with them, hand in hand, linked by a row of tiny hands, until we reach the winter house, until we're all safe inside the catalogue-papered walls of the porch.

Within a day or two, I'm back in the routine of things. The youngsters demand my attention, wanting to know all that happened: *Did dat hoit? Did youse bawl? Ronnie git caught robbin Grampas baccy! Randy bite my finger haff off while youse wuz gone! Teacher put e in t carner!*

Mummy lit me sleep in yer bed wile youse wuz away, said Geddy.

On and on they prattled until I was told almost every single thing that had happened to them while I was away. Daid was not at home when I arrived back from the hospital. I doubt if he even knew I was home or that Mum went back there herself. I hadn't seen Daid at all since the day he left the hospital to go back to Basin Island, since the day I told him about Gabe Wobbler's visit.

Gabe demanded that I tell Daid it wasn't his dog that attacked me. He said he needed his head trace dog for the winter. I was so emotionally distraught I couldn't stop bawling. All I saw were the lips curled back over the teeth so close to my face and gnawing away at my flesh. All I saw was Gabe's teeth so close to my face, gripping my shoulder. I felt like I was being attacked all over again.

I wud know dat dog hinny weers! I sob.

Youse wont nebber hab ta warry bout dat dog nor Gabe ever agin! Daid said to me then left. And that was the last I saw of my father until late November or December.

In the weeks that followed Daid's visit, while I recuperated in hospital, I heard the story of what happened that day. It was said Daid went back to Basin Island, took the gun down off the rack, and went straight to Mister Wobbler's place. It was said Mister Wobbler nearly died from fright when Daid walked through the doorway with the loaded gun in his hands. It was said that Gabe shot his head trace dog while the gun was pointed to his head. It was as good as a concert, they said. A short while later, Daid moved the family from Basin Island to the winter home in the bay. He moved away from the island for the last time. It seems he was more disturbed by the near loss of me than anyone could ever imagine. No doubt my father lost all faith in man and dogs that day.

NOVEMBER 08, 1959

In the wee hours of morning, James was born. I didn't know that my mother and the baby were fighting for their lives. I didn't know that until late afternoon when Cass and Uncle Kels came back from Long Point by motorboat.

The sun was dipping below the rim of Jack's Cove, glinting off the water in front of the boat as it slowly made its way across the bay. I watched Cass leaning over the stem of the boat looking for rocks below, as his father maneuvered the motorboat in and among the rocks still visible above the rising tide. I remembered then the letdown I felt when everyone else came to visit me at the hospital, everyone except Cass.

People came from far and wide, as far away as Plum Point in Newfoundland, to visit the girl who survived the savage attack of five husky dogs. Every night, the visitors came. I had no idea who they were, all of them flocked around my bed, gawking at me, as if I was some kind of freak on display. And there I was, hooked up to wires and tubes and covered in bandages. Sometimes there was standing room only in my room. The crowd reached as far as the doorway, all trying to see the mangled mess in the bed. Most of them were from the Labrador side, none of them I knew. They were there no matter what the reason, all except Cass. For the entire time I stayed in hospital, Cass never came.

I feel again a pang of loss, as I did back then. I tried not to let it bother me but it did. I couldn't ignore the strange feeling inside of me. Whenever I was in a painter's length of him I got warm all over. Perhaps it was because he was different from all the rest. Perhaps it was because he never made fun of me. But for five whole weeks while I recuperated in hospital he never came.

Now I watched him from the window facing the bay as the boat passed near the bank's edge below our house. He looked up suddenly. I see the flash of blue in his eyes as he smiles. My heart did a crazy backwards flip. Too eagerly, I wave back.

His father yells, *Keep 'er hoff! Keep 'er hoff!*

Cass jumps from the boat into the water; the water runs over the top of his hip rubbers. I see the muscles flex beneath his checkered shirt as he heaves with all his might to push the boat off the rocks. Uncle Kels glares in my direction. Quickly, I leave the window and get back to the task at hand.

Smiling to myself, I don Mum's white apron and pull a pair of laundered bloomers down over my thick brown hair, tucking it behind my ears. Then I dig a hole in the center of the flour and fill my hand with salt, enjoying the feel of it as it leaves my palm like sifted sand.

It was such a lovely day. The air was so still, too still for November month. Ronald and Brian had gone to Muskrat Brook to check their traps. Raymond and Clyde were down on Israel's Point with Uncle Ernest's boys, roaming along the landwash. The others were near the chopping block, playing. Some were in the brook sailing their wooden boats. I check to see if Riley is there, to see if they were all there before I put my hands in the breadpan.

Dont go nar t landwash, dat tide is comin in, I call out.

So quietly Cass opened the door I heard no squeak. Rather, I feel the breath of cool air on my face as it follows him in. It's too late to remove the bloomers. He's standing there in the doorway. Red-faced, I continue mixing the dough, pretending I don't see him. I expected him to burst out laughing, but he doesn't. He stood there staring at me, saying nothing. It seemed forever yet it was probably just a few seconds before he spoke. When he did speak, I'm unprepared for the message he conveys.

I feel tis only right fer youse t know dat yer mudder n t baby are fightin fer der lives. T cord twas knotted round t babys troat. Yer mudder wuz too weak to deliver im. Es only a couple of pounds, I think. I thought youse shud know, dats all, jest in case someting awful happens t dem. Dey was taukin about dat in the shop down-along. Is youse lissening t me, maid?

My mind is racing. I can no longer hear Cass speaking.

Flashbacks of the vision I'd seen kept tumbling over and over inside my mind. I should have known it would come to this. I should have known that God only let me live to he could take them instead. I should have known that when I saw the cord wrapped around the baby's neck. Cass leaves and grief and anger struggle for their rightful spot inside my soul. I battle the pain the only way I know how, by having it out with God.

Suffer t little chilren t come onto me! I mocked, pounding the dough in anger. *Wots dat spose t mean now? Dat youse can pluck dem up in t'sky when youse feels like? Why dint youse take me when youse had da chance? Naw, Gawd, youse jest wanna play games in my ead. Dat baby has nar gawddamn sin on him!*

Furiously, I pummeled the dough with my fists. As my tears dropped unchecked into the pan I mixed them under with the flour. I couldn't control my bawling. I couldn't waste the gawddamn flour either. *Bread tis manna frum heaven, she sez. And Gawd, did you sees dat? I kint doos nuddin right cuz I m not her. I m not her. I m not her.*

Gawddamn! And gawddamn!

By force of habit, when the bread was kneaded down, I turned it upside down and punched the sign of the cross in the middle with my fist, shouting in anger.

In t Name of t Fodder! (Gawddamn) t Son! (Gawddamn) t Holy Ghost! (Gawddamn) Amen! (Gawddamn) Amen! Dere, now, Gawd, es youse satisfied? Yere not Gawd, dats fer gawddamn shur! Cus, cus if youse wuz Gawd, youse wudden take dem away. Now, would youse Gawd?

I threw the pan of dough on the chair beside the fire. Venting out my frustrations, I yanked the flannel blankets savagely over the pan and covered it while the dough was still stuck to my hands.

When it got too dark outdoors, I called the youngsters in for the night. While Randy and Clyde did their homework, I washed the others and put them to bed. I didn't kneel beside the little blue bed to recite their nightly prayers. Prayers seem so futile now.

It was late before Ronald and Brian came back. After their mug-up they too went upstairs to bed. I didn't tell them about the baby, nor did I tell them Mum was hanging on the face boards of death's door. I don't know why I didn't tell them, I just didn't.

The lamp, turned down low on the kitchen table, cast an eerie glow across the yellow painted walls. I felt a disturbance inside the walls of the house as the wind picked up outside and moaned in the eaves. The light from the lamp flickered from the draft filtering through the cracks in the door. I stood on the chair and lowered the rolled up flour bag blinds.

Guilt pricks at my conscience as I notice the blackened lampshade. I remembered the familiar sound of her wedding ring clicking rapidly against the glass. I picture her soaping it with the dish mop in the washbasin. I could hear her humming, even though it was already late, as she swiftly wipes it dry with a clean white cup towel, a crisp ironed cup towel that smells like the wind. I catch the sudden sparkle of clean glass as she holds it up to the fading light outside. Satisfied, she sits the lamp back on the corner shelf above the radio. I remember the peaceful feeling settling down around the house after all the chores were done. I remember the smell of freshly baked bread sitting on the tank cover and the warmth in the house as the sun went down. It meant she was content when she was humming. Unlike her, most afternoons I seldom remember to clean the shade. Without her, not once did I ever get all the chores done. I can see her hands moving swiftly over those walls, over the ceiling, washing the soot away, swiping at the cobwebs clinging to the picture frames before straightening them up.

Between the two windows facing the bay there's a large painting of a woman holding a rose against her cheek. Her gaze follows me everywhere. Above the kitchen window there's a framed photo of Dr. Wilfred Grenfell, sitting in an armchair, like the queen upon the throne I know so little about. Parmenas says the photograph is of Lloyd Trassy, someone Daid goes hunting with.

A picture of the guardian angel hangs above the kitchen table, protected behind glass. It hung there long before I was born, it hangs there still. The angel's long bird-like wings are outstretched as she hovers above two small youngsters playing near a bridge while the powerful current sweeps underneath. The little girl, so like Geraldine, holds a bunch of wild flowers, while a little boy like Clyde, with a straw hat and chubby cheeks and wearing coveralls, reaches out to catch the escaping butterfly. They are unaware of the guardian angel standing over them, protecting them with soft glowing light, funneling down around them like a teepee, shielding them from the sudden death awaiting them below. I wonder if a guardian angel stands over my mother and the baby keeping vigil on them this night.

As I tiptoe around the kitchen, hanging the vamps upon the line, and arranging the boots along the partition to dry, I noticed the empty pipe rack above the stove. I wonder where my father is this night. I know his longliner is pulled up on the slip on Fishing Point. I'm assuming he's inland trapping with the Indians, like he's always done every fall since as long as I can remember. Why did he have to put her in the family way again? I feel it's all his fault she's hanging on the face boards of death's door. Why couldn't he be there with her just this once?

A shudder goes through the house as the wind picked up outside.

When the flankers die down in the stove, I shut off the drafter key, take one last look at the angel with the golden tresses and wide wingspan, and go to bed. Before I sleep, I kneel beside my mother's bed to pray. I ask God to send me a sign so I might know if they lived or died. *Gawd, please send me a sign like youse did when Mum wuz bleedin t deat dat time. I knows dat bread is never gonna rise after after all dem oaths I put on it, but if it doos I know tis a sign that dey lives. If it don t, I knows youse let dem die, and I won t never pray again. Have we got a bargain, Gawd?* I plead.

When my prayers are said, I take the youngsters up from the bed, one by one, to pee in the pail. Once they settle back again, I crawl under the already pissed-soaked quilts beside them and sleep.

Sometime towards dawn I awoke. I'm still exhausted. I don't want to get up from the bed, yet I know I must. Listlessly, I make my way to the kitchen. I don't have to look at the dough pan. I know it's flat, an un-risen lump. What's the point of checking it? I know what I'll find. I deliberately averted my eyes until I had the fire going in the stove. I fill the kettle to the brim and put it over the damper hole to boil. It's then I noticed the bulging dough hanging down over the pan, just inches from the floor. Stunned, I ran forward to grab it, feeling the elastic softness between my fingers. Quickly, I squeeze it in half and place it in a bowl. Its a miracle! God heard me! I was dancing clean off the floor, my spirits soared so high. I knew they lived, from deep within I knew, they lived! Swimming in happiness, I fried a huge stack of flapjacks while yelling at Ronald and Brian to get up. I ushered everyone from their beds, one by one, until they were all sitting down at the breakfast table. I couldn't wait to tell them the good news.

Soon, I say to the littlest ones, *Mummie and the new baby is comin home. Wees habs a brand new wee baby bruddy now.*

Who tole youse dat? asks Ronald. He never ever believed a word I said.

Not ready or wanting to share my innermost secret with anyone, I quickly and not so untruthfully said, *Cass did.*

Nothing deters me now. I toil from dawn til dusk. The water barrel is never empty, the wash is always done, the youngsters always clean and fed. I paint the cot and have the bed ready made and waiting for her return. The soft yellow flannel blankets hang over the back of the cot. I make new flannelette napkins on her sewing machine from the material I found in her quilting bag.

The youngsters are caught up in my enthusiasm; eagerly they help me with the many chores. They carry the wood to the bin, they stack the splits, all eager to be a part of mother's homecoming. Not a night went by that I didn't kneel with the littlest ones beside the little blue bed to pray, reciting all the prayers my mother taught me. I added a new one of my own, *Tank youse, Gawd, fer saving Mum and t baby. Keep us all safe this night and forever and forever. Amen.*

The morning she arrived back from the hospital was the same kind of morning it was on the day the baby was born. Still, cool and crisp. Most of the youngsters were in school, all except Geraldine, Elliot and Riley. I was outside getting another armful of wood for the fire. I lingered there absorbing the freshness of late November air. Three weeks had passed since the baby was born. Since that morning, not one living soul came to visit us. No one ever came back to tell me if she or the baby still lived, it was just a feeling I had, a feeling of faith in God.

Patches of snow lay here and there on the hilltops, yet the ground was frozen solid and so are the ponds on the marsh. Ice crystals gather along the shoreline. Winter hangs in the stillness as I stand there absorbing the purity of another perfect day. The air is so still I can hear the sound of tires scrunching on the gravel a couple of miles away. I knew the trucks had stopped dumping gravel near Big Head Bluff some time ago. The road ends near Googin's Bridge. This could only mean one thing, that somebody got a lift as far as the bridge.

I ran inside and beater upstairs to look out the back window facing Big Head Brook. I see two women alight from Godfather's blue car. One carried a tiny bundle, the other a small box. I know one woman is my mother. I recognize her green coat.

Darting from the loft, down into her bedroom, and into the kitchen, I make sure everything is done, no dust on the sills or the wardrobe. I checked the stairs for dust as I flew down, gave the kettle one last shine, and swooshed the wood chips off the stove into the fire with the duck wing. Afterwards, I threw another junk of wood into the stove and swept the floor again. The last thing I did was wash the three youngest ones' hands and faces. Everything had to be perfect for this moment. It had to be, I told myself, as I flew around the house, stirring up the air around me.

About a half hour later, I heard voices near the corner of the house along the footpath. Quickly tying my long hair back with a tattered yellow ribbon, I ran to the door to greet my mother. Finally, we're face to face. There's a short distance that spans the narrow bridge between us, but I don't run to her. I never could. I just stand there in the doorway waiting for her to cross the bridge. I'm overcome with gladness, even though her green coat hangs loosely on her skeleton like frame. I'm so happy to see her standing there in front of me alive. That's all that mattered at that moment, that and the bundle she's holding.

Yere, she says, *take care off im, es yours now.*

The little ones rush past me in the doorway.

Mummie! Mummie! They shout, hands clapping together with glee.

Aunt Violet yells, warning them not to knock her off her feet. Eagerly, I take the bunting bag from my mother's hands. While Aunt Violet helps my mother inside the house, I carry the baby straight to the rocking chair, with the youngsters following me in quick pursuit.

Sissy, let me see t babba! Let me see t babba!

Gently, I undo the blankets. He's sleeping, but I can't help notice his tiny jaundiced face. I remove the yellow bonnet and sweater while holding his fragile body gently in the crook of my arm. Bending down, I kiss him on the forehead for good luck, making a prayerful wish. The youngsters do the same in turn. One holds his little fingers, which are so tiny, so frail. He moves. My heart silently inflates inside my chest, so happy I am to hold him close to me at last.

Aunt Violet hands me the already prepared nurse bottle then goes to pour the steeped tea for her and Mum, who sits on a chair near the table watching the youngsters and me holding the baby. While the baby drinks, the others arrive home from school. Everyone is so glad, so happy that Mum is home. When the baby is fed, burped, and his napkin changed, I carry him to his waiting cot. Carefully I lay him belly-down, like she taught me, *Babies offen die of crib deat face up,* she once said.

Pulling the soft blankets up to the nape of his tiny neck, I secured the ends under the mattress. His fine textured silken black hair covers his miniature ears, reminding me of little Indian boys who once came to our house with their fathers. I kneel beside his cot to pray.

Dear Gawd, I say, *don t let er have anudder baby, let e be t last.*

Help me dear Gawd to take good care of im and t rest, jest like she wants me to. Help me dear Gawd ta keep dem from harm, to protect and cherish the baby, whatever dat means, give er strent, make er bedder agir, but, please, please Gawd, don t lit er hab nar nudder baby. In t Name of t Fodder, t Son, t Holy Ghost. Amen.

Still weak from giving birth. Mum went back to the hospital almost as soon as she returned. While she was away the baby grew, his jet-black hair fell off and grew back a mousy brown. His gentle smile warmed the cold spots of fear that engulfed my heart. Each night before going to sleep I knelt beside the bed and asked God to make her well again. As time moved forward and she didn't return, I dreaded to think what the coming Christmas would be like without her. I worried who would get the tree from the foothills if Daid didn't come home either. Who would bring the candy and gum from the merchant's store for their stockings, who would bake the pies?

My father spent most of his time inland over the mountains trapping with the Indians. He seldom came home during the fall and winter months. But like every other year, Daid arrived back from the country, not on

Christmas Eve, but two days before. Life went on as if nothing had happened to me or Mom or the baby. Nothing was asked and I didn't tell him what I knew. Once the venison he'd brought back with him was hung in the pantry, and his pipes were in the rack once more, and his guns blued and hung on the rack above the kitchen sink, he left. I assumed, and hoped, that he was going to the hospital to get our mother.

When Christmas Eve drew nigh, I helped the youngsters write their notes to Santa Claus on brown bag paper and watched their faces light up as the burning notes went up the stovepipe. But I knew within my soul I wasn't able to fill my mother's shoes. I did all this not knowing for sure if she'd be home this Christmas Eve, or whether she'd even be alive this Christmas Eve. I was aware there were special things to be done that only Mum knew how to do.

The new baby occupied my every waking and sleeping moment and, along with the daily household chores, I tried so hard to keep ahead of all of it. But I knew that without Mum no new mittens or socks or scarves would find their way under the tree, there would be no freshly painted toboggans, or pencil boxes or spin tops. What would I do if Mum didn't come back?

But then it happened, on Christmas Eve morning, I heard the sound of runners over the frozen bay. I heard the husky dogs barking and my father shouting at them to go faster. I saw him coming across the bay near Big Head Brook and noticed the coach box on the komatik.

I can't remember a more joyous moment than when my father brought my mother home from the hospital for Christmas. Even though she was frail and weak, she took charge of the household as soon as she arrived, preparing for Christmas Day.

Daid unlatched the Carnation milk box from the komatik and dragged it into the porch. Mum instructed me to hide the box filled with Christmas gifts underneath her bed. It seemed that Santa would come to our house that year like he always had. Suddenly, I felt all grown up.

In the afternoon, I scrubbed the floors while she starched the tablecloth and attended the pies baking in the oven. The heavenly scent of peeled apples and venison pies filled the afternoon as I strung the red and green crepe tissue paper across the ceiling, criss-crossing them, and hanging the green crepe paper bells at each end, with the huge red one in the centre.

I can still hear my father's laughter as Mum cursed him for dragging the tree across the freshly scrubbed floors. For the first time in a very long time happiness seemed to extend high in the rafters. I can hear the sound of Daid's laughter as he stuck the oversized tree in the corner of the bedroom. It was music to my ears. I recalled that it was the happiest I had ever seen my parents. At that particular moment, it was probably the happiest I had ever been, or would ever be again.

It wasn't until late Christmas Eve night, when the chores were all done, the mittens and vamps hung on the line to dry, the kindling sitting on the oven door, the vegetables peeled and sitting in a bowl of water on the countertop beside the pudding can, ready and waiting, and the stockings hung on nails on the enclosed stairs leading to the loft, that I noticed the paleness in her face.

I was so wrapped up in my own happiness and having her home it didn't enter my twelve-year-old mind that my mother was ebbing away like melting snow in front of my eyes. While climbing the stairs to my bed that Christmas Eve night I had a sudden urge to tell my mother how glad I was that she was home again.

As I turned around to tell her so, there framed in my memory is a picture of her sitting in the rocking chair near the stove, gently holding the baby close to her. There was something in her face as she held the baby close that made me unable to utter a word. For those precious few moments, I watched her in silence as she softly sang one of her Christmas favorites:

Away in a manger
no crib for a bed
the little Lord Jesus
laid down his sweet head

The soft sound of her singing mingled with the sound of the kettle simmering on the back dampers of the stove. Quietly, I turned and stepped on the landing and went to bed. Before I climbed into bed, I thanked God for bringing my mother back home and for keeping us all safe.

But then so much of the gladness I've felt in the last two days dissipates. I'm thinking that on the dawning of another tomorrow, I'll be alone with the youngsters again. I toss and turn in my bed, unable to sleep. As the house settled down around the night, I hear a soft tingling sound like chimes floated up from the room below. I recognized the sound of tiny tin icicles touching together on the tree. I knew she was down there quietly puttering about in the lamplight, filling the stockings, just like she did on every other Christmas Eve. She was tying the tin icicles on the tree with red and green worsted, and re-arranging the green and red paper candlestick holders that the youngsters had colored with crayons especially for her homecoming here and there on the branches. It soothed some of the torment going on inside my mind knowing she was down there preparing a special Christmas for all of us again this year.

On Christmas Day, all of the youngsters hurried downstairs at the crack of dawn to see what Santa had brought. There were mittens and socks for all of us, pencil boxes, a whittling knife for Parmenas, a parka for Ronald, books and apples and Doublemint and Juicy Fruit gum. And there was a special surprise for me.

Mum gave me the blue guitar I'd always raved about, the one in the Eaton's catalogue. Daid must have hidden the box in the pantry while I was putting the Carnation milk box full of gifts underneath her bed. I was astounded. I never expected her to give me the one thing I wanted most, a guitar so I could play like Cass. But I was not musically inclined. The precious gift gathered dust, left unused except when Cass tuned it for me. I never found the time to practice or learn how to play. I just loved the thought of owning a guitar. Just like I had always dreamed of owning a six-gun like Annie Oakley. It was only a whim, an impossible dream. And now that it had happened, I didn't know what to do with it. Yet I was so proud because it showed my mother did care for me, after all.

Daid brought her back to the hospital on Boxing Day. And there she stayed for most of the winter months. Almost a month went by before Daid came back home again. I assumed he was gone hunting, although he never came back to prepare his grub-box for the weeks or months he would be inland hunting. His toboggan he got from the Indians was still hung on the pantry wall from the winter before. He came back only long enough to vaccinate the huskies against rabies. He pinned the dogs between his knees and injected the fluid into each one with a long pointed needle. I hated the sight of a needle! Later, he left again. I can't remember if he stayed home one single night.

I was accustomed to him leaving now. I had long since stopped yearning for him to come back. I was as accustomed to him going as I was accustomed to being alone with the youngsters, and making all the decisions for the family while him and Mum were away.

Yet, I wasn't completely alone. Ronald, older than me, did his share of the chores. On the days the weather was fit, he went to the hills to cut firewood. Daid hadn't bothered to cut any before he went away to wherever it was he went. It was all left up to Ronald to cut and haul wood, and me to take care of the youngsters until our mother got back from the hospital.

The nights seemed much colder. Layered frost on the single windowpanes was two inches or more thick. At times, the walls of the house were like an igloo and the bitter cold settled in when the fire died down. The baby cried into the night. I get up from my bed, not wanting to, yet I knew I must. I leave the warmth of the heavy quilts. Half asleep, I change his napkin. Shaking from the cold, I stick the pin in his tiny side, not realizing I was doing so. He cried so piteously in the dark of night while I prepared a bottle of warm milk from the thermos. I carry him to my mother's bed and settle him down in the crook of my arm. I somehow managed to soothe him and me back to sleep.

As the nights pass, the baby seems to fret more and more. I didn't know what to do to stop him from crying. I go to the cupboard in the middle of the night, and reach for the Castor Oil bottle as my mother would have done. I didn't know how much I should give him. I had never done this before but I'm prepared to add a bit to the milk. It's in the spoon, the eyedropper is on the countertop beside the bottle. There's something, I'm not sure what, telling me not to give it to the baby. I know I should read the directions on the label. I carry the bottle to the table and screw up the wick in the lamp so I can see the label. And then I get the smell. It's a Castor Oil bottle all right, but it's not Castor Oil. I'm sure of it now! It's the vaccine the doctor gave Daid to inject the dogs. I don't have to look; I know the needle is there in the cupboard too. Anger rises up inside of me. I curse my father to the bowels of Hell for his carelessness. I know I've come close to poisoning the baby. In my rage, I smashed that goddamn bottle against the cold iron stove. I leave it there and climb back in bed with the baby in the crook of my arm. Sometime before dawn, we both fall into a sobbing and exhausted sleep.

CHAPTER 10

⌂ **CURSED**

After the dogs attacked me, Daid moved our summer home across the ice by dog-team from Basin Island to the mainland. He used two komatiks latched together like pontoons on a floater plane. He plunked the house down on a snowbank in Lanse Kinard, a cove next to Uncle Willie's place. There it sat until the snows melted. When the bay ice broke up and drifted out to sea, he shored up the house with square deals, planks he found along the shoreline from a schooner loaded with lumber that sank off Lance au Clair. He shored it up on the spot where he'd dumped it, close to the landwash.

Late June, he moved us from the winter home to Lanse Kinard by motorboat. Shortly afterwards, he left. I stopped wondering when he'd be back again. The memory of him saving my life was diminished by day-to-day matters that had to be dealt with. From time to time, I hear the put-put of the engines, and see his longliner going up between Basin Island and the mainland. For three summers now, he's been transporting the doctor and nuns back and forth to their chalet in Belles Amour.

The caplin rolled just below our cottage on the shore. Caught up in the moment of silver flicks upon the water, all of us, including my mother, wade in and flicked the tiny fish ashore with our hands. Enough to fill two washtubs. Uncle Willie gave us a bucket of coarse salt from his stage. Two days later, when the eyes turned white, we washed them and spread them out on the rocks to dry. For days we had fresh fried caplin, the heads and tails still attached, fried in pork fat. Tea, molasses drenched bread, and caplin was savored by all of us. Dried caplin was stored in cardboard Carnation milk boxes for the winter ahead.

As the summer approached, slowly but surely Mum regained her strength. She was more like her old self again. Like a butterfly free from of its cocoon, she flitted here and there, trying to do everything at once. I sensed the change in her, she was different somehow. She seemed to be flying on the wind. She seldom showed me that long ugly scar anymore.

Instead she pretties herself up in the evenings and heads in the direction of the ridge, towards Uncle Willie's place, with a pack of Players cigarettes tucked up her sleeve. Most evenings she would go to visit Aunt Violet, or Mr. Teacher's wife. And on the weekends she'd go to Long Point, partying with her other friends. Sometimes she went to a cowboy show. More often her name was linked with the man from Long Point, the man Daid once almost killed her for.

Her spirit seemed to soar in the clouds. The fact that we had moved to the mainland and the dream of having a new home was perhaps enough to set her on a course of optimism. No sooner were her frilly white cotton curtains hung on the window frames, the new linoleum tacked to the floor boards, the cottage arranged the way she wanted it, than she too, like Daid, disappeared up over the ridge. She'd comb her thick brown hair, cover it with the new black hair net, grease her face with Pond's cold cream, smear lipstick, ruby red, on the rim of her upper lip. Involuntarily, I smack my lips together when she does and my nose wrinkles when she wrinkles hers in the mirror compact she's holding. *I wish youse d git outta my way, my maid! Yer always angin over me shoulder*, she snaps, impatient to be gone. Perhaps driven by the desire to fill an empty void in her life, she left our house every single evening, rain or shine. I watched her hurry up over the hill until she was no longer in sight. She wore her pretty dresses. Most of them had puffy sleeves, sashes around the waist, and colorful flowers. They were dresses she made with her own hands; all except for the bright red taffeta one she owned that summer. I had never seen a prettier dress. Sometimes, while she was gone, I reached into the wardrobe and took it out, just to admire it, to touch it. Yet never once did I put it on. She wore the red taffeta dress many times over the course of the summer, then at the end of summer she wrapped it up in tissue paper and put it in the trunk with all of the other dresses she owned. I had no idea where she got the red dress. I just know it was a special dress, a dress to fit her happy mood. She looked like the first robin of spring flitting around the kitchen floor, pinning back her long hair before she pulled the black hairnet over her hair.

Mind dem youngsters wile I m gone, my maid, she'd say. *I m goin down-along fer a spell! Don t fergit to mix dat bread!*

While Mum and Daid escaped to God knows where, and Parmenas, Ronald and Brian followed in their wake, I was trapped there alone in the small hut, with no one to talk to but the youngsters, the dogs, and the wind. I had many misgivings about this place, this barren treeless land where blackberry bushes crept over the surface of the flat rocks from the shoreline to the top of the slope. Our tiny house was almost hidden below the slope of the hill, nakedly exposed to the open sea. It was a strange and lonely place. Very few people came to visit us. Once in a while I'd get an unexpected visit from Mr. Teacher Sir's daughter. Sally and I had always been friends. After they moved to Bradore Plains, I would send her notes, written on brown paper and folded and tucked to the shape of an envelope. I wrote her name in pencil because we didn't own an ink pen. On Monday morning when Mr. Teacher Sir arrived back in the village he always brought a note from Sally. It was special to me, a secret only she and I shared. I hungered for her infrequent visits, so little I saw of other girls my age. I was slow to adjust to our new surroundings. The only other thing I had to look forward to were my visits with Uncle Willie, who lived just beyond the ridge.

Ronald went fishing with Uncle John in Long Point, Parmenas went fishing with Uncle Nrst and our cousin Eldon. Brian cut cod tongues for Uncle Willie's sons and spent many nights at his place. He was paid two dollars a day. Grub was plentiful that summer. We had fish almost every day, fried, stewed, boiled. We had bread. The flour barrel was filled to the brim in the storehouse beside the cottage. I mixed a batch of bread on the nights Mum commanded and lugged water from a pond nearby. The youngsters played down along the landwash, catching tiny lumpfish and thorn-fish. They spent their days playing in the water. Sometimes, they strayed away from home. Oftentimes, when the supper dishes were washed and put away, I'd make an excuse to go to Uncle Willie's place, taking the water bucket with me to get spring water from his brook. The youngsters were always in tow, the baby, Riley and Geraldine and Elliot. I enjoyed my evening visits with Uncle Willie. It helped to pass the time away while I waited for my mother to come home. Most times, Aunt Violet was gone down-along too.

When I returned to our tiny hut I performed the nightly rituals that were mine alone to do now. Brian and Raymond usually wandered off until after dark. Ronald and Parmenas came back late into the night. Most all summer long, they went fishing, except on the weekends when they too went down to Long Point to a cowboy show. Geraldine, Elliot, Riley and James were my responsibility. When it was time for them to go to bed, I'd wash behind their ears and scrub their hands and feet. On Saturdays, I'd wash and pick the nits from their hair. Afterwards, while they slept, I listened for her footsteps. As I waited long into the night, I'd read copies of *"Reader s Digest* or *"Chatelaine* that Mum had brought back from the hospital. Or sometimes I would write an order on the form at the back of Dupuis catalogue, an order that I never sent. Sometimes I embroidered an apron, or a new set of pillowcases for my bed, or knitted a pair of baby socks from a ball of soft yellow wool, all of it just to past the time away. There were times when I just gazed at the moon glimmering across the swell. Sometimes I thought about Alfreda, Aunt Carrie and Cass. Sometimes I just cried.

It was late August when the tide turned and took me along on a course I had no desire to follow. The bakeapples ripened on the stalks and were so plentiful that I was able to pick many cases on the nearby marshes while Brian and Raymond wandered farther inland to do the same. Mum sold the berries to Godfather's shop for three dollars a case (25 cents a pound). Godfather supplied the bottles to put the berries in.

I used some of the money I earned to order things from Dupius catalogue, a skirt I always wanted and a new pair of shoes. Aunt Violet promised to have a dance in her storehouse when my birthday came. But it was a Saturday in late August when she had the dance. Whenever there was a square dance, either on the plains or in any other village, people came from everywhere to socialize and dance the night away. Most times the dances went on until dawn. Like everyone else, I was excited. I could hardly wait. I knew Cass, Alfreda, and Uncle Nrst's crowd would come to the mainland by motorboat and I could hardly wait to see them. Surely goc Mum would let me go, after I'd spent most of the summer alone with the youngsters.

Finally, the day was here and the sunshine sparkled off the water. All day long Mum and I scrubbed and cleaned. In late afternoon, I had a sponge bath, washed my hair in rainwater, and dressed up in my new pleated skirt and my shiny new shoes. I tried to leave without her seeing me. As soon as she went to the bedroom for something I made my escape. But before I got around the corner of the house I heard her shrill voice, *Youse be back yere befer dark, my maid, youse gotta mind dem youngsters, cuz I m goin to t dance at Violets place.*

I didn't heed one single word she said. Instead I ran with all my might up over the ridge and down the path to Uncle Willie's, so eager I was to be gone. Andrew was playing the accordion when I arrived. Already, there were a few people from Long Point there. My cousin Will and I dragged all the chairs up from the house to the storehouse and lined them up along the walls. Aunt Violet sent us to the stage for an old bench. I didn't want to go to the stage and get the bench. I didn't want to dirty my new skirt. But I thought I'd better keep on her good side, especially if she'd put on this dance for me to celebrate my already long past birthday. I was in for the surprise of my life when Aunt Violet turned to me and in front of everyone demanded that I go on home now so my mother could come to the dance.

Red-faced, I left the storehouse. But instead of going straight home, I walked down to the point, near the landwash, and there I stayed until it was nearly dark. I skipped rocks across the swell, venting my anger towards Aunt Violet and my mother.

I m not mindin dem youngsters agin, I m not. All I ever doos is mind dem youngsters. Why doos I hab ta mind dem youngsters agin? After all, I had a birthday t udder day, and no one remembers dat.

I had expected a cake, but when that didn't happen I tried to make one myself. But without eggs or baking powder, it didn't rise. There was no icing sugar either. We ate it anyway, but no one remembered it was my birthday and I didn't say. It was just a cake.

When it got too dark to see across to Basin Island, I knew no one would be coming over as there was quite a swell on. And if Cass and Alfreda and the rest were not going to be here then I might as well go on home and mind the youngsters. I crept along the shoreline, out of sight of the storehouse, but when I reached the cove I lingered. I was still angry with Aunt Violet and my mother. I didn't want to stay home and mind the youngsters. I wanted to be thirteen. All I could think of was that she would be out there kicking up her heels again while I stayed home minding the youngsters. I was so sick of minding the youngsters. All I wanted was to celebrate my birthday. I was hurting more than I was angry. No one cared if I was thirteen.

I fumbled in the dark for the latch and quietly let myself in. I didn't want to wake the baby. I knew I would have to rock him to get him back to sleep again. So quietly I entered, my mother never knew I was there until it was too late. She was sitting in the rocking chair, wrapped up tightly in the arms of the man from Long Point. Perhaps it was the cold night air; then again it could have been the sharp intake of my breath that made her realize I was standing there. Whatever it was, she jumped guiltily to her feet and smoothed the tail of her red dress down around her legs to cover her exposed parts. Perhaps it was the anger in my face that made her talk and act the way she did. Rushing past me like a silly child playing her silly games, she called over her shoulder to the man from Long Point as she scurried from the house, *I m goin now, youse kin stay dere with Clarissy if youse wants, but I m goin to t dance.*

There was no mistaking what she meant as the drunken ass staggered to his feet with his fly still open, coming in my direction. Perhaps she should have told him, like she had told all the others before him, that I was gone in the head. Perhaps she should have told him how many nights I waited up with the axe beside the door, in our winter home in the bay, just in case someone got a notion to come to our house when my father was gone.

As the man from Long Point staggered towards me, I grabbed the kettle up off the cold stove and struck him in the face before he could advance any farther. *Git outta dis house*, I screamed, *befer I beat yer face right off yer Catlick ead, youse son of a bitch.*

Shock registered in his drunken eyes as he staggered towards the open doorway, trying to make his getaway before I beat the face clean off him. That's what I would have done if he hadn't gone. After his footsteps had faded into the distance with hers, I went to the porch and latched the door.

All the youngsters were asleep and as the night closed down around me a terrible sadness washed over me. There's a pain so great inside my chest that I can hardly breathe. How could she do this to me? What did it matter how much I did for her, or how well I took care of the youngsters? She didn't care about me. Just as long as I was there to do her bidding, as long as she could run free, she knew I would take care of them. I couldn't take the pain of all that I knew. I couldn't deal with her or this shame anymore.

With tears streaming down my face, I unlatched the door and quietly let myself out. Unable to deal with what had just happened, I walked to the shore and waded in. I didn't want to go on as if nothing had happened. I wanted her to see me as more than a dog to be kicked whenever the need arose. I wanted my mother to love me.

The tide was still rising as I walked into the sea. As the water crept up around my legs, I heard the baby crying. His crying so loud in my ears, I wish he'd stop. I didn't want to rock him back to sleep. I just wanted to be left alone. I wished he'd stop. Gawdamm it, I wish he'd stop. In anger, I turned towards his crying, wishing he would stop. I was unaware of the water streaming from my new buckled shoes as I walked out of the swell and back to the shoreline. Back to the house and to James, standing in his crib and sobbing uncontrollably.

He had grown so much. He was my brother and yet he was my son too. She had given him to me at birth and I had promised to take care of him when she was gone. I reached for him then. Wrapping a quilt around him, I carried him outside. Down to the landwash I carried him, and there on the ledge I contemplated his life and mine. I saw the futility of it all. I knew we'd both be better off if we were dead. I don't know how long I wrestled with my insane thoughts. I don't know how long I sat on the ledge rocking back and forth, telling God that I didn't want to live anymore while soothing the baby back to sleep. It was late into the night before I carried his sleeping form back to the crib. Neither she nor I ever spoke of that night again. I buried it, along with all the other forbidden thoughts. But I never forgave her, not even in death.

Fall came. Parmenas went to school in Lance au Clair. I assumed Alfreda went back to St Paul's River. I didn't see her at all that summer. Daid went inland fur trapping with the Indians. Ronald went to the foothills with Uncle Willie to cut firewood. And, like the winter before, I hardly saw the inside of the schoolhouse. I stayed home to mind the youngsters. School for me was over now.

That winter was much the same as the last one. Daid was absent for most of it. He was gone for so long that I often forgot what he looked like. Sometimes, when he arrived back home, he was clean-shaven, other times he returned in full black beard. Like a winged eagle, he swooped down upon us for brief periods of time. Then, he'd leave again, so alive while Mum's fate hung on the advancing wind.

I began to feel the strain of everyday crises and chores. Everything seemed to pile up at once. I had so little control of the household. Ronald was the only one I didn't have to worry about. Like me, he hardly went to school at all that year. He spent most of his time cutting wood to keep the fires burning. When he came back from after a long and tiresome day I'd help him saw the wood on the sawhorse and stack it in the porch. I don't remember if we had a tree for Christmas that year. I don't remember if my mother came back from the hospital. I can only remember the jannies, or mummers, coming to our house. I remember black soot all over their faces. They looked like evil dead straight from Hell.

During the holidays, Parmenas did very little with the spare time on his hands except torment me and bring our many cousins back home to carry on and drag their snow caked boots across my freshly washed floors. He'd had a taste of life on the outside now. He was older too, sixteen. He was a man like Daid. He could come and go and do as he damn well pleased.

My cousins, Eldon and Ovila Wobbler were men too. They discovered moonshine during Christmas, just like all the other men in the village. It was a known fact that men from other villages came to buy the moonshine Mister Wobbler's sons kept in kegs in the cellar hole. On one particular evening, while the youngsters were outside randying down the hill, the boys came to our house. I was clearing away the dishes from the supper table when they sidled in like dogs pushing one another to one side. They loitered in the doorway, refusing to close the door, letting in draft on Rolly, who was playing on the floor. They squatted here and there on the steps. They laughed at me when I shouted and cursed at them to get out. When I saw Ovila, I knew it was all Parmenas's doing. I'm sure he's leading Ovila to believe that if he can have some show with Selina, then he have some show with his sister too. He was constantly tormenting me about Ovila. He thought Ovila should be my boyfriend. He knew I didn't want him hanging around the house. I knew Ovila couldn't be trusted. I saw him knock his sister out cold when she called him dogfish mouth.

All of the youngsters were outside randying down the hill, except for Geraldine, Riley, and the baby. Geraldine played at the top of the stairs with the dolly that was once mine and was now hers. I marveled at how quiet she was while combing her dolly's hair. I stacked the plates on the table, poured some hot water into the pan from the two-gallon kettle steaming away on the stove and, with a fork stuck in a cake of Sunlight soap, I danced it up and down in the water until the water lathered. I washed the dishes with the mop and drained them on the cup towel.

I tried to ignore the boys. Eldon stands near the door, snickering. Ovila climbs up a few more steps. He sits there dangling his logans and kicking the walls, taunting me just to see what I would do. I wanted nothing more than for them to be gone. How dare they think they could come inside and get away with everything just because my mother wasn't home? I was seething so much I could have strangled Parmenas with my bare hands. I could have pounded him with my fists. It was all his fault.

I wasn't afraid of Eldon, only Ovila. Parmenas finally went outside to randy down the hills with the others, including Selina with the curly ringlets. He left the rest there with me, laughing louder now, getting braver by the minute, trying to see how far they could push me. I continued to wash and dry the dishes.

Tired of playing with her dolly, Geraldine moved down a couple of steps. She became fascinated with the red button on Ovila's checkered cap. She slid down another step to study it, stopping just short of reaching distance. He was so occupied with calling me names and tantalizing me, trying to get my attention like a rutting pup, he didn't realize she was there until she reached out to grab the cap from his head.

So swiftly he turned, striking her in the temple with his closed fist, knocking her off the stairs from eight steps up. I dropped the plate I was drying and rushed forward to catch her before she hit the floor. It's too late. I heard the loud sounding thump and saw her lying there limper than the rag doll she had been playing with.

Hysterically, I plucked her up off the floor and shook her, trying to bring her around while the boys stood there, their snickering turning to hoots of laughter. I ran to the washstand to get a facecloth and placed it on Geddy's forehead. Daid always brought Mum around that way whenever she fainted. The boys' laughter gets louder in my ears. I know now why they howl. I'm wiping Geddy's forehead with a dry cloth. I ran to the water barrel and dipped it in the icy water to bring her around. I'm screaming now for Eldon to help me. He stands there with Ovila, still laughing. I think he's afraid of Ovila. It seemed forever before Geraldine opened her eyes. I continue to wipe her face until I'm certain she's okay. Then I carried her to my mother's bed where it's safe, where the baby sleeps.

From the bedroom doorway I can hear Ovila bragging about his right uppercut and see him swinging his fist upward once more, showing Eldon exactly how he brought Geddy down. I'm sure he thinks he's Rocky Marcioni, the boxer.

I grab the steaming kettle off the stove. It's in my hands and they recognize my madness. They move together towards the closed door. As swiftly as Ovila raised his fist to strike my sister, I covered the distance between them and me, *Youse gawddamn sons of bitches, I ll scaw youse t deat fer hittin my sister if youse comes nar yere agin*, I yell.

They barely escaped as the kettle smacked against the door facing.

Scalding hot water spewed all over the walls, the ceiling, onto the floor. Out of control, I turned back to grab the poker to chase them outside. Out there on the snowbank I danced with spite in the Devil's shoes, while they scurried away over the snowdrifts like rabbits in the darkness.

Back inside, I secured the rope latch behind me. Then I went to the bedroom to get Geraldine, she was sobbing still. Cooing to her I say, *If dey comes back yere agin, Sissys gonna chop dem hup in little wee junks and burn dem in tstove. Jest wait and see if I dont!* Eyeing Parmenas's tomahawk standing upright against the wall I continue, *If dey tinks dey can hurt my little wee sissy and git away wit it, dey got anudder tinkin comin, bejeesas!*

From that day until he went back to school, I saw Parmenas as nothing but a hindrance. All he ever did was taunt me about Ovila. I wondered where he thought I got the time to chase stupid boys with all the work I had to do. I had no idle time on my hands like him. It wasn't me that got the opportunity to go to school; I had to stay at home tending to all the youngsters' needs. I wasn't special like him. She never cared for me like she cared for him. He could do nothing wrong, he was always Mummie's boy.

Why doan youse git t Hell outta my sight and go hoff in dem woods wit Ronnie and elp e git some wood fer dat stove, I snapped at him.

Some of the youngsters were sick with the flu. I was afraid the baby would catch it and die before Mum came back home again.

Tis all yer fault, I screamed at him. *Dat Ovila hit Geddy. If youse wuzzent a coward ass, yud beat tsculpin mout clean hoff es face instead hoff tarmentin me aw day long.*

The next night, I finally lost control. It was suppertime again. Some of the youngsters sat at the table scratching their heads and watching me slice bread, some were whining, others squabbled, some were coughing. One of them kept running back and forth from the kitchen to the porch, leaving the door wide open. Parmenas was standing on the stairs chanting over and over, *O-bi-la! O-bi-la! O-bi-la-la-la!*

Shut yere gawddamn mout! I snarled. He continued. The racket going on in the house was enough to drive me up Komatik Path and over the hills to Injun Pond and never come back. Perhaps it would have been better if I had, then I wouldn't have been made to face the consequences of what happened next.

So swiftly the knife left my hand and like an arrow it found its mark. It dangles from Parmenas's leg, the long shadowy outline spreads across the yellow wall by the light from the Aladdin lamp. Parmenas screams. Ronald, stacking wood in the porch in the dark, rushes in to see what the shouting is about. Shock registered on his face at the sight of the knife sticking out of Pim's leg. He ran forward to yank it out. I saw the puckered open flesh wound before the blood squirted.

Now, see wot youse done, my missy, see if youse doan git a lickin when I tells Daid, screams Parmenas, as the youngsters all gather around, gaping at the open wound.

The impact of the awful thing I'd done suddenly hits me. *Oh Gawd. I stabbed Parmenas!* I ran straight upstairs to my room. In the darkness, I burrowed down under the quilts of my bed where it was safe. I felt such shame I couldn't stand the sight of myself.I had blood on my hands, my brother's blood. *Oh Gawd*, I thought, *I ll be labeled a murderer just like that man from down-along who shot his sister.*

All evening long I stayed upstairs, alone in the darkness. Ronald helped Parmenas bandage his leg with pillowcase strips, and then sent the little ones to bed. Thank God the baby was tucked in before I did that despicable act.

Around midnight all was quiet, except for me. I couldn't settle down. Worse still, I heard my father's voice calling to the dogs. I didn't know he was coming home. I wasn't sure I could face him but knew I had to owe up to the awful thing I'd done. I waited for him to hang up the traces and feed the dogs before going downstairs to tell him. Ovila's brother Raoul beat me to it. I heard him tell my father all about it as he untangled the traces and hung them in the porch.

She habs to be gone in t ead, he said to my father. *She went and stabbed er own brudder and yesterday she nearly scawed Obila t deat. She jest went fullish like.*

Daid grunted and told him he'd deal with me in the morning. I knew I was dead, but the strangest thing about it was that I suddenly didn't care anymore. I knew I deserved to be beaten to death with the belt for what I did to Parmenas. But Ovila, I knew I'd scald his face clean off the next chance I got.

Parmenas rushed down the stairs to produce his swollen leg as soon as Daid entered the house.

T'isn t dat bad, I heard Daid say.

Tis my bad leg, Parmenas whined. *T one I had polio in. She s gonna git it t marra, ain t she, Daid? Aint she?*

Wees will settle dis in t marnin. Now, git up t bed.

All through the long night I tossed and turned, wanting it all to be over with, wishing it never had happened, wishing I could block it from my mind forever but I couldn't. Each time I closed my eyes I saw the puckered flesh. I found no solace in the fact that Parmenas had drove me to it. What if I had really killed my brother? What if he had bled to death? What would Mum say when she came home?

Towards dawn, I heard Daid cursin and moving about below. The baby is crying, but I can't bring myself to go downstairs to Mum's bedroom to get him with Daid sleeping there. Finally Daid got up to give the baby the bottle himself. A short while later I hear the splits cracking in the stove. The fragrance of steeped tea soon waffled across my nose as it traveled up through the knothole in the bedroom floor. The nail heads popped with the heat from the stovepipe. I guessed it to be half past six. I knew I had to face him sooner or later. It might as well be before the youngsters got up, I thought. Silently I crept past the boys' beds in the loft and tiptoed down the stairs on trembling legs. Daid spied me before my feet touched the bottom step. It was as if he was waiting.

Now my maid! he roared, *I tinks youse hab sum explainin ta do. Wots dis I heers bout youse stabbin yer brudder wit t knife. Youse bedder tell t trut!*

Like a dammed up river, the truth came spilling from my mouth.

Parmenas is always tarmentin me bout Ovila. E never elps me doos nuddin since Mum went back down t hospital. I habs t do all t work my ownself. E won t even elp Ronald cut any wood. All e eber doos is carry on while I habs t mind dem youngsters myself, wash t clothes, cook t grub, everything. All e ever doos, day in, day out, is tarment me bout dat big mouth! I d kill e to deat if e ever comes yere agin. Tis all Parmenas s fault that Ovila knocked Geddy out. E got e ober yere dirtin up the house all t time. I knows I shouldn t done dat but e nebber shuts hup, I said in one long breath, wiping my nose on my sleeve. *So hit me if youse wants, I deserve a lashin. Jest like Raoul said last nite, I m a murderer, just like dat man from down-along.*

Wot youse mean e knocked Geddy out? Daid asked.

I told him then, leaving out the part about how I tried to scald Ovila with the hot steaming kettle.

Parmenas. Git yer gawddamn ass outta dat bed right now and git down yere, Daid shouted.

Reluctantly, Parmenas came down from the top landing where he was listening all the while. He slivered down along the side of the wall.

Is dat true wot yer sister sez? Daid bellowed.

We-eel, tis all er fault, youse knows, he whined. *She stabbed me wit dat big knife. I didn t stab er. Besides, tis er place t mind dem youngsters, not mine.*

Smack!

Permanas goes sprawling in the corner.

Tis yer place t elp er when yer mudder is gone. Youse is t eldest now. Befer youse gits any grub in yer guts dis marnin git outdoors and chop up t wood then haul dat komatik to Narse Brook and haul back a drum of water. From now on, while youse es ome, youse will elp yer sister and if youse ever tarments er agin, I ll beat youse wit t belt!

Parmenas limped upstairs with tears streaming down his face. He hissed over his shoulder when Daid wasn't looking. *Youse is gonna git it when Daid leaves agin. Jest youse wait, my maid.*

It didn't matter much. I was sorry I had told Daid everything. I didn't want him to hit Parmenas. I just wanted Parmenas to stop tormenting me. Even though I had owned up to the awful thing I had done, it didn't exonerate my guilt.

Maundy Thursday fell on April Fool's day. When I arose from my bed in the morning I turned over a new leaf on the John Leckie calendar. The picture of fishing boats framed in rope was fresh and clean. I felt relieved that my mother was home from the hospital again.

Mum insisted that I scrub the soot-covered walls on Maundy Thursday. She had the scrub bucket ready when I came downstairs from making the beds and dusting the loft. I washed the soot from the ceiling and then the walls. By late afternoon I was near dropping from fatigue. My back and stomach hurt and I was so contrary that I could have taken the heads off all the youngsters as they tracked mud and snow across my freshly scrubbed floors.

While Mum baked bread and prepared supper, I retreated to my room to take a much needed sponge bath. When I discovered I had the curse I thought it was an April Fool's trick. Then I got scared, thinking that I was hemorrhaging like Mum had. And then I remembered what Naomi said one day, *All girls gits dat, wees women now, but yer not, my maid, cuz youse doan have nar tit yet, youse gotta have tits first, looks like yer nebber gonna git yeres, my maid.*

I looked down at the bumps on my chest, with brown wart like molds sticking out from the center of them. I was elated I had the curse. I felt so proud, like a real woman. I couldn't wait to write a letter to Alfreda, or to tell Naomi I had the curse. I had something to brag about at last, just like they did. I called downstairs to Mum.

When she finally came up to my room I danced around in front of her, waving my soiled navy bloomers like a flag. *I got dat! I got dat! See, I m a woman now jest like youse*, I whispered, so pleased to share my most private matter with her.

Wot in Gawds name is youse tryin t put thru yer head, my maid? she asked in frustration.

Youse knows, I whispered again.

First she turned white, then red, then white again. She really had me scared now. Perhaps it wasn't such a good thing to get the curse after all. She reached out and grabbed me by the shoulder. In a lowered voice she hissed, *Yer a long ways frum a woman yet, my maid, now dat youse habs dat stupid curse youse bedder not lit me catch youse playing wit dem byes. I m not habin youse comin back yere knocked up like dem other harlots in dis hole. Stay yere! Don t move til I gits back.* She swung around on her heels and went back downstairs.

Move? I was too stunned to move. How could she think that just because I had the stupid curse I was gonna chase after the boys. It wasn't something girls had to show to the boys, surely Gawd!

While unspoken questions tumbled over and over inside my mind she returned. In her hand were elastic bands attached together, with ends dangling down from either side with buckles attached. In her other hand she held what looked like a cotton swab wrapped in cheesecloth.

Here, put dat on yer ass, she said and quickly left the room.

Dumbfounded I stared down at the unsightly thing I was holding, wondering why I should have to put it on my ass when the curse was coming from the other place. Eventually I figured it out.

I didn't ask for the gawddamn curse, I told myself, it came to me all by itself. *Wots t madder wit Mum? You d tink she wud be proud dat I wuz all grown up now but naw, she jest had to make me feel dirty all over. I m not dat stupit. I knows I m a woman now, didn t I aw ways help er when she miscarried? Didn t I always have t burn dat stuff in t stove, didn t I wash dem sheets and keep all dat hidden away frum t byes?*

I was so sure she would understand. I thought you were supposed to tell your mother, but all of a sudden all I wanted to do was hide behind the wardrobe at the foot of my bed, not ever wanting to face her or the world again.

I wasn't imagining things when I came down for supper. Mum had herself so worked up she was in an awful state. She slapped the youngsters for carrying on then proceeded to tell Daid all about my most private matter. It humiliated me past all reasoning when I knew it was only women like us who should know about those things. Daid grunted and said nothing while she ranted and raved, banging the dishes together, shouting to the rooftop how she was cursed herself now that I had that gawddamn dirt. Hurriedly, I did the dishes and ran from the house to escape her prattling tongue. I headed straight towards Naomi's house certain she would understand. I told her everything as we walked along the snowbank to her brother's place.

Easter Sunday came and went. Mum gave me a lovely satin dress, with puffy sleeves and a crinoline underneath, as well as a tube of lipstick and a pair of nylon stockings. She even gave me a garter belt. Gawd, did I feel special! My mother was treating me like a real woman after all. I wore my dress on Easter Sunday. On Saturday night, my mother twisted paper in my hair. She tied strands of my hair in paper bag love knots all over my head. I slept upright in my bed all night long and in the morning, when I removed them, I had a head of curls. For the first time in my life I had a full head of curls, springy, like slinky toys, bouncing up and down. Easter wasn't so bad after all.

On Easter Monday, after supper, the men went to Gabe Wobbler's house to play cards. I wanted to be there in Gabe's house, like all the rest, standing around watching the men playing poker. I wanted more than anything to be there, I knew Cass would be there and I was sure he would notice that I was a woman now. But I soon learned what it meant to jump from the frying pan into the fire. I should have known Naomi couldn't wait to spill her guts, the bloody long tongue!

After supper, I met Naomi at her house and we proceeded to go on to Gabe's place, to join up with Matilda. We sat together on the stairs leading up to the loft. Cass was there, stretched full length on the settee, leaving little room for anyone else to sit but on the floor or the steps. Naomi and

I sat in the steps, in our jumpers, with slacks underneath. We never removed our boots. No one removed their boots; the floor was always wet with snow. The mop stood in the corner, near the entrance, and everyone took turns mopping up the melting snow.

The men were barely seated around the table dealing the cards when the whispering began. Soon they were snickering and making snide remarks. Gabe said, *So, Clarissys got t curse, she tinks shes aw woman now, eh?* That's how I knew Naomi had already spilled her guts, I knew I was their laughingstock for the night. I knew I was going to die with shame right there and then if I didn't get out. As I stood red-faced, attempting to make my escape, Gabe threatened to remove my bloomers and see for himself if I had the curse or not. The doorway seemed so far away. I knew that heartless bunch all too well. I knew they were capable of doing what they said they would. I knew I shouldn't have come here in the first place. I wasn't one of that crowd.

My mind flashed back to Basin Island and one Sunday afternoon when Naomi and Gabe tore Alfreda's bloomers off and hung them on the broomstick. While they flapped there in the breeze Alfreda danced around in front of them half naked, crying in shame. I was unable to help her that day; scared they'd do the same to me. But as I stood in the centre of the floor surrounded by men and boys reaching out to grab, tease and try to pin me down, I felt as though the dogs were attacking me again. A fierce pride welled up inside of me. A madness I recognized only too well caused me to leap in the air, grabbing the mop handle from where it stands in the corner near the door. Bringing it above my head I make contact with Gabe's face while my teeth sank in another man's arm.

Touch me ya mangy sons of bitches and I ll kill ebery last one of youse where youse stands, ebery last one of youse befer I lit youse tear my bloomers off like youse done wit Freeda. Now, BACK HOFF! BACK HOFF.

Everyone shrank back, shocked by my sudden outburst.

Wees only tarmentin youse, my maid, they said.

Suddenly, Cass began to laugh, muffled at first, and then his mouth burst wide open like a bloody rain cloud. Words spilled out while tears of laughter ran down his cheeks.

I tole youse, he laughs again, *I tole youse that youse wuz nar match fer er, Annie Oakley got nuddin on er, so elp me Gawd, I nebber seen t likes, she licked t lot of youse jest like I sez she wud.* At his words, the men laughed. They were soon rolling around on the floor and howling like dogs before a storm.

I reached behind me, lifted the latch from the door and made my escape. While they howled, I dashed across the frozen bay towards our house. Once inside I beater up the stairs to my room, to the welcoming darkness, hoping it would swallow me whole or, better still, that I'd wither away to nothingness before dawn.

CHAPTER 11

⌂ IN A DIFFERENT LIGHT

Time moved us forward. So much had happened since the night my father so viciously attacked my mother. I no longer waited for him to come home. I was only too glad to see him leave again. The fear was always there that one day he would kill her. The screaming and fighting never stopped. He d throw things at her and she would escape his madness somehow and then he would leave. Whenever she could escape she would, and I d be alone with the youngsters again. Somehow I became the parent, caring for the youngsters and taking care of their every need. I tried so hard to put all of the things that had happened up until now from my mind. Yet, even though time has a way of healing the trauma in our lives, I knew I would never be able to trust him or her or anyone else ever again. There was no penetrating the wall I had built around me. Although there wasn t anyone who cared, it didn t matter none. I locked the invisible shield around me and kept the door in my mind closed tight to squelch the fear that crept up inside of me at night as I burrowed beneath the quilts and hid from reality.

Mum discovered an open sore, just above her empty brassiere cup.

Like a scared and frightened child, she lays her chest and her soul bare for me to see. It was always me, never Daid, or any of the rest. It was only me and the younger ones at home. Who but me could she tell, who but me?

I could never be sure when it was we changed roles, but we did.

The doctor informed her the cancer was spreading. In no time at all it seemed to occupy the whole area of the left side of her chest. Her once healed scar was full of ugly scabs, like a monstrous crab attached to her. All summer long, she went back and forth to the hospital. And as the days and nights went by, she began to weaken from the onslaught of the pain that racked her body. I knew the time would come when she would be too weak to come back to us again.

As the scabs spread stealthily across her chest, she prepared for her death. She knitted from dawn til dusk, madly clicking the knitting needles while complaining about the unfinished house Daid was building on the hill. She kept repeating over and over that she'd be in the grave before it was covered in.

In the few short weeks she was home, she paced the floor, always staring up at the new house with a yearning look in her eyes. Perhaps she was yearning for Daid to come home so he could finish the house for us before the winter came. Or perhaps she yearned only for him to come back. Perhaps she never gave up hope that one day he would come back down over the ridge especially for her. He never did.

Now, wud youse take a look at dat pitiful sight. I ll be long gone befer e gits da windows in. Weers e at agin now, ya spose, wots goin t appen to the lot hoff of youse when I m dead and done? Gawd only knows.

JULY, 1961

Bishop Brown came to Bradore to confirm those of us who were old enough. Mum came back from the hospital for our confirmation. Along with a few others from the village, Brian and I got confirmed. During June month, we spent many hours reciting the Ten Commandments, the Lord's Prayer, the Belief. I already knew it by heart, but Brian couldn't remember any of it. I spent most Sunday evenings helping him with the Ten Commandments, urging him to repeat them over and over again. It was frustrating trying to get him to memorize the words.

Raymond and Brian were inseparable. Wherever Brian went, Raymond followed. If Brian went to Uncle Willie's or down-along somewhere, perhaps to visit with his new school chums, Raymond tagged along. They were like twins, glued together, side by side, and so it would be that Raymond would recite the Ten Commandments instead of Brian. He knew them all by heart by the time Bishop Brown arrived, but he was still too young to be confirmed. He would have to wait another three years before the bishop came again.

Brian was such a showoff. He loved to make Raymond giggle. The more he went on with his foolishness, the more Raymond laughed.

Raymond stood near the dropped leaf table with chin in hand, watching Brian and laughing at him trying to recite the Ten Commandments from the Catechism book while I sat in the rocking chair near the stove with the baby, demanding that he pay attention. Darkness came, and the night closed down around the four of us while we recited the Ten Commandments over and over again. The others carried on in my mother's bed. Nobody wanted to sleep, not even the baby who fussed and whined while I was rocking him. As Daid used to say, they were brewing up a storm.

Gimme dat book! I say to Brian. *Now, repeat after me. Thou shalt have no other Gods but me.*

Dow shud hab nar udder Gawd but me, he mimics.

Thou shalt not make to thyself any graven image.

Dow shud not make to dysel hinny graben himage

Nor the likeness of anything that is in the heaven above, or in the earth below or in the water under the earth, thou shalt not bow down to them, nor worship them. For I, thy Lord thy God am a jealous God, and visit the sins of the fathers upon the children unto the third and fourth generation of them that hate me and show mercy unto thousands of those who love me and keep my commandments.

Now youse es rattlin yere head hoff, my maid. Hows youse spec me ta larn like dat?

Okay, I say. *Jest leave dat one and go to the turd one. Dat one is shorter. Thou shalt not take the Name of the Lord thy God in vain; for the Lord will not hold him guiltless that taketh his Name in vain.*

Tis aw rite fer youse ta say, youse know dat aw reddy. I kint larn nuddin in dis gawddam book.

Dere, see now. Luk wot youse jest done. Youse broke the turd commandment. Youse took t lards name in vain, and dats not all. Youse cursed with dat prayer book wide open.

Dat dont madder. Tis jest a stupit book hinny ways.

Now, my son, watch yer mout. If youse dont watch dat tongue of yers, as shur as jeesas made mum's little h apples the Devil will come after youse.

Ya, jest let e come after me. I ll fix e some quick. I might trow dis gawddamn book at em if e comes after me. Aw dats in dis stupit book is farks and knives.

Raymond giggles and giggles, Brian giggles, and shamelessly so do I. While giggling helplessly and trying to explain to him what an awful thing he had said, a knock came on the door, a quiet knock. I'm thinking that Uncle Willie is out there listening to Brian curse on the prayer book. I'm thinking he's trying to scare us, making us believe the Devil is after us. I decide to play along with Uncle Willie. *If yere white come in, if yere black, stay out!* I shout. Nothing happens.

I'm waiting now, but nothing happens. I repeat the words again and this time the door opens just a crack. *Okay Uncle Willie, come on in now, befer youse scares dem youngsters,* I say.

Nothing happens!

I look at Brian and Raymond, they're both staring at the door, their eyes bulging out of their heads. My imagination takes over. What if we had conjured up the Devil and he's out there in the porch? Or worst still, what if the orangutan Uncle Willie had always said was in a cave under Queen's Hill was out there in the porch?

Holding the baby on my lap with one hand I twisted around in the rocking chair and grabbed one of Brian's logans near the stove. I threw it at the door and the door shut. Whatever is in the porch makes a terrible racket before it runs outside. We could hear it running around the house. It stops near the window. Brian, Raymond and myself stare at the blackness but see nothing. Then it's running again, around and around the house. It stops once more. This time it's in the porch again. A knock comes on the door, a quiet knock, like the first knock.

Now Uncle Willie, stop dat, youse is scarin we t deat. If dats youse cum on in now, I say.

Nothing happens!

Again I say, *If youse is white cum in, if youse is black, stay out.*

The door opens a crack, just like it did the first time. I wait only a few seconds before I spring into action. This time, when I grab the logan and throw it at the door, I run with the baby still in my arms and secure the latch. Whatever it is, or whomever it is, runs around the front of the house again, stops near the window for a short while, and then continues on around the house.

Oh m gawd, deres hair on es back, coal black, shouts Brian.

I'm no longer in the rocking chair. I'm in my mother's bed along with all the rest. In the darkness, I'm trying to figure out a way to get everyone up in the loft before that thing breaks the latch free from the door. I know it's in the porch. I hear it moving about, it's fumbling with the latch. Then suddenly there is no sound. A long time passes before I get up the nerve to go back into the kitchen and turn down the light. As I snuggle down under the covers with the youngsters, including Raymond and Brian, I remember that I hadn't mixed bread. The flour was out in the storehouse and could stay there for all I cared. Nothing would force me to open that door for the rest of the night. The mystery was never solved. Brian had convinced himself the Devil was after him for making fun of the prayer book, while I truly believed it was Uncle Willie's orangutan that had strayed from the cave.

It was a special time when the Bishop came. Godfather's wife decorated the pathway with plastic flowers and fir boughs from her walkway to the schoolhouse, where the confirmation was to take place. We had no church. Protestants were poor. We represented the good in the Book. There was never any money for the collection plate. Unlike the Catholics from Long Point, paying for their confessions to the priests in long black robes, the villagers gave in other ways. Giving coppers made us feel like purity instead of poverty. We never had two coppers to rub together, as the saying goes, but we always had one to put in the collection plate every three years when the Bishop came. So poor we were that Mr. Teacher Sir's wife made holy bread. She gave it to the Bishop. He cubed it, then blessed it, and placed it on our tongues for us to eat. Being confirmed meant you could get an extra helping of bread. Not getting real holy bread was as disappointing to me as finding out there was no Santa Claus.

When the archway was finished, it was high enough for the Bishop to walk through. He was a tall man, with thick white bushy eyebrows. After the ceremony was over, I stood near the arch beside my mother in my white nylon dress, with the crinoline underneath, my white gloves, and my white veil with the white flower attached to a comb that she stuck in my long brown hair.

It felt good not to have those damn yellow ribbons tied around my hair, lice catchers my mother called them, now that I refused to wear them any more. I'm wearing long white stockings too, and pretty black buckled shoes. The stockings feel so nice and I'm hoping they never run. They are not the first pair I owned. Mum gave me a beige pair for Easter, and no sooner had I put my foot in them than I got a run all the way up my leg. I stopped the run with fingernail polish, bright red. No one could see it; it was hidden beneath my dress. Mum used the stockings in the mat she was hooking when Easter was over.

If only Mum would stop talking with the Bishop, so I could go home and put my clothes in the box before she brings the youngsters back. I wanted everything to stay heavenly white forever, tucked away in that box underneath my bed where wood smoke couldn't turn it that sickly yellow, like everything else in our house that was exposed. I didn't want this moment to end. I felt like a princess standing there. This feeling of goodness reaching from my toes to the top of my rainwater washed hair. Brian is there beside me looking pure and saintly in his black suit and white shirt, the little bow tie he keeps twiddling around and around with his thumb, and his shiny black shoes. He's jumping from foot to foot, wanting to be gone. I'm sure there's something else he'd rather be doing now that it's all over. Thanks to the Devil in the porch, he knew his Catechism so well. Luckily, he didn't have to wait three more years before he got confirmed.

He elbows Raymond. Raymond curses. My mother yells at them to stop their carrying on, her face beet red because the Bishop is standing right there. I'm sure she wants to give Raymond one of her backhanders, but she can't. The Bishop is standing in front of her and she can't chastise her heathen offspring while he's standing there, as big as God Himself, in long white robes, a golden sash around his neck, with the cross and chalice cup embroidered on the ends, telling her what a fine son and daughter she has. They knew their Catechism well, such good Christian children, he says.

I stand beside her, so saintly in my white dress, staring up at the tall man in front of me, thinking if he's so close to God why is there a louse crawling over his eyebrow, the right one. He flicks at it with his hand, thinking probably that it's one of the many black flies swarming around us. Mum sees and knows I'm about to tell him about the louse. She breaks in on my thoughts, *Clarissy, yere, take t baby and dem youngsters and go on ome now. I ll be ome t once.*

Summer passes; once more the bakeapples are plentiful. Brian and I picked many cases of bakeapples and Brian took them to Godfather's shop and sold them. With the money we earned, under my mothers instructions, I placed an order in Dupuis catalogue for clothes we needed. And before I carried the letter to the post office I added another item to the list, a pale yellow kimono and nightgown for my mother. I wanted to give her something special for her birthday. I refused to believe that she would leave us before then. The *Northern Pioneer* would arrive with what we'd ordered before her birthday, I surmised.

Over the course of the summer I saw my mother twice, not counting the time I took the youngsters to the hospital to see her. She was in good spirits and her voice was strong. I could tell by her voice she was glad I took the youngsters down to see her. I placed the baby on the bed beside her and she held him close. When all the rest decided to climb upon the bed beside her, the nun came and ushered us out of the room. Perhaps it was then I convinced myself that she might get better and come back home to stay.

The first week in October, on a Sunday afternoon, Daid brought her home. One of Uncle Willie's sons helped him carry her down over the hill on the hand-bar. She wanted to come home one last time, to see for herself that we were okay.

I saw them coming down over the ridge, a frail and pitiful creature sitting on the hand-bar between them. My heart was pounding in my chest when they stopped in front of me. We never spoke. I just opened the porch door. Daid scooped her up in his arms and carried her inside. I followed behind them with an armful of wood for the stove. He sat her down in the rocking chair. It was a day that shames me still. It's a day when I didn't sweep the floor or wash the dishes. It's a day when I didn't do much at all, except chop the wood that Uncle Willie brought to us from Jack's Cove. It's a day when I stayed outside with the youngsters all morning, idling the time away. It's a day I rebelled against the dish mop and the dishpan. The dishes are piled on the table, the floor is not swept, and the beds are not made.

I stand near the stove, not sure of what to do. I'm in a dilemma as to what to do first. So I do nothing but stand near the stove with my arm resting on the white enamel back, the shelf that holds the vamps and mitts and the dirty cup towel. No matter what I do at this moment, I know I'll never be able to erase the desperate look from my mother's face.

She's so weak, so frail. She sits there on the rocking chair hardly moving, her cheekbones plainly visible on her white and hollow face. Daid is already outside in the fresh air, while she and I stare at each other in the limited space between us. The tears run unchecked down her face; they seem to soak right through her pale skin. Her voice is barely a whisper when she began to speak.

I had to cum ome ta see how youse wuz makin out wit da youngsters, my maid. I had to cum back yer one last time before I dies, she gestured with one hand. *I had t know youse and t youngsters is gonna be okay. My days es numbered now.*

I didn't speak. I didn't say one single word, instead I walked towards the door like my father did and left her there alone in her weakened state. I didn't want her to know I felt her pain. I didn't want her to see me cry. I didn't want her to see my guilt. Just by the state of the house, the unwashed dishes, the unswept floor, I knew I had already let her down, like him, like Daid.

Weakly, she calls my name.

I wait a moment to compose myself before going back inside. I was afraid of what she might say. I didn't know what to do. Yet, when I enter, I find her sitting on the edge of my bed with lid of the trunk open. How she got from the chair to the bed I'll never know. Beside her is an assortment of colourful mitts, vamps and sweaters, and scarves, all tied together with worsted and labeled. Ten bundles, one for each one of us. I didn't see her put all of it into the trunk. It didn't come to me to look inside her trunk while she was gone, yet I knew she knitted madly all summer long.

When the final bundle is lifted up and placed on the bed beside her, I see a black dress beneath it. The dress lies folded on blue tissue paper at the bottom of the trunk. I had never seen the dress before, never one so lifeless and dead black. Bright printed dresses were the only kind my mother had ever worn. If I could go back and erase the thing that happened next I would, but I can't. I should have been more prepared but I wasn't. All summer long, whenever she came back from the hospital or when I went there to visit her, she talked of little else but her pending death. She prepared for it like it was some long journey she was going on and she would wake up from it one day. She needed to know that I would take care of everything for her while she was gone. Her words came back to me as I stared down at the dress.

I wanna be waked in dis house. Don t nobody take dat ring hoff my finger. I ll come back t haunt youse if youse do. As shur as jeesas made dem little green h apples I m comin back to yer fodder as a bird. I ll fix im for nebber coming ome.

A horrible thought enters my mind. It enters my mind so quickly I don't have time to rearrange my thinking. She means for me to wear that dress to her funeral, that long black dress with the lace white collar she made with her own hands, with pretty pearl buttons offsetting the dead black front. My heart jolts against my rib cage. The shock of it sets me reeling. I see the dress. I see her death. I see me standing in the dress. I felt her pulling me into the grave with her. Yes, it was exactly how I felt.

Wots dat fer? I shouted, pointing accusingly at the dress. *Hope youse doan expect me t wear dat ting when youse dies, cuz I m not. I won t.*

The shock of horror on her face, the terrible look in her eyes. Her face falls, her thin shoulders sag, her features twist in emotional and uncontrollable physical pain. It was as if the sky had opened up and all the rain ran down her face at once Silently at first the tears ran, then sobs wracked her fragile body. Unable to stand the sight of me any longer, she buried her face in the folds of a sweater she was holding and motioned for me to leave her.

The instant those awful words are spoken, I'm filled with regret.

For one brief moment emotions ran deep. I wanted to run to her, perhaps I wanted to throw my arms around her, perhaps I wanted to tell her I didn't mean to hurt her, that tomorrow she'd be well again.

Helplessly, I stand there in the middle of the floor staring at her, witnessing her pain right down to the very root of her soul. I didn't know what to do. I was frightened by what I saw.

I ran outside into the sunshine. I ran away from my dying mother, leaving her to suffer alone. I ran until I reached the long blades of grass, death-brown and bent over in the autumn wind, near Daid's boat that lay high and dry on the slip in Lance Kinard. And there I hid behind the rudder. I hid from that terrible haunted look in my mother's eyes, from the unforgiving look I know must be in God's eyes too, and I cried. How could I possibly ask forgiveness from her or God? Why did I say those awful things to her? I feel such shame. She was too weak to fight me like she used to. I was so mixed up. Why couldn't I tell her that I didn't want her to die and leave me here alone? I know she has to go. I know this is her way of saying goodbye. But I'm not ready Gawd.

CHAPTER 12

⌂ OCTOBER WINDS

Some inner force propelled me to my mother's side. I hadn't seen her since the day she showed me the contents of the trunk. I was too ashamed to face her. By the time I arrived back at the cottage that day, my mother was already gone. Daid took her back to the hospital, this time for good. I hadn't seen her since, but as the day moved forward something within urged me to go to her, I knew I must.

Parmenas stayed with the youngsters while I started out on foot alone, swiftly covering the four miles to the hospital. The sun hung in the sky, reflecting off the dancing waves as I walked along the shore road. My thoughts were such that I hardly noticed the briskness of the October wind or the gathering clouds sweeping across the afternoon sky. By the time I reached the hospital my heart was racing with fear of what awaited me behind those doors. Like reaching hands they seemed to beckon me. And I felt even more imprisoned by the quiet click of the lock as the big oak doors closed slowly behind me. The sound of the wind is gone; only the sound of my rapid, heavy breathing and my footsteps on the stairs rise up from the hush that hangs within those halls. It took a while to reach the top landing on the stairs that seemed as high as Jacob's Ladder. Opening the second door, I walked quietly down the long corridor towards a statue of Mary facing me with outstretched hands, before turning the corner towards the nursing station.

Sister Martha, writing dossiers at the front desk, glances up as I tiptoe past the station. Quickly, she walks towards me and whispers that my mother had been transferred to the upper wing of the hospital. I nod, and then climb yet another flight of stairs on legs that threatened to fold beneath me. I'm so afraid, so very afraid of what awaits me in Room 309. I knew only too well what it meant if they had transferred her to the upper floor. On trembling legs, I propelled myself down the next long corridor. I can't go back.

I mustn't let my fears show for her sake and mine, I mustn't. It's vital she knows that I'm not like him; I'll never be like him. For one brief fleeting moment I fool myself into thinking that perhaps she will get better and come home again, but reality slaps me in the face when I reach the partly closed door and enter ever so quietly, without her knowing. A thousand words cannot describe the scene before me. I've seen my mother at her best, at her worse, but nothing shocked me as much as the sight of her now. Destiny's cruel joke is upon us both.

Propped up in the hospital bed is a skeleton figure with long bony fingers hanging over the side, with tears streaming from sunken eyes and down over hollow cheek bones. The white gown hangs loosely over her left shoulder exposing the thick ugly crusted scab that covers her entire chest. It moves up and down, up and down, like a crab upon a sea drenched beach beneath the tidal wave of her emotions. She stares down upon my father's brown, healthy, weatherbeaten face as he dozes upright in the black leather chair near the window facing the sea. A thick bluish grey cloud of smoke rises in haloed wreaths above his head from the cigar pursed between his lips. Wrenched in sorrow, broken, old before her time, beaten, withering away to nothingness, with intense pain etched on her furrowed brow. It's there in the contours of her pale face that I see her again as a bird with broken wings, abandoned and waiting for death to claim her. Her chest rises and falls with every painful breath she takes. Her heart is silently shattering in all directions as she stares down upon my father dozing upright in that black leather chair.

Mum senses my presence, she turns towards me then. A gasp escapes me when her sunken eyes, like knotholes on dead barkless trees, besiege mine. My mother's loneliness, desperation, and fear surround me like thick molasses in the polluted air around us.

Oh Gawd, dont die. I came as soon as I heard you calling me. I m here beside you now, always have been, always will be. I won t let him put you in the grave like you said he would. The words I'm thinking never leave my lips; I bite them to stop their trembling. Unable to bear the pain in my mother's eyes any longer, once more I look away. A skeleton hand rise from the sheets, beckoning me closer. Trembling violently, I move towards my dying mother. I'm so afraid, so very much afraid. That's not my mother, screams my inner self. Yet no matter how hard I try to block it from my mind I can't escape reality. Please dear Jesus, I pray, don't let her see how afraid I am.

I concentrate on the long bony fingers with uncut nails hanging over the side of the bed instead. They lay stark white against the white cotton spread that covers her above the waist. Her nails have never been this long. They are not my mother's hands. Hers have popping veins, bright red from use of Gillette's Lye, from scrubbing shitty long johns on the washboard in the wee hours of the morning. Anger mingles with fear now.

Wots t madder wit dem nurses? Kint dey cut yere fingernails hoff? I speak inside my mind.

It's then I see the wedding ring. The thin gold band lay on the side of a narrow strip of bone, a mockery of her wasted life.

Doan none of youse take dat ring hoff my finger when I dies, she'd said. *If youse doos, I ll come back t haunt youse, as shur as Jeesus made dem little green h apples, I will!*

Who is gonna want to do t likes of dat, not me, dats fer gawddamn shur! I'd replied.

I shudder now at the past conversation forgotten perhaps by her but never by me. I hear the echo of it once more as it clashes against the lampshade while she cleaned it, early in the evenings when the fire was quiet, just hot cinders in the stove, the kettle humming, see-sawing back and forth on the back damper. I hear echoes of days when life was good and I felt secure knowing my mother was there beside me, putting the house back in order before nightfall. Has it been that long? How many months and years have gone by since I heard such peaceful sounds? Why God has allowed her to be in this state, I'll never know. I'm jolted back to reality by my mother's rasping painful voice.

Youse came. I prayed youse wud, deres so much I hab to tell youse now. My time is short, she sobs. *See yer fodder, Clarissy, see im fer wot he is. E s not gonna elp youse like youse tinks. I knows I gotta die now but look at im. E can ardly wait to shove me in t ground. All I asked Gawd twas to let me live til James wuz ten, t wont be long now. Promise me, my maid, youse won t let e give youse all away after I m gone. Promise me, youse will rear dem youngsters. Youse is fourteen now, a woman almost. You re dere only hope. Promise me, my maid.*

Caught up in the web of her emotions, Daid's face becomes a blur through the unshed tears I try desperately to keep in check. Her pain and grief devour me. I always knew. She didn't have to tell me that he wouldn't help me raise the youngsters. Where was he all those days, months, and years that I stayed alone with the youngsters? Where was he all summer long? It wasn't him who watched her come to this. It wasn't him who saw the scab creep stealthily across her naked chest. It wasn't him who listened to her day after day talk about little else but her pending death. The anger I feel towards him mingles with her pain and my own. It scorches my soul like a singeing iron. Even then, while her frail voice rasps, whispering desperately like one lost and dead already, he hadn't noticed. He sat there with eyes closed as clouds of smoke rose above his head. He hadn't noticed that I was here beside her. Any illusion I harbored about my father helping me when she was gone died then. I knew from that moment on I stood alone.

Then inside me I found a strength I never knew I had. I found myself saying, *Youse doan have t worry none, Mum. Wees gonna be okay, jest youse wait and see. Parmenas is gonna finish high school jest like you wants. E s gonna get a job after dat. Fer now, wees can live off Family Allowance jest like youse told me to. I promise. Uncle Willie will get some wood fer we for t winter, im and Ronnie can go in Jacks Cove by motorboat. Youse knows I kin rear dem youngsters like youse wants, I'm mindin dem now, aint I? We will be all right. Deys all gonna get der learnin too, jest youse wait and see,* I whispered urgently, nearly choking on the anger vented out in his direction, yet I dare not openly defy him to his face. My voice was lowered deliberately so he didn't hear. Hers was desperate and pleading, fearful I wouldn't heed her final words. And I was afraid that she might die thinking I'm like him, that I would let her down like him. I prattled on nonstop in urgent hurried tones. Her next words stopped my prattling tongue, breaking the link of misery that united us as one.

I m scared t deat wots gonna happen to youse when I m dead and gone, she rasped. *Look at t way youse is dressed t day, my maid, comin all the way down yere wit nar coat on yer back and dat wind so raw and cold. How often doos I hab to tell youse bout goin roun half dressed? Youse gonna get yere deat of cold yet. Now, go to t wardrobe and get my coat. Put dat on yer back, I won t be needin dat no more.*

So quickly I condemn her. Some inner part of me cried out, *No Mum, doan make me wear dat ugly ting. Youse knows how I hates dat coat.*

I'm suddenly reminded of empty, dark and lonely nights with the wind howling outside, the youngsters sleeping soundly in their beds, while I strain my ears for sounds of her feet upon the hard caked ground of ice or mud or snow. I see her again smearing the red lipstick over her thin lips, aware it was there in the pocket still, and donning the ugly green coat, knowing full well within minutes she would run out the door. How often I watched her dash up the hill and over the ridge in search of something, perhaps it was her lost dreams.

Her eyes follow me as I walk on wooden legs toward the closet to remove that green coat from the hanger. The coat collar is stained with makeup and years of use, the Red Cross pin embedded in the lapel showing signs of rust around the edges. I held the coat in front of me like a sculpin on a cod jigger, looking down at it with mixed emotions.

Put hit on, she rasps, before weakly lifting her hand to wipe the tears off her chin. Slowly I slide my arms through the sleeves as shivers cascade down my spine.

Tis late, she said, sucking hard at the polluted air. *Go home now.*

Gawd, I say to myself, *I dont wanna leave my mudder Gawd!*

The sister comes hurriedly to her side, at the same time motioning for me to go, for Daid to put the cigar out. He's fully awake then. Her rasping fills the room. She fights the nurse to take the machine away from her.

Take good care of dem dem youngsters, my maid. Dont ever fergit me, she rasped. *Gawd go wit youse now.*

Don't leave my mudder Gawd! I say as I walked down the long empty corridor to my destiny and away from hers, I felt her eyes burning holes in the green coat. I don't look back, I can't. Those eyes, haunting, despairing, lost, will stay in my mind forever. As I get farther and farther away, her death clamps down upon us both.

Once I'm outside the hospital walls and those big oak doors swing shut behind me, once the sun hits my face and the wind sings in my hair, I run with all my might. I run away from the hospital, away from the village, trying desperately to outrun the terrible pain behind me. When I'm certain no one can see me from any windows I take the green coat off and keep running, the coat hanging from my fingertips like a burning birch. I want to drop it, yet I hold on to it for fear of snuffing out the last burning embers of my mother's life.

When I reached Lance au Din Hill, about a mile and a half away from the white hospital teetering on the cliff, there on the layered rocks I finally let out my frustration and pent-up grief. Insanely I cried to God in the heavens above to take my mother out of her misery. *Hey, Gawd! Is youse listenin ta me? If youse is, den take her fer chrissake, take er now. Dont make er suffer like dat. She dont have another sin tsuffer fer. Wot kind of Gawd is youse anyways, to make er suffer like dat? Jest take er offa dis gawddamn earth. I can't stand ta see er suffer no more. No more. Gawd. No more!*

I don't know how long I lay there on the rock, but I sensed a power far greater than me there beside me. As the sun moved down towards the horizon and dark clouds moved across the sky with the wind, I stood up to make my way across Lanse au Din. On a flat rock in front of me, there's a gull with broken wings. It stares back at me with wide startled eyes. Instinctively I reach for it, but it waddles away. I reach again, trying to shield it with my mother's coat, just as a red truck appears on the road coming from the direction of the airport. The white-collared minister is sitting in the back of the truck. His eyes meet mine as the truck sped past enroute to the hospital. As I reached down to help the injured gull I see pain and the fear in the bird's eyes, the same fear and pain I saw in my mother's eyes the day I tried to reach out to help her. The day my father beat her mercilessly. The gull hops out of my reach, wanting to be left alone like her. The sight of the gull, and the minister going towards the hospital brought me acceptance. I know I can't turn back the clock or change the course of her destiny or mine. Gathering strength from the promise I made her, and holding her coat against my face, I turned in the direction of home. I hardly noticed the rain and the wind as I ran along the road towards Lanse Kinard and to the legacy she left me. As I hurry along, I'm very much aware of my mother's broken spirit running along beside me

CHAPTER 13

⌂ **THE BURIAL**
October 9, 1961, 7 P.M.

My mother gave up the will to live. She died in the middle of the October storm with no one there beside her except the good Sisters of Lourdes, and perhaps Daid.

Parmenas and I took turns standing by the window staring out at the black of night, searching the hill for signs of someone coming down to us. We sensed her passing to the other side. It was there in the rain slashing against the windowpanes like streaking tears. I could feel it in the angry wind as it rushed against the sides of the shack in forceful spurts, threatening to pluck it up off its wooden uprights and dump us in the pounding surf below. Even the elements seemed to be lamenting my mother's passing.

Numb with grief and fear, I sallied around the kitchen doing the evening chores. Saying nothing at all while I washed the dishes and swept the floor. After I washed the youngsters' faces and hands and put them to bed, I went near the window to stare out on the black of night with Parmenas. Neither of us spoke, we were terrified of the unspoken truth. While the others slept, we watched and waited, praying someone would come. Surely someone would.

Around midnight, headlights from a vehicle appeared on the lip of the hill shining like beacons through the darkness. As we watched and waited one lone circular path of light moved down over the hill getting nearer and nearer. As it neared the corner of the house where the footpath leads to the door, we left the window and stood in the middle of the kitchen floor. Our hearts were pounding as we stood there trembling, unable to move, awaiting the knock upon the inner door. We never spoke a single word, only stared at the latch as it lifted from the slot and the door swung inward and knocked hard against the kitchen wall.

Godfather stood before us, dripping water all over the kitchen floor. Rain ran off his yellow mackintosh, forming tiny ponds around his rubber boots. I don't lift my eyes. I can't. There's nothing I can do but wait for the answer to the silent question burning inside my skull. I didn't want to know yet, like Parmenas, I waited, unable to speak. Godfather must have sensed our fear.

Youse knows why I m here? he asked. We nod in unison. *Yer mudder passed away at seven o clock dis evenin. She s out of er misery now, poor ting.*

Silence follows. And still I stare at the floor. I feel his eyes upon me before he lifts the latch turns on his heels and leaves. I heard no sound but the roar of the wind behind him as his footsteps fade away. Parmenas rushes forward, securing the latch into the slot, then came back to stand beside me. We stare at each other now, afraid, so very much afraid of death. Parmenas's shoulders began to sag. Tears ran like tiny brooks down his face and into his mouth.

Still, I'm unable to move or speak; only nodding when he sobs out loud. *I s gotta go ober ta tell Aunt Violet, she habes ta know dat Mum es gone, I gotta go ober dere.* He rushed out into the darkness, yanking the door shut behind him.

I heard his footsteps pounding on the ground and the sound of his wailing only seconds before all was swallowed by the angry wind.

The sudden flicking of the flame in the lamp casts dancing shadows across the green walls. The house shudders and I'm acutely aware of the pounding surf on the rocks nearby and the angry unrelenting wind that seems to blow stronger now. I'm so afraid.

Once more I feel her pain. I feel the depths of her loneliness, her desperation, the sorrow etched on her face, deep inside her sunken eyes, haunting, despairing, pleading, lost, like a frightened child. I know I've seen inside my mother's soul. Her pain becomes mine. It burns deep within me while I stand in the centre of the kitchen, alone and shuddering with my unspent grief. By force of habit I kneel down beside the rocking chair, but I'm unable to pray. I don't know whether to thank God for taking her out of her misery or to cry to have her back. I try to pretend she's up there with God, so she doesn't hurt any more, yet the lamenting wind tells me otherwise. I know her spirit is here beside me.

All during the storm-filled night I pace the floor, fighting the demon darkness, not knowing what else to do as the past comes tumbling through the windows of my mind. There's so much to contend with now and there's no one here to talk to. I try to remember the good times, so few they were for her, and imagined what I would say on the dawning when I have to tell the youngsters that Mum isn't coming home.

No one came to our tiny shack on the shoreline to be with us, except Uncle Willie. When dawn broke over Lanse Kinard, he was there beside me. He came, just like I knew he would and Daid would not. All the pent-up grief I'd held in check all night long came to the surface as Uncle Willie sat on a chair near the stove, sucking on the stem of his pipe and listening to me wail. I told him about the visit with my mother that day, how I asked God to take her out of her misery.

She made me promise, Uncle Willie, I wailed. *She made me promise t keep t youngsters all together. She tinks Daid is gonna give we all away. E kint wait to shove er in the ground, she tole me, she wants to be waked up yere in dis shameful piss-pot house. I cant let Daid take er corpse back yere, I kint let dem youngsters see er like dat. Dats not Mum I seen dar in dat bed. Oh Gawd, Uncle Willie, wot an awful state she wuz in. Find Daid. Tell im e kint bring er back yere. If he doos I ll leave dis gawddam shack. I ll take dem youngsters and go to Injun Pond, onest t gawd, I wud, I wud!*

Hush child, doan bawl, youse nor dem youngsters don t hab t go through dat, I can tell youse now, my maid, yer fodder will have to deal wit me if he tinks es gonna plunk er corpse down ere fer youse to look after. Gawd knows, my girl, youse been tru enuff, he said, knocking the ashes from his pipe against the damper.

Then the only person I had ever trusted left.

Before the door shut behind him I hear him say, *Dem poor younguns, wots goin appen t dem now, youse spose! Poor poor May.*

Eleven o'clock on Wednesday morning, they lowered my mother into the ground. Daid reached down, scooped up a handful of dirt and threw it in her face; that was how I saw it. The youngsters were urged to follow suit. I couldn't bring myself to throw dirt at her. I didn't see the coffin lowered down. I saw my mother, limp like a dead dog, thrown down into a hole, covered up with dirt and hidden quickly from our sight like someone with the plague.

Perhaps if she hadn't told me so often, perhaps if I hadn't seen or known of so many things, I might not have believed that Daid would nail her coffin shut. Earlier, as I washed and dressed the youngsters and walked hand in hand with them across the plains towards the little schoolhouse, it crossed my mind again and again.

We stood outside; the youngsters stand beside me, huddled together. Some cling to my legs, afraid to go through the doorway. I too am afraid. I can see the coffin sitting on two chairs. I try not to shake for their sake and mine but fail. I'm forced against my own will towards her corpse waiting there.

The teacher, Godfather's wife, and Aunt Violet come to meet us, taking the youngsters by the hands and leading them up ahead of me. I walk behind, clutching the baby tightly to me. Aunt Violet stands beside me, lifting the youngsters one by one so they can look down upon Mums cold still face. She tells them not to be afraid, but to touch her one last time. She tells them Mum is now in Heaven with God. She leads each one back to the empty seats beside Daid. He sits there, head bowed, dressed in his death black suit. He sits there sniveling, a picture of sorrow for all to see. Bitterness gnaws its way through the lump of unspent grief inside me. I can't stand the sight of him right then.

It's comforting to know that Uncle Willie is there, along with his sons, sitting on a row of chairs to the right. They are all wearing black armbands.

I stand alone beside her coffin; the others have taken their places next to Daid. The teacher reaches out and takes the baby from my arms. I couldn't bring myself to touch my mother. How could I when I never touched her in life? Instead, I jam my tightly closed fists down deep inside my coat pockets. I could see the pain still etched between her brows, even though I knew she was beyond suffering now. I wanted to believe she knew I was there. I wanted to tell her that I will keep the promise I made to her just a short while ago. I wanted to tell her that I would never be spineless like him. I never would. For a moment I forgot anyone existed but my mother and me. When Mr. Teacher Sir began the final prayers I was unable to move away. I saw the v-shaped crease etched between her eyes and the pinched skin around the thin blue lips, now devoid of the red lipstick she loved to wear. She wouldn't want others to see her like that, I thought. Yet she did look befitting in her black dress with the pearl buttons down the front and the white lace collar she had crocheted with her own two hands.

I truly believed she had put the dress in the trunk for me to wear. I knew the difference now. She was at peace at last and I was saved the horror of dressing her corpse, thanks to her friend, who had tied her hair back with the bright yellow ribbon she loved so much.

At that moment, there was no one but her and me in that schoolhouse.

Like anchors weighing me down, I felt the weight of the responsibilities she'd left me with. I wasn't ready to go on alone. I wasn't ready or able to let her go in peace. As I stared down upon her face, a terrible loneliness and fear of the unknown swept through every inch of my being. Aunt Carrie came to stand beside me, burying my face in her bosom. She knew, she understood my torment, just the way she had all through my growing years. She picked me up when I fell and fought Mum for my dignity and made me believe in myself.

I kint go on without er, Aunt Carrie, I wailed. *I kint.*

Hush child, yere mudder t will always be wit youse, yere not alone. Youse have to go on, fer er sake and deres, youse have to.

In a high pitched voice, she began to sing the hymn that was my mother's favorite, the one she asked me to have sung at her graveside, *Rock of ages, cleft for me, let me hide myself in thee*. Like a drowning child, I clutched her tightly around the waist as she led me away from my mother's still face. At the graveside she soothingly tells me, *Youse have ta be strong fer der sakes, my maid. Youse is der mudder now, youse always was, Clarissy. I knows dat and Gawd knows dat. Gawd will bless youse some day. Take dem on home now and raise dem like yer mudder asked youse to. Gawd won t fergit youse, I promise.*

CHAPTER 14

⌂ TARPAPER SHACK

Our winter home that once nestled beneath the hills of Norse Brook seems so faraway now, perhaps it was there only in my imagination. Daid dismantled the structure in the spring of 1960 and carried the planks, beams, and windows up to Lance Kinard by motorboat. Uncle Willie's sons helped him carry the planks from the shore and up the hill. Within a week the foundation was shored up and the house shaded in. For a while it seemed he would keep the promise he'd made to Mum, her one final recuest, the one she'd begged, pleaded, cursed and screamed at him for. All she ever hoped for in her final days was to see the house finished so we would have a warmer place to live after she was gone.

But all too soon he got itchy feet again. When the migrating ducks swarmed across the skies, when the fishermen moseyed down to their stages to mend their cod-traps and gear up their nets for the season, he left.

All summer long, the square butterbox eyesore with the four-sided roof stood unfinished. The tarpaper hung from the sides like lapping dog tongues scraping noisily against the exposed planks. As time went on the wood, pounded by heavy winds and slashing rain, turned a wintery grey. No one but me saw her fretting and carrying on so about the unfinished shack on the hill. Even now, there are times I can hear her voice echoing in the rafters still.

Now, wud youse take a look at dat pitiful sight on dat hill? I ll be long gone befer e gits dat finished. Weers e at agin t day ya spose, down on t Labrador no doubt, chasin after dem udder skirts. Gawd knows e won t have long t wait now. Some state youse are all gonna be in when I m dead an gone.

That lost and tormented look in her eyes was always there, day after futile day, as she stared up towards the ridge for signs of him coming home. The crease between her brows got even deeper that last summer of her life. The earth was barely settled on her grave before he left again. Actually, he never really came home at all.

Why he was there when I arrived back home that afternoon, I'll never know. Perhaps he thought that by putting the bread in the pans while I was at the graveside, it would make up for his leaving again. Perhaps he thought it would make things right between him and me. The bread was rising in the pans on the table when I got back. I just assumed it was him that did it. How could he possibly put the bread in the pans while still wearing the fine suit he wore to her funeral?

I had no illusions when I saw him standing there in the doorway. Why would he stay at home with us now when he didn't come to us on the night she died? How could I ever forgive him? Seconds later, he hurried up over the hill with the wind pushing at his back. He went without so much as a backward glance, without uttering one single word. With my face pressed against the window, I numbly watched him hurrying up over the ridge to catch his ride to Lance au Clair, down on the Labrador, just like my mother had done so many countless times before. I watched him scurry away, leaving me to carry the burden alone, leaving me cold and dead inside. As I saw the door of the blue truck swing shut with him inside, I vowed with a vengeance that I would find a way to keep us all together like I had promised her I would. If I hadn't been so naive, if I hadn't been such a jesus hardhead as she always said I was, if I hadn't been so numb with grief, I might have wondered how.

Weeks went by before he showed up again. He swooped down upon us like some vicious dog, snarling and throwing things about, shouting at the youngsters to get out of his way, shouting at Ronald to go inside to the foothills to cut the winter wood, shouting at me to darn his vamps and boil some water for his tea, shouting at Brian as he wailed for molasses we didn't have to put on his bread.

The next day, after the rain stopped, I heard banging and sawing up on the hill. I knew he was up there trying to do something with the house. And I knew it meant one thing, he was gearing up to go fur trapping. I knew he'd be gone for quite some spell. This time, I listened to the banging and sawing alone. There was no joy knowing he was up there trying to finish the house now that she was gone. I saw it as another way for him to mock her still. I had no desire to leave Lance Kinard and move into that unfinished tarpaper shack without my mother.

He would return once more before going inside to hunt. He came back when the ground was frozen and snow was on the hills. Hurriedly, he tarred and tacked the felt down on the roof and shoved the windows into the openings and nailed them to the struts. Once more, he was like a madman possessed, seized by violent bouts of temper, striking out at the youngsters whenever one of them came within arm's reach. I couldn't help but wonder if perhaps Mum had come back from the grave in the form of a little bird, like she said she would, if he didn't get the house finished before the heavy snows came.

Ronald, dear gentle Ronald, always wanting to shine in Daid's eyes, climbed up on the rickety ladder to the roof to lend him a helping hand and got thrown off for his effort. The injuries he sustained plagued him for many years afterwards.

Only one room was ever partitioned off inside the house, and that was Daid's room, yet I refused to call it his room. As far as I was concerned it was her room, the one she should have slept in long before she had died. When the many lengths of galvanized stovepipe leading up through the roof were attached to the stove and the door to the main entrance was hung, he went inland to hunt. We would move ourselves to the winter home or not at all.

No tilt or lean-to was slapped together so poorly or looked so undignified as the tarpaper shack on the hill. I often thought if Mum could have seen the half-finished dog-pen he expected us to live in she would have died all over again. No paint was ever bought for the ceilings and the pantry cupboards were open boxes nailed to the wall. The sill-less windows made from scraps of lumber looked like gray square eyes without lids.

Parmenas and I dragged the table and chairs and the beds from the summer house up over the rocks and snow to the shack. We placed the beds along the walls, away from the drafty windows, dormitory style, upstairs on the bare planked floors. I placed my own bed along the far wall in the opposite corner. Our first winter in the house, the undivided loft was always cold, the one pipe leading up through the floor to the roof served little purpose against temperatures that fell to 40 below at night. On stormy days the snow piled up like sand dunes beneath the windows. On the few nights when Daid came home, the littlest ones and myself slept in the loft like the rest, but as soon as he disappeared beyond the ridge I moved us back to the room downstairs to keep warm. Always then, I felt like the possum I'd read about in one of the youngsters' readers, with my brood constantly clinging to my tail. There were days when I mourned the death of our winter home in the bay the same way as I mourned my mother's passing.

By early December, the ponds and coves were frozen over and most were safe to travel on. When the first heavy snows came and packed down hard on the frozen ground, the men on Bradore Plains harnessed their dog teams and went to the foothills to haul wood. The sticks, previously cut in early fall, were piled in cords beside the dog path awaiting the first snows. In early autumn, before the boats were hauled upon the slips, some men went to Jack's Cove to bring back their wood by motorboat. They spent days carrying it down to the water's edge on their backs. Most men cut their firewood in the fall. Everyone prepared for the harshness of winter ahead, everyone except Daid. He was so occupied with his other life on the Labrador Coast he cared little enough to come home and stack the wood beside the door before winter set in.

We were too far away from Komatik Path to go there and carry wood back home on our backs. Instead, most days, Ronald, Brian and Raymond combed the landwash for pulp-junks like we used to do on Basin Island. They carried them back to the chopping block, where they sawed and split them and stacked them in the porch. It was barely enough to stave off the freezing cold.

One cold, sunny morning the men on Bradore Plains went to the foothills to haul back the winter wood. The dogs were barking all through the village. There was a stir of excitement in the air. The komatik runners rumbled loudly over the crusty snow as the dog teams raced past our house, down over the ridge, and across Lance Kinard en route to the foothills. Ronald kept pacing back and forth from the door to the window, and I sensed he wanted to be gone with all the rest. A short while later, he harnessed the few remaining dogs Daid had left behind. I watched him lash the chocks (frame to hold the wood on the sled) and the axe to the sled. He set off in the direction of Komatik Path, following those gone on ahead of him. I saw him running along beside the team urging them to go faster. The half starved dogs could hardly pull the empty komatik behind them. It wasn't long before more teams caught up to him and passed him. I was glad he was making an effort to get some wood, and I was equally glad that he wouldn't be in the woods alone.

I remembered back to another time when he followed the men into the woods on a day like this when he was twelve and we were still living in the bay. As he was securing the traces with a full load in the chocks, the dogs bolted and he was dragged for several miles, holding on to the nose of the komatik while he was pinned between the runners. If the man who married Great Aunt's daughter hadn't happened by just in time Ronald could have died that day. The man managed to stop the bolting dogs and free him. Ronald was brought back to my mother bloodied, bruised and torn.

Now, on this day, by mid-afternoon, I had finished scrubbing the rest of the vamps and went outside to pin them on the line. I heard dogs barking, a common thing I paid little heed to at first. I could hear the occasional *Atta, atta, rudder, rudder* coming from the other direction. I figured some of the men were already back with their first load of wood. I knew it would take Ronald all day before he got back from the woods. I wondered if any of the men would be kind enough to help him chop down enough to fill the chocks.

I was looking in the direction of Deep Cove when I saw two dogs coming along the cove. I surmised that someone's dogs must have slipped their traces. As they got closer still I recognized Bren and Rover, with traces trailing behind them and ice hanging from their fur. I knew it couldn't be sweat. It meant only one thing, that they had been in water somewhere. I knew Ronald had to be in trouble.

I began running towards the bay, across Lanse Kinard and onward towards Deep Cove. Up ahead of me I saw him coming, being towed along the path by Spark, the head trace dog. *Jeesas! Jeesas! Ronnie! Ronnie!* I cried.

Spark was bent almost to the ground. He was struggling to break free from the hold Ronald had on the trace that was still attached to him. By securing the trace around his wrist before slipping the knot that held the sealskin traces to the komatik and setting the other two dogs free, Ronald had saved his own life. In a savage attempt to make it to safety, Spark had dragged Ronald out of the icy water. Both boy and dog stumbled and fell, stumbled and fell, as Spark headed in the direction of home, dragging Ronald along behind him.

Wot happened? I screeched, as I ran along beside him. The ice was caked to his parka; his face and mitten-less hands were turning blue.

I fell in da ice, lost t komatik, he wailed.

T hell wit t gawddamn load. At least youse didnt drowned t deat, I wanted to shout at him, but didn't.

When we finally reached the house, I ran to the stove and added more wood to the fire while Ronald stood nearby, shivering. I hurried down to the storehouse to get a bundle of new shingles to throw on the fire to make it burn faster. I'd never touched the shingles before, but right then I cared little what Daid would say when he discovered they were missing. I had to make Ronald warm again. I kept stoking the fire, jabbing at the shingles to make them burn faster and cursing my father.

If dat lazy son of a bitch had came back yere to cut the wood youse wuddent be in t woods. Tis all his fault youse nar drownded t deat. Where in t name of jeesas do youse spose he is at all dis while? No doubt down on t Labrador like mudder sez e wuz. I wish e was dead instead of er. Wees all goin to die if e gits es way. Gawddamn im! I say. Gawddamn im.

I was still cursing my father when Uncle Willie came through the doorway. He helped Ronald out of his wet clothes and wrapped him in quilts, rubbing his hands and feet to bring the life back into them. Later that afternoon, Pern and Andrew went to Deep Cove and retrieved the komatik and brought back a full load of wood, which they dumped near the chopping block. The next day, Uncle Willie brought his axe and saw and he and Ronald sawed the wood and we stacked it in the porch.

The wood lasted for a week or so.

By the time Daid arrived back home we had all but run out again.

When he saw that no wood was standing near the chopping block like tepees, he went into a violent rage. He took off his belt and nearly beat Ronald to death. I screamed at him to stop. I tried to make him listen to me. I told him how Ronald had almost drowned trying to get the goddamn wood. He didn't care at all. Viciously swiping him across the back, the face, the legs, Daid forced Ronald to harness the scrawniest of the dogs, hitch them to the komatik and drive them towards the foothills. Somewhere in the back of that cruel and twisted mind he truly believed it was Ronald's responsibility to keep us from freezing to death. Just like he took it for granted it was me who should raise the youngsters and not him.

There was a terrible pain inside my heart for Ronald as I helplessly watched him limp off towards the hills beside the dogs. I continued to watch until he was out of sight. How many times, I wondered, had he beaten Ronald? Why hadn't Mum ever tried to stop him? Why couldn't I?

Ronald was in excruciating pain. There were bloody welts across his face and hands, and ones I couldn't see all over his body. All I could do was stand beside the window looking out and wanting to run after him. I stood staring after him, moaning like someone in great pain.

Once again, the past came rushing to the forefront of my mind.

It was Easter Sunday. Daid and Mum decided to go to Bradore Plains to visit Aunt Violet and Uncle Willie. While Daid harnessed the dogs, Ronald cried to go with them. There was no reason why he couldn't go, ncne of the others wanted to go along. Daid said no, and then threatened to lash him with the belt if he attempted to follow them like he said he would. But Ronald didn't heed his threats. Sometimes I think Ronald was more of a jesus hardhead than me!

The frozen bay stretched out for miles, to the Plains and beyond. I watched as the dog team became a speck in the distance. I could still see them as they topped the ridge where our house now stood. It was a perfectly clear day. About a mile behind them Ronald was running hard, fo lowing in the beaten path leading across the three miles of ice towards Uncle Willie's place. He was determined he wouldn't be left behind. He knew where he was going; he had been there before. I dreaded what would happen when he reached Uncle Willie's porch door. I watched him like I did just now, until he was out of sight.

Shortly after the supper that I, then aged ten, prepared, the dog team returned. Mum entered first and then Daid came through the doorway dragging Ronald by the hood on his parka as his screams filled the room. Daid dragged him upstairs, stripped him bare, and beat him savagely with the leather belt, as Ronald's screams raged through the rafters. I was so afraid that Ronald would die; yet I was too afraid to help him. I hid behind the stove, weeping silently, while Mum paced back and forth, wailing out loud and pulling her hair, but doing nothing to stop the beating. The next day, the floorboards were stained with Ronald's blood.

Daid left home like he always did after one of his violent rages. Mum attended to Ronald's many wounds. He didn't go to school for a week. Ronald, tiny and puny looking, was strong in his mind, while I was stocky and weak. I told myself I couldn't go up the stairs to save him. I was only ten, yet the guilt remains that I didn't help him. Like Mum, I was afraid.

I couldn't help Ronald then, just like I couldn't help him now. There was no reasoning with my father. I wished I were running beside Ronald, instead of being trapped inside the tarpaper shack doing Daid's every bicding like my mother before me. Only one thing was for certain as I watched Ronald hobble out of sight. If Daid lifted a finger to hit me now I would turn on him like the mad dog my mother always said I was. As sure as Jesus made her little green apples, I would have struck him dead. With what, I might have wondered, with what?

Git t jeesas outta dat winder, and git dem vamps darned if youse knows wots good fer youse, he yelled at me. *Youse will be t next one t git t belt if youse don t doos wot I sez.*

He allotted out the rations hed brought back with him; some he took with him, some he left for us. He then harnessed his other dogs, latched the grub box, snowshoes, gun and tomahawk onto the toboggan and left, shouting over his shoulder for me to go to Godfather's shop to get some grub on tick until he got back again.

By the time Ronald arrived back from the woods, he was changed somehow. I saw the defeated look in his puffed and swollen eyes. He seemed so lost, so forlorn, like mother in her final days. Broken, with no will to go on.

Ronald left home that same night. Later, I heard he was living with our cousin in Long Point. Perhaps I would have done the same if there was somewhere else for me to go, or if there was anyone to take care of the youngsters. I knew in my heart that sooner or later Did would have beaten Ronald to death. I breathed easier knowing he was safe at last, but I mourned his leaving just as I mourned Mum's death. I knew neither one of them would ever be back.

I figured my father was living elsewhere, because he no longer brought back furs to skin and stretch over the molds to dry. I can't remember seeing any of the molds in the storehouse after we moved to Bradore Plains. This time, I knew he wouldn't be back from the country until he got some venison. I knew he'd be gone for quite a while. Perhaps he'd never come back.

At night, while the youngsters slept, I stayed up sewing by the light from the coal-oil lamp until the oil ran out. I cut out pajamas from existing ones, using flannel I found in Mum's sewing bag. I sewed them up on her Singer sewing machine. The pajama tops had sleeves either too short or too long and the buttonholes were uneven, but I was proud of what I'd accomplished. The pajama bottoms were easier to make than the tops. I used the elastic from old pajamas and reaved it through the band folded over and sewn in place around the waist. I made a nightdress for Geddy too. I could hardly wait for Christmas Eve when I'd dress the four littlest ones in their warm flannel nightclothes.

In the afternoons, while the youngsters were in school, I pieced together a patchwork quilt. All four sides were uneven, but the patches were brand new ones Mum had left behind. The youngsters had warm mittens, vamps, and scarves for the winter ahead. Mum had made sure of that before the cancer weakened her frail body. I tried so hard to do everything the way I thought she would have wanted. I tried so hard, yet I knew I'd never be able to fill my mother's shoes.

CHAPTER 15

⌂ THE MUG AND THE CROSS
Christmas - 1961

Christmas without our mother was a Christmas I've never forgotten. Days before Daid arrived back from the country, we ran out of supplies. Most villagers got supplies on tick or credit at the general store until spring, when the seals were harvested and sold. Daid hadn't gone sealing the spring before, and it was evident by the empty molds in the storehouse that he hadn't trapped much in the fall. And since he had stopped fishing two summers before there was very little of anything to bargain with at the general store, except for the Family Allowance that came from the government each month.

Mum, who was sure Daid would desert us after she was gone, had arranged with Godfather to take the Family Allowance when it arrived at the Post Office, and give me grub whenever I needed it.

While I waited in vain for Daid to come back, Aunt Violet urged me to go and see Godfather as my mother had instructed. She hardly had enough grub to feed her own crowd, and as much as I dreaded going to Godfather for help, I knew I had no choice.

The day before Christmas Eve, I bundled up the youngsters, put them on Parmenas's komatik, and took them with me to the shop. It was the first time I'd been across Bradore Plains since my mother died, and getting grub to sustain us was reason enough to cross the Plains towards the graveyard in Eddy's Cove. I had rehearsed what I would say when I was face to face with Godfather. I wrote what I needed on a note before I left the house.

I dont want it on tick, I said to him when I arrived in the shop. *Mum sed I could come to youse and youse could take dat Family Allowance dats at t Post Office by now, I spose. I only wants a couple of tings, jest wot I have on dat note, and p rhaps some candy and a stick of gum or two fer da youngsters stockins, jest in case Daid dont git ome dis Christmas Eve. E s gone inside huntin agin. Youse knows e shud be home t once.*

Godfather barely glanced over the note before he crumpled it in his fist. *Yer mudder and fadder already owes me more than dat Family Allowance yer mudder gits, my maid.*

But Mum said I could come ta youse if I needed grub.

Yer mudder is dead, my maid, so git dat foolishness outta yer ead. Yer mudder is dead and youse got nuddin ta do wit dat Family Allowance.

But, I have nar scrap of grub to feed we wit. Perhaps if I can hab some flour and a pack of yeast — hinny ting, til Daid gits ome. Youse can hold onto the Allowance til Daid gits back. Tis at the Post Office, I s pect.

I kint give youse nuddin, so go ome now. I kint give nuddin more.

Ow can I feed we wit nuddin? I shouted.

Dats yer fadder s problem, not mine, now go on ome like I sez.

As I stood there glaring at him, determined not to leave empty-handed, he shoved a tally book across the counter.

Here, see fer yere owntself, he said. *Dis is wot dey owes me already. See, now youse knows why I kint give youse hinnyting.*

I saw pages upon pages in the tiny notepad he flipped, amounts totaling some hundreds of dollars or more at the bottom of the last tally sheet, all of it owed by my mother and father.

I asked and pleaded no more.

I walked away from Godfather's shop, back across Bradore Plains towards the tarpaper shack, as empty-handed as I had come. How would I feed so many hungry mouths without one single morsel of bread, without a single copper to buy any flour and yeast? What if Daid didn't come back with venison for us to eat? I knew it was pointless to go to the Post Office to try and get the Family Allowance. I knew it wouldn't be given to me, nor could I cash it anywhere. In my mind I knew that Godfather had already applied the sixty-three dollars against the balance owing him. I wasn't concerned any more whether or not we would have a Christmas like I had promised her. My concern now was that we would all starve to death.

Somewhere in the Bible it says that man does not live by bread alone, yet without the bread that Aunt Violet gave us almost every day we might not have made it. She had so little herself and each time I went to her I felt guilty for having to put her in the position to help us survive. She cried and cried, while I stood in the doorway all cried out and listening to her curse my father to Hell and back again.

Jest youse wait and see when e gits back yere agin, I ll fix is wagon fer littin youse by yourself wit dem youngsters wit nar bit o grub in t ouse. I ll tell e to git off es lazy ass and git some grub to feed dem youngsters isself, I got me own crowd t feed. Here, take dat, she sobbed, shoving another loaf of bread into my waiting hands along with a half a cup of molasses. *Yer mudder will be turnin over in er grave by now. Don t let dem youngsters waste it now, my maid. Make sure it lasts youse fer a day or two, dats all I have to give youse. Perhaps yer fadder will be back tamarr, surely Gawd.*

The next morning, Christmas Eve, I stood near the window looking across the snow-covered land towards the storehouse down in the cove. There was little I could do but pray for a miracle to bring him back home that day.

Youse knows I habs to take care of dem youngsters dis Christmas Eve jest like I promised Mum I wud, I said, looking up to the sky. *Youse knows we gotta have grub. Don t madder if I don t hab nar candy fer dem, jest as long as I habs grub. Dats all I asses fer, dats all, Gawd.*

I had no desire to sweep the floor with the duck wing stub, or scrub the floorboards with seine netting without any soap, or scrub vamps on the washing board. There was no reason to prepare for Christmas Eve. All I could do was stare down at the storehouse on the shore, willing him to come back. I knew I was beating my head again the naked struts but, as much as I dreaded him coming home, still I wanted him to come back this Christmas Eve.

While I stood fretting near the window, I barely noticed his dogs among the other dogs roaming around on the snow banks with traces trailing behind them. My father had arrived. Dressing the youngsters, I ran with all my might down over the hill to face him, with one youngster on my hip and dragging the other two linked together, holding hands. As always, the rest had wandered off.

Two caribou were lashed to the toboggan with ropes, tongues hung down over bark colored teeth, lips drawn back in death, antlers spread wide, their once proud heads no longer erect.

Wees don t have nar bit of grub left in t house. Godfadder wudden let me have none and I m tired of bummin frum Aunt Violet aw ta time. Mudder s cheque is spose to be at the Post Office by now. I tole im ta take mudder s cheque an give me some grub, but he wudden give me nar scrap cuz youse and mudder owed e everyting. Daid, youse hears wot I sed.We got nar scrap of grub, I shouted frantically at his turned back.

He was sitting on an upside down two-gallon galvanized bucket busily sharpening his dagger on a leather strap. *Git up t house. I ll be up t once,* he snarled.

We re aw gonna starbe t deat, jest like Mum sed, I yelled back at him, getting the last word in as I hurried back up and over the ridge.

All that mattered at that precise moment was that he had come back to be with us for Christmas. While I waited for him to come up from the storehouse, I unharnessed the dogs and hung the traces in the porch. I swept the stairs with the stub end of the duck wing, melted snow on the stove and scrubbed the floor with a piece of seine netting. Later, when he was gone, I would scrub the youngsters down, pick the lice and nits from their heads, and dress them in the new pajamas I had made them before Christmas. I had it pictured in my mind how he would go to the Post Office, get the Family Allowance and go to Godfather's shop to get some grub. I fooled myself into believing that everything would be all right now that he was home. It was early afternoon when he came up from the storehouse, holding a huge caribou liver and heart.

Get me a bowl, quick, he snapped, as I rushed forward to take it from his bloody fingers.

I added more wood to the fire and built it high. While Daid sliced the meat and fried onions and pork fat together on the stove (leftovers from his trip in the country), I went outside and packed the kettle with clean snow to brew the tea. About an hour later, most of us were sitting at the table eating our first cooked meal in more than two weeks. He didn't ask where Parmenas and Ronald were, or Brian, and I didn't say.

Later, while I was washing the tin plates in soapless water and drying them with an old pillow slip, he left. There was still hope. After all, where would he be going if not to Godfather's shop? I envisioned contentment on the youngsters faces when they got up the next day to find candy in their stockings. I looked forward to tomorrow's dawn with a lighter heart.

Brian arrived back home. When I told him that Daid was gone down along to get grub and presents for everyone for Christmas he drove nails into the post that stood near the stove and hung the stockings on it. I can see the little vamps still, seven vamps on seven nails, from the tiniest one on the bottom nail to the biggest one on the top nail, climbing up the rounded post that kept the ceiling up.

Hurry up now, quick, say yer prayers n get under the quilts, quick.

Santa is up dere on the roof waitin fer youse ta close yer eyes, I told them, so overcome with optimism that I think I believed myself that Santa was really coming to them that night.

It took a while for the little ones to settle down. Even Brian and Raymond stayed home and went to bed early. When everyone was asleep, I took the pudding can down from the cupboard shelf and the only white tablecloth from the tray in Mum's trunk and spread it corner ways on the kitchen table. I had contemplated staying up until Daid got back so I could peel the turnip and potatoes and put the salt beef to soak, in preparation for dinner the next day. I hoped he remembered baking powder and raisins for the pudding.

When more time had elapsed and still he hadn't returned, I added more lard to the rag in the sardine can burning on the kitchen table and went upstairs to bed. I remembered other Christmases past and I didn't want to be up if he came home with moonshine on his breath.

In the dark, I knelt beside my bed to pray, *Please Gawd, tell Mum she don t hab t warry now; tell her Daid is gone to git t grub, and dat we hab meat too. See Gawd, we re gonna be okay now. Please Gawd, bless us all dis nite and Mum up dere in heaven, even Daid.*

Even though we had no tree, and there was no smell of freshly baked pies or a clean smelling house or new toboggans or pencil boxes, Mum would still be proud as she looked down from heaven this Christmas Eve night, I thought. At least, we were all together, except for Ronald and Parmenas, and all of us were safe.

Towards dawn I awoke. Clyde was standing over me, fear and mistrust in his eyes. *Sissy lied,* he wailed. *Santa dint come. Sissy lied.*

Still half asleep, I jumped out of bed, hastily pulling my sweater and slacks on before going downstairs. Six pairs of eyes looked at me accusingly. Some of the youngsters were whimpering, some neither spoke nor cried. I rushed past where they were squatting on the unfinished stairs. Daid's logans were sitting on the floor near the stove, I didn't have to look to know that not only was there nothing in their stockings, but worse still there was nothing at all to eat. The countertop was bare.

A mocking voice kept going off inside my head, *See, I tole youse, youse jeesas ard ead, youse wudden t lissen t me. See, I tole youse he wuz gonna starve youse all t deat.*

Parmenas's voice, sharp and loud, bellowed down the stairs.

Wot the lard dyin is t madder wit youse youngsters, huh? Sometime during the night he had come home without me knowing.

Sissy lied, the youngsters said in unison. *Santa dint come.*

Wot do youse mean, Santa dint come? he shouted, his eyes fixed on me. '*E better not have fergot youse youngsters. If e did, I'll fix im befer dis marnin is over, by jeessas.*

In two leaps, his feet landed on the kitchen floor. His eyes went first to the boots, then to the closed bedroom door. Rushing forward like someone gone mad, he began to pound upon the door with clenched fists.

Is youse in dere, Hitler? If youse is, youse bedder get up. By the lard dying jumpin jeesas, if youse tinks youse can ferget dem youngsters fer Christmas youse got a nudder ting comin. Now, come out here befer I goes in dere where youse s at. Gawddamn youse. Tis t marnin youse is gonna meet t maker. Now come out here, I sed.

All the youngsters stood by, their eyes popping. Surely they must have thought that Santa was hiding in Mum's room. The baby, Riley, and Geraldine clung to my legs in fear. Not on that terrible, terrible morning, but much much later, it came to me that the youngsters must have thought Parmenas was going to kill Santa Claus.

I too was trembling, but for a different reason. I knew that Parmenas would meet with death as soon as the bedroom door swung open. I stood there like an animal trapped in headlights, unable to move, unable to stop what was about to happen.

Though only a few seconds passed, it seemed like an eternity before the bedroom door was yanked open. I could see the anger and the torment in Daid's eyes; I saw his raised closed fist. Parmenas was dancing up and down in front of Daid with his own fists swinging, his feet lifting off the floor with rage. Daid took a swing at him and missed. My heart stopped when Daid reached for the dagger sitting on the ledge of the stove and angrily raised it above his head.

Parmenas, enraged even further, was shouting louder now.

If I dies dis marnin, youse measly son of a bitch, I m taking youse wit me. Dem youngsters wud be bedder hoff if youse wuz dead, Parmenas shouted, daring him to kill him, repeating over and over. *Youse might kill mudder and get away wit it, but if I dies, youse is comin wit me. Youse is comin wit me, you lazy no good son of a bitch.*

Then the strangest thing happened.

Daid threw the knife in the corner, sat on the backless chair near the table, put his head upon his arms, and wept.

Parmenas, still enraged, gathered strength from Daid's weakness. He screamed over and over for him to dry up those crocodile tears.

Dats all dey is, jest like the way youse bawled at er grave. I wish youse wuz dead instead of er.

On those final words, Parmenas turned on his heels, yanked on his logans, grabbed his parka off the hook, and ran from the tarpaper shack. Some of the youngsters followed suit, still in their pajamas and with bare feet in rubber boots. Half dressed, they ran down the path towards Uncle Willie's place, running for all they were worth, not looking back, and crying over and over, *Wait, Pimmy, wait.*

Stunned, I watched them go down the path. I knew Aunt Violet would share her bread with them once more. She wouldn't leave them outside in the freezing cold.

I neither spoke nor cried as I went towards the stove to scrape the ashes into the ash pan and empty it outside over the snowbank before putting a fire in the stove. I continued to do the necessary chores as if nothing at all had happened. I lit the cardboard under the splits and stared at the tongues of flame as they licked and curled around it. When the fire was started, I put vamps on the feet of the three remaining youngsters.

Daid was still sitting near the table sobbing, his face hidden in the crook of his arms. I didn't have to ask. I should have known better. How could he repay anyone if he hadn't fished all summer, or trapped in the fall? Did he expect Godfather to carry us on his back for the rest of his life now that Mum was gone?

The fire began to slowly burn. I stood staring down upon the splits in the belly of the stove, watching the flames build higher as the shavings caught on fire. I added wood to the fire, opened up the drafter, and put the damper back down. Powerless to do anything about our situation, I kept looking everywhere and anywhere just so I wouldn't have to see him there with his head down on his folded arms.

Unable to listen to his sniffling any longer, I took the youngsters and went back upstairs to bed. There was nothing else I could do, nothing else I could say, to change the fact that he had come home empty-handed in the middle of the night. How was I to forgive him for this terrible, terrible day? How was I to know that Godfather refused to give him any grub on tick? How did I know if he even went near Godfather's shop at all?

Sometime during the next few hours, he went outside to chop wood. Uncle Willie's sons had brought another load of wood when we ran out. I could hear the thud of the axe as he split the wood. I could hear him stoking the fire and putting more junks in the stove. I could hear him put the damper back down. I heard him go back and forth to the porch each time he carried an armful of wood to the bin. I heard him put the lifter back up on the rack on the stove. I heard him close the oven door. Later, when I came back downstairs, there was a roast of venison in the iron pot in the oven. I should have been glad that he put the roast on but I wasn't. I was still too upset to speak. I puttered around the kitchen doing the things that I had already done the night before, hearing only the sound of my mother's voice.

See, my maid, see, I tole youse. Youse is aw goin ta starbe t deat.

Daid demanded that I go to Aunt Violet and ask her for yet another loaf of bread. I did as I was told. Uncle Willie was sitting near the fire smoking his pipe when I entered. Aunt Violet handed me the bread. Neither one of them said anything. Parmenas sat on the settee near Uncle Willie, his eyes swollen from crying. I often wondered what would have happened to the lot of us if Daid hadn't moved us from Basin Island to live near Uncle Willie and his crowd.

Around noon, the roast was ready. I set the odds and ends of plates and saucers on the table along with the bended forks and knives, some with broken tops. I sat the baby in the highchair with his blue plastic bowl. Riley and Geddy sat silently at the table watching Daid carve the roast with his dagger. I poured tea in Daid's mug and sliced the bread and put it in the centre of the table on a tin pie plate before sitting down to eat. There was tea, venison and the liquid substance to soak the bread in. When Daid and I finally sat down at the table to eat, we said no grace, like my mother would have done. Instead, there was only silence. The deadly silence fell down around us, like dust particles trapped in a shaft of sunlight. A coldness is in my bones. Since the early morning conflict between Parmenas and Daid I hadn't exchanged one single word with him.

What was there to say? I had no more illusions. I couldn't imagine how we were going to survive without any grub. Where would he get any? Who would be foolish enough to give him anything on tick if he owed so much?

I would have welcomed the clatter if the baby had flung his plastic bowl to the floor as he always did, but all three of the youngsters sat quietly at the table, lapping up the meat, gravy and bread. It was as if they too understood the gravity of our situation.

Daid's eyes never left his plate. I watched as he cut through the meat with his dagger, and wolf it down, loudly slurping on the strong black tea from the oversized mug. The mug with the blue and pink flowers and the gold rim that I had kept safely out of reach of the youngsters all this while, just the way she would have done. As black as tar was how he loved his tea and that's how I steeped it for him, just the way she would have done. I tried doing everything exactly as she had done. I see her sitting next to him, sipping from her gold-rimmed cup with the neat little saucer while he slurped loudly from that oversized mug. How often, I wondered, did she wait for him to arrive back from the country tired and hungry? When I was little, how often had I watched him drink mug after mug of dog-black tea and a full loaf of bread before he got up from the table? I could watch him drinking and eating all day, so happy I was my Daid was home.

Her voice cuts through the memory.

Look at dat savage E can eat t Devil and snap at Hell.

Always, he laughed at her when she said that, his laughter ringing in the rafters above us. It was so very long ago.

His mug seemed the symbol of what her relationship with him really was, a slave to do his every bidding, someone to be left alone to bear more unwanted youngsters while he trekked the mountainside with the Indians, and to be there when he got back. Why was I still guarding that goddamn mug? How could I take it down from the upper cupboard shelf and put it on the table beside his plate on this dismal and futile Christmas morning? Through blurred eyes, I hear her voice. *Don t youse break dat mug, my maid, e ll be like t savage when e gets home if e don t hab dat chrissly mug to drink wit.*

Those happier carefree days stand so vividly in my mind, those days long before my mother got ill or he or she did despicable things, long before he beat her senseless in front of me.

I remember once being half-afraid as I watched him chase her around the room. I didn't know what was happening behind the closed bedroom door until I heard their muffled laughter, and then I would continue playing with my paper dollies, contented, both of them forgotten.

On the day she knew he was coming back, all day long she would pace back and forth in front of the window facing the bay, looking for signs of the dog team.

Git dat mug frum t cupboard, my maid, and set it near es plate, she'd say. *E ll be ome t once lookin fer es chrissly tea.*

A vision of the long spouted white enamel teapot sitting on the back damper of the polished nickel-plated stove, see sawing back and forth, flashes across my mind. I remember the smell of steeped dog-black tea waiting for his arrival. That was my cue to go outside to sit on the bank to listen for the sounds of barking dogs in the distance. As the sun slid down the other side of Queen's Hill, I'd sit on the snowbank beside the house with my arms wrapped around Blackie, the pup my father gave me, waiting in anticipation for my Daid to come home.

It was the most exciting time of my life when Daid and the dog team broke over the ridge, with him barely visible against the snow in the white canvas cossack my mother had made for him. He was a spectacular sight running alongside of the komatik, his voice like music on the wind calling to the dogs, *Atta, atta. Rudder, rudder.*

I hear the sound of runners over the hard packed snow, the dogs yapping their heads off. Blackie would spring from the snowbank and run across the bay ice long before Daid reached Big Head Bluff. I'd run too, not heeding my mother's voice as she screamed at me to come back. Bringing the dogs to a halt, Daid would lift me up and perch me on top of the komatik box, holding me in place with his mitten hand while I triumphantly rode the rest of the way back home with my Daid. My Daid.

I was always in his way when he tried to unharness the dogs. I was so eager to tell him everything, practically stepping on his sealskin boots as he went to the porch to hang up the traces, lifting me high so I could hang them on the six-inch nail. Then he'd order me to go inside while he climbed the scaffold to throw frozen junks of blubber meat down into the meal tub below for the hungry snarling dogs. Parmenas and Ronald were always there doing their share, but I never acknowledged them, only Daid. I wouldn't let him out of my sight. I wasn't afraid of him then. Once he removed his cossack and sealskin boots he'd sit at the table, where that huge mug was sitting on the right hand side of his plate, filled to the brim with dog-black tea. I can see her so plainly fretting, making sure his plate was filled with fish and potatoes, or whatever else there was to eat, before his tea got cold.

It was celebration time when Daid came back from the country.

After the supper dishes were cleared away, my mother's cousins and their sons would come to the house, anxious to see the kill and to hear about his hunting trip. I'd sit quietly on the steps listening to him talk until my mother shooed me off to bed.

I was so contented, so at peace, as I absorbed the smell of Oracle pipe tobacco filtering through the air and rising in haloed wreaths above his head as he sat at the kitchen table, still drinking tea from his oversized mug. Before going to sleep, I always said a special prayer thanking God for bringing my Daid safely back home.

The vision vanishes and now only the stranger remains, sitting at the table slurping tea from his oversized mug. I stare at the hand that holds the mug, those hands that nearly beat Ronald and her to death. I see that goddamn mug as a mockery of my childhood days. The urge is there to reach out and smash that goddamn mug against the filthy, soot covered walls, or better still against his goddamn head, for her sake, for their sake and mine. The urge is so great that it takes all my willpower to get up from the table and run outside. In desperation, I vent out my frustration and anger on the un-chopped wood near the chopping block.

Never had I felt so helpless and so alone. I grieved for the loss of Ronald. I was certain now that Parmenas would leave again, this time for good. Brian seldom came home as it was, and Raymond usually followed Brian wherever he went. I felt them all slipping away, one by one. I knew we couldn't survive without Mum. I knew it was futile to think I could hold us together without a single morsel to eat or one red copper to buy anything with. Suddenly, I didn't want this responsibility anymore. I just wanted things to be as they used to be. I wanted so much to be that little girl again, to go back to when we were safe and I didn't have to carry the burden alone on my shoulders. I wanted to be able to piggyback ride on my father's back. I wanted to slide down Uncle Labb's Hill in the bottom of the bay with him and Parmenas, Ronald and Brian, with not a care in the world, feeling safe beside my Daid. I wanted to hear my father's laughter upon the wind and hear her voice screaming at him not to randy down the hill with us from that far up. I was never afraid, I trusted him. Just like the day he risked his own life to save mine, I always knew my father would save me.

I wanted to feel the wind on my face and see the blue in the sky as we sped down the icy slope to the silent marshes rushing up to meet us. I wanted that more than anything else in this world because I knew then my mother was there, looking up at us from the doorway, and not down there in the cold, cold ground.

But now the stranger sitting there, sniveling on his sleeves near the kitchen table was the real image, the one she had tried so desperately to make me see for the past three years. The one I knew I would never trust again. Her words kept tumbling over and over inside my mind. *See im, Clarissy, see im fer wot e really is. Youse knows he s not goin t elp youse. Youse es aw gonna starve t deat when I m dead an gone.*

I carried the chopped wood inside the porch and threw it in the goddamn bin, acknowledging the fact that the father I once thought I knew I will never know again. Perhaps he existed only in my imagination. I went inside to add more wood to the fire. Daid was still sitting at the table, with his eyes glued to his empty place. I washed the baby's hands and put him on the floor. I cleared the table and added some scalding water to the dishpan. Daid got up from the table and went to his room. As I walked around trying to do everything with nothing, I got more frustrated by the minute. I wanted to escape from those dingy walls. Perhaps if I hadn't promised her, perhaps if I hadn't cared whether they lived or died, I might have walked away like Parmenas and Ronald.

Suddenly, he's standing there in front of me, with a tiny square box in his hand. *Ere,* he sobbed. *Dats yers.*

I doan want nuddin, I cried. *All I wants is some grub t feed dem youngsters wit. Youse knows we kint live on nuddin. I doan want nar present, only some grub. I tole youse dats all I want.*

Here take dis, I sez, take dis, he cried, shoving the box in my direction.

There was no explanation as to why he couldn't bring back any grub. There was only the terrible torment in his eyes and the tiny white square in his outstretched hand. If I hadn't been so upset, I might have wondered how he could buy me a present if he couldn't bring back any grub for us to eat. While I stood there facing him, Geraldine came to stand beside me and the baby and Riley followed suit, all three of them looking up at me with hungry eyes, expecting something too.

I reached out and took the box from his fingers. Inside the cover on soft cotton batten lay a pretty pink rhinestone cross, the cross Id seen in Godfather's shop the last time I went there with my mother. The time before she went back to the hospital for good. Only my mother knew how much I'd wanted that cross.

I took the cross from the box and held it up to the light; all nine rhinestones sparkled from the sunlight coming through the broken window. Through blurred vision, I pressed the centre white stone to my eye and began to read.

Our Father, who art in Heaven, Hallowe ed be Thy Name, Thy Kingdom come, Thy Will be done on Earth as it is in Heaven. Give us this day our daily bread.

See, Sissy, see, said Geraldine, before I threw the cross against the wall, before I screamed at him. *I dont want anudder cross t bear. I jest want some grub to put on dat gawddamn table. Dats all I wants, dats all I ever wants. I wish youse wus dead instead of er. Gawddamn youse, I say. I hope youse leaves and nebber comes back.*

Pushing the youngsters out of my way, I ran upstairs to my bed where I sobbed uncontrollably again. How could he think that I could forgive him for this terrible, terrible day? Did he think I was going to suddenly conjure up the grub I needed to keep us alive? Did he think that a cross I once wanted was going to make all the difference? I hate him now, hate him for being so spineless, hate him like Parmenas for his crocodile tears. I hate him for what he did to Ronald. I hate him for putting my mother in the ground. I hate him with every breath of my being. I hate him.

A short while later the youngsters came upstairs. All three of them climb in the bed beside me. Geraldine's frightened little face is close to mine. Clutched tightly in her tiny fist is the rhinestone cross. *Daiddys gone,* she says. *Kin I have yer cross forever?*

Unable to bear the futility of it all, with no grub to feed the youngsters and me, with no soap or lye to wash the pissy sheets, with no broom to sweep the floor, with no coal-oil for the lamps, with nothing and no one to turn to, grief consumes me. I sob out loud. *I want my mudder, Gawd.*

CHAPTER 16

⌂ **MANNA FROM HEAVEN**
January 1962

It might have been a combination of many things that forced me to behave as if my mother was coming back again. Perhaps it was the scene at the hospital on the day she died that gnawed away at my innards and wouldn't let me forget her. Then again it could have been the dingy walls, the empty coal-oil lamps, the bare pantry shelf, the empty wood bin, or the enormous responsibility placed upon my shoulders. Who knows why I began to pretend that she was coming home? Who knows why I behaved the way I did? Not me.

In the mornings, when I pummeled the feather beds, fluffed the pillows and dusted the stairs with the stub of the wing, I could swear she screamed at me for not digging out the dirt in the corners. On days when I thought I couldn't bear the futility of it all, I'd tell myself that Mum would be home soon. There were countless times I stood near the window looking up over the hill to see if she was coming yet. I hoped when she did that she'd be carrying a gallon of coal-oil in one hand, and a bar of Sunlight soap and Gillette's Lye to boil the pissy long johns in the other. In those times when I pretended, I'd set her pretty cup and saucer on the table and prepare some tea for her. Her baby finger always stuck off while she drank from her cup. His mug no longer existed. I smashed it against the stove with such ferocity that for days afterwards I found pieces in all four corners of the kitchen and around the stove.

There were times I saw her sitting in the rocking chair darning socks or mending patches on the boys pants and I'd hear her singing her favorite hymns. I too sang with gladness then. In my mind, I'd scrub the floor, wash the clothes and bake the bread, all things I would really have done if only I had the necessary things to do it with. Everything always fell into its rightful place whenever she came home again.

While I waited for her return, I tidied up her room, got down on my hands and knees to dust the corners and under the bed with the stubby duck wing, then swooped up the dust and dirt with a piece of cardboard. Using a piece of seine netting and a worn down bar of Sunlight soap Aunt Violet gave me, I scrubbed the wooden plank floor. I turned the piss stained feather bed over and over until it was puffed high in the middle just the way she would have liked it. If it were a windy day, I'd pin the quilts and pillows on the line to air them out.

The day finally came when I got up the nerve to lift the lid up of her trunk. With tremors riveting down my spine, I reached inside and took out the spread she'd made with her own hands, feeling as though I was reaching inside the tomb of Jesus and removing the sacred cloth from its resting place. The spread was brand new and soap smelling clean from months of being in the trunk. Inside the spread, wrapped oh so carefully, I found the Guardian Angel. Mum must have placed her there with all the other treasures she owned. Like a long lost friend I held her to my bosom before I hung her on a nail above my mother's bed. I felt so certain she would protect the youngsters while they slept, just the way she always had. So carefully, I unfolded the spread and draped it across her bed. As I stood back to admire the spread, that pretty embroidered spread, my mother's life began to unfold before me. I remembered the first days when she stamped the designs in the centre of the spread. So often I'd watch her from the darkness, bending over the lamp, her nimble fingers weaving magic through the broadcloth. Sometimes she smiled to herself. Could it be she was dreaming about the house on the hill? Feverishly, she worked at the spread, and then bit by bit it took on a life of its own. Orange, yellow, red roses, green leaves and soft brown miniature baskets began to grow into the cloth. In the center of the spread was one large basket filled with tumbling roses, spilling over the rim like tears, reaching down and intertwining with the many others all along the outer border edges.

Even when she knew her days on earth were numbered, she continued to work at the spread. She refused to give up until she had embroidered the final stitch. Longingly, I gazed at the spread, tracing every inch of the pattern with my fingers. The cloth felt like silk, better than silk. On the nights she weaved her soul into the cloth she wove a part of mine along with it. As I stand back to admire it, I see beyond the beauty in the spread. All the interlocking roses, the splashes of soft brown, remind me of Great Aunt's square, so beautiful, and then so soiled with my mother's blood. Bewildered, with fear standing so vividly in her eyes, she stands there, in the pool of blood around her feet, looking down on me, sitting on the bottom steps. Pain and fear run deep inside my chest. I know her soul is woven inside that spread I've laid across the bed. A terrible sadness envelops me, drawing me back to the day we buried her. She never had a chance in life. Pain, suffering and misery had rained down on her. She was destined to die perhaps before her time, if not from giving birth or disease, then by my father's cruel, cruel hands. Her death was a combination of so many things. I try not to think of the terrible loneliness she must have felt, the terrible pain I knew she endured before she passed out of this world on that dark and angry night. I try not to think of her down in that cold, cold ground. Not down there in that cold, cold, ground. Not down there, not my mother, God!

FEBRUARY - 1962

Howling winds and heavy snows slashed across the treeless plains in all of Hell's fury. There were times the roof nearly lifted off from its rafters and perhaps it would have been better if we had perished in the night. Even the elements seemed to have turned against us.

Daid hadn't returned since Christmas Day. I never expected he would. When he left, he took most of the venison with him. One shoulder hung in the storehouse. Day after day, Brian and I took turns hacking the frozen meat from the bone with the axe and I boiled it in the pot with coarse salt Aunt Violet gave me until it was all gone. Aunt Violet gave me more bread and molasses to keep us from starving while Uncle Willie tried in vain to bring my spirit back.

He brought the youngsters back home late that afternoon after Daid had gone. He built a fire in the stove and urged me to get out of bed. He stayed with us late into the night. He told us stories of other Christmases past, his own hardships and happenings. He kept telling me over and over that everything was going to be okay.

He came to visit every single day. Always, he'd build the fire in the stove. At night, the youngsters, wrapped in quilts or wearing their parkas, would gather around the stove, enthralled by Uncle Willie's storytelling. We looked forward to his visits so much so that on stormy days Brian, Raymond and I took turns blowing our breath on the heavy frosted windowpane to see if he was coming up the path to be with us. Whenever he left us to go down the path towards his place, I longed for him to come back.

Uncle Willie's son, Manuel, brought us some grub once a month, whenever he received his dole from the government. He'd bring me half a sack of potatoes, some fatback pork and turnip. He'd stand in the doorway and hand me the potato sack, saying, *Don t madder none if youse cant pay me back. Aunt May dun enuff fer me. Ere, dis is frum Ma too.*

Aunt Violet would send enough flour to make a batch of bread and a half a packet of yeast. Pern and Andrew, Uncle Willie's two oldest sons, brought firewood and dropped it off near the chopping block. Uncle Willie would bring his own axe and chop the wood. The youngsters and I lugged it in the porch and stacked it in the bin. To save the wood, when darkness settled down around us and Uncle Willie had gone back to his cove again, the youngest ones and myself burrowed down under the heavy quilts on my mother's bed, tattered now and rank smelling of piss, to keep warm. The oldest ones climbed the stairs to the loft to sleep. They too climbed in one bed to keep warm.

In fall, before the cove froze over, I'd carry the piss soaked flannel sheets, quilts and shitty napkins to the landwash and beat them on the rocks, then rinse the tattered rags in the pond nearby before hanging them out to dry. Once winter set in, the pond and shoreline froze and I had no way to scrub the quilts and put them out to dry.

Without Uncle Willie, Aunt Violet and their crowd helping us, I don't know what we would have done. I doubt if we would have survived the winter of 1962.

Tings will git bedder, Uncle Willie would say. *Doan give up, child. Dem younguns is dependin on youse.*

Wot can I doos when Gawd forgot we too? I cry. *E doan ansser my prayers no more.*

Dats cuz youse dont pray no more, my maid. Youse gotta have faith. Yer fadder will come back wit some grub jest youse wait and see. Wait and see.

All I ever doos is wait n see. Nuddin is gonna happen,youse knows dat, Uncle Willie. I hopes he dies and nebber comes back. Wheres e at now? Down on t Labrador, chasin dem skirts jest like mum said befer she died, huh? Where is e? Not here wit we, dats fer gawddamn shur, I say with derision.

After the next major storm, the snow birds came. They flew down from the sky by the hundreds, flying past the curtainless window as I lay in my mother's bed with the youngsters. I could hear their gentle but frantic chirping as they scurried around the ground in search of food.

Depressed, not wanting to get up to start the another futile day, I stayed in bed with the youngsters. There was nothing to feed us with and I was tired of having to go to Aunt Violet and beg her for yet another bun of bread. It would appear that Daid had vanished off the face of the earth and by doing so had finally sealed our destiny. I had no desire to wake the youngsters up to a cold, empty, miserable shack. If Parmenas hadn't come home at that precise moment, I doubt if I would have gotten up at all that day.

Bolting through the doorway, he shouts, *Deres manna fallin frum t sky.*

Wot in jeesas name is youse tryin t put in yer tick skull now, huh? I snapped at him. *Go on, my son, doan be so foolish, I knows now deres bread fallin outta t sky.*

Youse doan believe me, doos youse, my maid? Come and see fer yerself. Luk now, wots dat if dats not manna? Deres tousands and tousands out dere, flyin everywhere, he shouted over his shoulder as he headed in the direction of the storehouse on the shore.

Soon he was back with some old boards and a piece of seine netting. *I kint find nar ammer,* he said, *I wunner if Uncle Willie got some nails. Jest youse wait and see. Befer dinnertime, we will have nough to eat, by Gawd!*

Parmenas made a two-feet square haul-down. He found some twine and tied it to the end of the stick to keep the haul-down up, and then he passed the other end through the broken window near the kitchen and fastened it on a nail. He sprinkled crumbs underneath that Aunt Violet had given him. Next, he instructed me what to do when enough birds were underneath.

All youse hab t do is jerk on dat line. When t stick falls down, youse run out dere and get dem birds, he said.

Wot eif deys es still alive? I m not murdurin Gawd s little birds.

Doan be so lard dying jumping foolish. Jest hit dem over the ead with t lifter, or a rock, dats all. Now get dem youngsters ready, I m takin dem t school. When we gets back youse should have dem birds stewed up fer dinner.

He took Brian, Raymond, Clyde and Elliot to school. They went there on empty stomachs.

I kept going back and forth to the window to see if the birds were underneath the net. There were a few but not enough, so while the fire was building in the stove I stood near the window, watching. My mind had wandered off and when I looked again there seemed to be at least a hundred little heads pecking wildly at the crumbs. I hesitated barely seconds before I plucked the string. When the haul-down fell, I ran outside to see how many I had captured. All the tiny birds were lying there, pinned beneath the seine meshing. Some were dead, some were chirping loudly, some had broken wings. They all looked so tiny, frail and so totally helpless. I had expected them to be dead already. I wasn't prepared for this. My stomach heaved at the thought of killing them off.

I lifted the meshing and tried to shoo the live ones away. Very few were able to escape. They fluttered about the snowbank, dragging their broken wings. A small rock was protruding out of the snowbank. I have no idea how it got there; perhaps Parmenas had placed it there. I hit the remaining few birds on the head. I had a flashback of moments when sparrows and wobblers hopped up on their nests as I silently watched nearby. I remembered the joyful feeling I had knowing those tiny feathered friends really trusted me, I felt certain that God would punish me for the awful thing I had done.

I went inside and got a bowl to put the dead birds in. One by one, I picked them up by their lifeless wings and placed them in the bowl. I sat the yellow plastic bowl on the countertop. I couldn't bring myself to take the knife and skin the feathers from their tiny still warm bodies. All of a sudden I couldn't stand the sight of them. I had to get away.

Wots t madder wit youse, my maid? Runnin wit dem youngsters like dat youse would tink Satan twas after youse. Where s dem youngsters mitts? Youse bedder start dressin dem youngsters bedder dan dat, Aunt Violet said, when I arrived at her door.

I couldn't answer Aunt Violet. My heart was leaping wildly inside my chest. How could I tell her the awful thing I had done? How could I tell her I was afraid that God would strike me dead for murdering those tiny birds? How could I tell her I was afraid the birds might come alive and attack me? I stood near the porch door and said very little while she cut a slice of bread and gave it to each one of the youngsters and sat them on the chairs near the stove to get warm. I declined when she asked me if I wanted some bread. I had no appetite. She made small talk while I barely listened. A short while later I was feeling a bit silly. I began to wonder if perhaps I should go back to the house to be there when Parmenas got back. I lingered as long as I could.

When the hands on the clock moved near to midday, I took the youngsters and made my way back home. I was afraid to open the door, but when I did the shack was silent and the birds were as I left them, in the yellow bowl on the countertop. I couldn't look at them. While the youngsters sat on the chair near the table, I added more alders to the fire and went to stand near the window, waiting for Parmenas to arrive back with the others.

Parmenas was expecting me to have the birds stewing in the pot when he got back. He looked shocked as he stared at the birds lying belly-up in the bowl with the feathers still on them.

Clean dem yer ownsel, I snapped before he had a chance to curse on me. *I m not touchin Gawds little creatures no more. If youse wants dem, youse kill dem yer owntsel frum now on.*

By t lard dying jumpin. Give me dat bowl quick. See if I doan skin dem. Dats only a mouthful youse got dere. Brian, see if deres some more under dat haul-down. Youse youngsters is not goanna starve if I kin elp it, not dis day, our Lord.

Parmenas cleaned the birds out on the snowbank and put them in the iron pot with coarse salt and water, each one no bigger than a prune and their tiny hearts the size of yellow peas. After they were cooked, all the youngsters gathered around the table while Parmenas ladled the food out. I sat and gobbled up the cooked meat with the rest of them. The hunger in my stomach overcame the sins on my soul.

Day after day, Parmenas continued to kill the birds, by the hundreds he killed them until the sky was empty again. And I cooked them. I was so glad Parmenas had come back.

CHAPTER 17

⌂ **THE STRANGER**

It was Easter before Daid came back home again. He never said where he'd been and I never asked. I had no desire to know. I could only surmise and heed the echo of my mother's voice.

When he returned, the large wooden box latched on the komatik was full of grub: potatoes and bologna, pork and beans, lard and Eversweet margarine and molasses, yeast and a full sack of flour. There was coal-oil for the lamp again, and matches to light the fire with. Sunlight soap and Gillettes Lye to boil the long johns in. I assumed he'd sold the furs he trapped in the fall, even though I saw no sign of anything when he arrived back from the country.

With the long and dreary winter behind me, my spirits began to lift. There was reason for me to get up in the mornings now. It wasn't long before I was doing the wash and hanging it outside to dry on the new clothesline Daid bought for me. It was a good feeling to see some of the tattered white sheets flapping stainlessly in the spring wind.

After three miserable months, alone with the youngsters and not knowing what would happen from day to day, I could hardly believe it was Daid down on the pond chopping a hole in the ice to fill the water barrel. I couldn't believe he was allowing the youngsters to go along with him instead of kicking them out of his way. For the first time in months, the water barrel in the porch was filled to the brim. The dipping bucket was hung back on the nail above the barrel. I watched him harness the dogs and go in the woods and bring back a full load in the chocks on the komatik. Even though it was late in March month, there was still plenty of snow on the ground. He sawed, split, and stacked the wood in the porch. I couldn't believe any of it. Could it be that Daid was home to stay? Could it be that he was making up for all the time he had left us alone?

When the first steamer arrived, there was a brand new wringer washing machine for me from T. Eaton Ltd. It had a gas powered motor machine that scared the hell out of me every time he started it. I hated the damn thing and as soon as he'd leave the house I'd push the red knob to stop it, hoping to God that it would never start again.

We finally had enough grub and other things I needed to do the household chores. I tried not to dwell on the day when he would leave again. I pushed it from my mind and relaxed in those moments when things seemed right again. But I knew it was only a matter of time before the restlessness stirred up inside of him and he'd be gone. Like always, he would go with the changing wind.

Spring finally arrived. Ice floes broke apart between Basin Island and the mainland and open water appeared. Ducks came flying over the islands, companies upon companies of them. All the men in the village came to Duck Cove, put their wooden flats on their komatiks and pushed them across the dangerous grey ice until they reached the tiny island about a quarter of a mile offshore. All day long, the ducks flew over the open water in front of the island. All day long they fell from the sky as the men emptied their shotguns. When Daid came ashore in the late afternoon, he had sixty ducks or more. I helped him skin, clean, and put them in cans. He crimped the lids on the cans and we boiled the pots late into the night. We would have ducks to eat now, as well as seal meat.

I could scrub the vamps, the sheets and the quilts and hang them outside to dry on sunny spring days, but I could do nothing with the bare floors and the soot covered, unpainted, and uninsulated planks between the struts. With a knife, I dug the dirt and grime from the cracks in the floorboards. I scraped out dog hairs and junks of dirt that had built up on the ends of the table legs and the remaining backless chairs. I dug out the corners of the table on the baby's high chair and scrubbed it clean. My white mop turned grey black the first time I dragged it across the soot stained floor. After using buckets of scalding hot water and Sunlight soap, the floorboards still didn't come clean. And there was no way to restore the shine to the dented kettle without Bon Ami or sand. The kettle sat on the stove with a partially burnt wooden handle and dented sides, reminding me of the many times I'd thrown It against the wall in anger and frustration. There were many things that could not be changed or repaired again.

Daid stayed home for April and May and part of June. I had expected him to be long gone before his footprints dried upon the planked floor, but he didn't.

He would bring me a broom, a mop, a gallon of coal-oil, a fine-toothed comb, a bag of flour, a gallon of molasses, a sack of potatoes and some pork, as well as other things, before he left again. Surprisingly, there were times he stayed at home with the youngsters while allowing me to go to Long Point to a cowboy movie.

In June, the bakeapple blossoms peppered the marshes and it looked like it was going to be a fruitful summer. I began to make a list of all the things I would buy with the money I would earn when the berries ripened on the stocks. Dupuis catalogue arrived in the mail and I circled the things I wanted to send for, just like my mother would have done.

Once more, Ronald went fishing with our cousin's husband in Long Point. Parmenas went fishing with Uncle Willie's crowd. Brian and Raymond spent days on the stagehead cutting cod tongues when the men came back from the fishing ground. I managed to keep the rest of the youngsters from straying away from home. I took some of the older ones bakeapple picking with me, when and if Brian stayed home to mind the two youngest ones. Or I'd take them with me to the shop to get some bologna, pickles, beans and pork with the money we earned. As always during the summer months, grub was more plentiful than in winter.

We had lots of fish to eat. When autumn came, Parmenas went back to Lance Au Clair. I sent the children to school with their new scribblers and pencils and their new rubber boots. Aunt Violet helped me patch the knees on their too small pants and the elbows on their too small coats. We would have new clothes when my order from Dupius catalogue arrived by the *Northern Pioneer* on her last trip to the coast for the year.

In early November, when the first snows were on the ground and the ponds were frozen over, Daid came home again. He was back to his usual self again, cursing and shouting and throwing things about. He stayed long enough to prepare for his trip to the country to hunt. He had very few supplies with him when he came back and he took most of it with him when he left for the country.

I mixed a batch of bread, while he made the baking powder biscuits and darned his vamps himself. The next morning, I watched him latch the grub box to the komatik along with his rackets and rifle. As he hitched the dogs to the komatik, he called over his shoulder that Grandpa was coming to stay with us for a spell, and for me to go to Godfather's shop if I needed some grub. I knew I would never go back to Godfather's shop. I would never relive that humiliation; even if it meant we'd all starve to death.

Our summer of plenty was over. There was no beef or pork barrel in the cellar, only a keg of red berries, and we had very little sugar left to make jam. The ducks Daid canned in the spring were all gone. We had hardly enough to carry us through until he came back again, if he came back before Christmas at all.

Grandpa arrived a few days later on a Sunday afternoon. I watched him hobble up the frozen path from the direction of Aunt Violet's place. I was leery about Grandpa coming to stay with us. It was the first time he'd come to visit since we moved into our new winter home. I remember him sleeping in the folding cot across the room from me in our old house, the same cot where other visitors slept when he wasn't there. Space was limited in our winter home and the extra space was in my tiny room only.

I can see the knobs of Juicy Fruit gum Grandpa stuck on the ledge above the bed. Parmenas always had a mouth full. He'd snatch that chewed up wad from the ledge every chance he got, while Ronald stole Grandpa's pouch tobacco. Sometimes he'd hide it in the little pillowcase on my doll's bed. As long as I could remember, Grandpa always came to our house when Daid went inland hunting with the Indians. Grandpa never gave us one red copper in his lifetime. But he sure was handy with the belt when he was around.

I knew his visit meant extra work for me. I didn't want to take care of him like my mother used to do. That old man smell of him was more than I could stomach. That's how I saw Grandpa, nothing but a seedy smelling hindrance. I prayed he wouldn't ask me to scrub his long johns while he was here.

I prepared a bed for him beforehand. He would sleep on the loft in Parmenas' bed. I helped him carry his small bundle of clothes upstairs. They were tied to the old cane he carried over his shoulder. He walked up the stairs ahead of me with his brand new cane with the gold plated handle, his old man smell wafting down around me. The next morning, being Monday, I was up before dawn. I knew by the full bright moon without a circle around it the night before that it was going to be a fine day. I needed to get the sheets out on the line to dry. I filled the boilers and pots and put them over the dampers on the stove to heat the water. I sorted the soiled long johns and vamps and piled them on the floor next to the tubs sitting on two chairs. By the time Grandpa got out of bed, the morning was half gone. The dishes were washed and put away and the second and third youngest were outside playing. The baby sat on the floor, babbling to himself. I poured Grandpa a cup of tea and put bread on an enamel place. I was already resenting his presence here. I didn't want to tend on him. I wanted to get the wash out on the line before noon. I couldn't go upstairs to change the sheets while he was sleeping and while the first two were soaking in the tub, I went to Mum's room to remove the piss soaked blankets from the bed. All the while, Grandpa was talking to me from the kitchen table, telling me that Daid would come back from the country this time with venison for the winter, telling me that things were gonna be okay. I'd heard all that before, I thought. I knew my father was back to doing what he always did. I knew that nothing was ever going to change. I noticed Grandpa didn't bring anything to help see us through either, not that I expected him to. I only half listened to him as I tried to untangle the cotton sheet that were caught in the bedspring on the inside of the bed. I pulled the bed partially away from the wall and leaned across it to untangle the sheet without tearing it.

I was so preoccupied with trying to untangle the sheet, I didn't see or hear Grandpa coming to stand beside the bed. As I slid off the bed I came up against him standing there. I jumped away from him as his hand reached out to grab me, to hold me there. At the same time he began to coo to me like a child, telling me to let Grandpa do it to me cause I had an ass just like my mother.

As I jumped away from him, distant images overflowed from some dark place inside my mind. And, with the images, rage broke free from where it was hidden like a violent torrential river onto swollen ice. I ran past him to the stove and grabbed the steaming kettle up off the damper hole.

Git outta dis jeesas ouse befer I scald yar jeesas face clean hoff.

Doan youse fire dat kettle at me, my maid. I ll give you a lashing wit t belt, if youse doos.

Ya, dis es t day youse will meet yer maker, youse gawddamn ole basturd. Git outta dis ouse and doan ever come back ere agin. I m tellin Daid when e gits back.

Doan youse tell yer fadder now. I m goin. Jest let me git me parka. Youse bedder not fire dat kettle, youse hear.

As I watched him hobble down the same path he walked up yesterday, leaning on his cane, heading towards Aunt Violet's place, many sickening visions raced through my mind. He stopped and turned and wrung his fist at me. In turn, I screamed more profanities at him. I don't know why I didn't throw the steaming kettle in his face as I threatened I would. I don't know why I didn't follow him and smother him in the snowbank. God knows I wanted to.

After he was finally out of my sight I went back to making the bed, but first I yanked that goddamn sheet with all my might and ripped it from hem to hem. I didn't care if my father knew I'd driven him from the door. I didn't care if my mother was looking down from the sky. I only knew that on this day my life took on another evil twist. And it was out of this day that this rage inside of me rose above the surface, never to be subdued again.

As days went by, the rage continued to grow. Before Grandpa arrived at our house, I had a routine with the youngsters. And I was so looking forward to Daid coming back from the country with venison for the winter. There was a part of me that hoped he would stay home this time and help me take care of the youngsters.

All summer and all fall I'd heard the rumours that he had a woman down on the Labrador. The woman my mother had told me so much about had a name now and I had convinced myself that's where he spent most of his time. I wondered if she had any youngsters and if he was taking care of them instead of us. But I still hoped he would stay home with us. With Uncle Willie and Aunt Violet's help, I managed to get through the fall months. As I stood on the threshold of winter I was suddenly faced with the cold hard facts of reality. Perhaps if Grandpa hadn't came, I would still be pretending that my father cared whether we lived or died. My mother's voice kept ringing inside my mind telling me otherwise.

Ronald was no longer at home, neither was Parmenas. I was used to Brian and Raymond wandering off but they always came home around dark. But suddenly, with the arrival of that seedy old bastard, all hope inside of me died. How dumb I was to think that my father would come back at Christmas and help me through the winter months as he did in the spring. The pattern inside my mind was quite clear. Daid would go in the country and Grandpa would come and stay with me, just like he used to with my mother. Only this time, perhaps Daid expected him to stay with us while he gallivanted down on the Labrador after that other skirt.

I doubted if my father ever knew the main reason Grandpa stayed at our house while he was gone. Perhaps we belonged to that seedy old bastard. Perhaps now Daid and him both expected me to fill my mother's role. As a child, I saw too much and now that my mother was no longer here the old bastard thought it was time to have a go at me. Did I hear her laughter, like the day she ran out of the house and left the man from Long

Point with me? Perhaps I did. As I watched Grandpa walk away, I hated her then more than I hated him. I hated my back-boneless father even more.

It's the middle of December and I'm lying in my bed listening to the sound of wind spurts moaning in the eaves. I lie in my bed not wanting to get up. Earlier, I lit the fire then went back upstairs to bed. I stayed in bed, not caring about anything or anyone anymore. Even though there was nowhere to hide from the truth, I found comfort in my bed. I couldn't stop dwelling on Grandpa and imagining the worst yet to come. One thing was for certain, it didn't matter how hard I tried to keep us all together, my father didn't care. No one cared if we lived or died, no one except Uncle Willie and his family. I couldn't tell Uncle Willie about Grandpa, but perhaps I should have.

I hear the youngsters squabbling among themselves; they fight and whine almost always now. They dress themselves and leave the house, the younger ones following the older ones. I knew if I stayed upstairs in my bed they would all go to Aunt Violet's place.

In the quiet that settles after they leave, Mum's voice is loud and crisp upon the morning air, *I tole youse to git yer carcass outta dat bed, t day is almost gone and youse got nar tap done yet. Git up, I sez, befer I goes up dar wit dat stick.*

Fully dressed, I jumped out of bed. The echo of her voice is there as I run from the filthy shack. Like the youngsters, I ran down to the sanctuary of Aunt Violet's place. She was pinning wash out on the line. I ran to stand beside her, to help her like I always did. And like always, Aunt Violet lectured me, trying to make me do more than I was doing. Perhaps she was worried about my state of mind. I doubt if Aunt Violet had ever known just how much I needed her. And even if it meant putting up with her lecturing me it was better than being alone with my mother's ghost.

I saw the stranger on the doorstep at almost the same time as Aunt Violet did.

Whose dat, youse spose? Run Clarissy, quick, see wot dat man wants. I nebber seen the likes of e befer. Run, urry up.

I quickly covered the distance between Aunt Violet's house and ours.

The tall, clean-cut stranger, wearing a high peak hat and a grey uniform with a revolver strapped to his side, turned towards the cutting sound of my angry voice.

I m Mr. LeDrew, he said, *and I m looking for the residence of Robert Smith.*

Youse found t jeesas shack, I snap, keeping my distance from the intruder.

Is your father at home? he asked politely.

Youse won t find t likes of e round yere. He s been gone for a long spell now.

Is your mother at home?

My mudder is dead, I answer coldly.

Who are you? he asks.

Clarissy.

Can we go inside?

Wot fer? Deres nuddin but misery in dat gawddamn shack.

Still, I think we should go inside, Miss, he said.

I don't know whether it was his assertiveness or the gentle tone of his voice, but I found myself lifting the latch and leading him inside the shack. Once inside, the hugeness of the man seemed to dwarf the kitchen space. I rushed forward and got the best chair, its legs tied together with rope and a few rungs still in the back, and silently hoped the legs wouldn't give away when he sat down. I don't know why I suddenly wanted to please this stranger. Quickly, I wiped the dirt off the seat with my sweater sleeve before I motioned for him to sit while I went to stand defiantly beside the cold stove. In the middle of the floor was a pile of ashes I had scooped up and left when I lit the early morning fire. A fresh pile of dogshit was in the corner too. It seemed to jump up at me. The shame of a complete stranger seeing the filth inside this shack washed over me. I began to make allowances for the terrible state around me. I let him know the house was in this state because I had nothing to work with. With pen poised above the notepad resting on his knee, he began to write. The more I poured out my soul, the faster he wrote. I told him how I hated my father for leaving me all by myself to raise the youngsters.

Wots him and mudder tink I is? I got nar scrap of grub in dis jeesas shack and nar stick of wood out dere nar the chopping block. Wees is all gonna die jest like she sez. She expects me to do everyting. All she ever doos is blame me fer everyting.

I thought you told me she had passed away.

She did. But er ghost is aw ways ere, hauntin me. I wish we wuz all dead wit er, then I wuddent have to worry no more. Hitler is gonna let we all starve t deat jest like she sed e wuz.

Bitterly, I explained to the stranger how Godfather was every bit as responsible for our dilemma as my father. I told him how Godfather refused to give me any grub on tick. I truly believed that he took the Family Allowance to pay off the debts owing him. I said I couldn't go and ask for grub like Mum and Daid said because so much was still owing to him. I told the stranger about my Uncle Willie and Aunt Violet. I told him about my cousins who brought me wood all the winter before. I told him how we would have died without Aunt Violet's bread and the snowbirds.

I told him about my cousin Manuel bringing us a bag of grub every time he got his dole in the mail.

Wees cant go thru anudder winter like dat agin. I kint let Daid give dem youngsters away. I promis er, I promised. All I wants is sum grub t feed we wit, dats all.

By the time the stranger left that shack he knew the inside of my tortured soul. I said everything I could except beg him to take us away from the godforsaken hole we lived in. I might have known that Uncle Willie was responsible for his visit, knowing we were heading into another winter like the last. I might have figured it all out if I could have coped with the turmoil going on inside my mind.

After the stranger left, I had a sudden desperate urge to clean up the filth just in case he came back. I scooped the ashes up off the floor with my bare hands and threw them in the stove, then I ran down to the landwash and bobbed the flayed ends of the thin mop up and down in the water until I got it almost grey-white again. I ran to the brook, fetched a bucket of water, and tried to wash the filthy floor. I succeeded only in smudging the sooty grimy floorboards as the wooden end of the mop scraped across it. I was rushing around the cold, soot covered, piss smelling kitchen trying to clean it with only cold water when Aunt Violet came through the doorway with four of the youngsters in tow.

When she asked me who the stranger was, I said I had no idea. All I could tell her was that I thought he was a policeman and that he was tall and had a gun. All I could think of was the shame of having the clean and meticulous stranger standing in the filth around me.

Perhaps dats sumboddy frum the welfare place. Perhaps deys comin to take youse away frum dis hole. Yer fadder shud be shot fer leavin youse in dis state. Deys kint take the youngsters, Aunt Violet. I wont let dem. I promised Mum dat I wud keep we all t gedder. Youse knows I promised.

Youse kint doos no more dan youse already done, my maid. Git dat tru yer tick skull. After all, youse is not Gawd.

CHAPTER 18

△ **RAGE**

Christmas week finally came, rolling in bleak and miserable, like a thick grey fog. Trapped inside the cold shack, with the smoke-covered walls, the empty cupboards and the filth evident in all corners of the house, I felt strangled. I had no will to go on, nor did I have the will to take care of the youngsters any more.

Day after day, I waited for the return of the stranger. As Christmas loomed upon me, I had all but given up. Had he promised he would return or did I imagine it?

With hardly a glimmer of hope, each new day was no different from the last. I did very little while I waited for Daid and the stranger to return, except keep the fires going, hang the dirt-caked vamps above the stove to dry at night, and pile the youngsters badly worn rubber boots on top of the splits drying on the oven door. The youngsters stank with the smell of stale piss on their clothes. Lice dropped from their heads as they continued to scratch. Snot dried on their tattered sleeves from wiping their runny noses. Dogshit was everywhere, except upstairs, and it was a constant battle driving the few remaining dogs away from the door. Daid hadn't brought home any bone meal to feed them with. They were starving too.

Days after I drove Grandfather from the house I was still seething with rage and fear. I had no one to turn to only the youngsters, and I vented my rage out on them. I didn't care if I ever woke up at all. Some days, I didn't get up from my bed. The youngsters wandered away and if they hadn't returned by late afternoon, or if rough weather set in, I'd go in search of them, carrying the broken axe handle in case I met up with stray dogs. As much as I didn't want to be anchored down with the youngsters, I didn't want them to be attacked by dogs like I had. Sometimes I walked to almost every house on Bradore Plains before I found them. Rounding them up like stray cats, I forced them to come back home with me. When they disobeyed and tried to run away I smacked them; sometimes I tied them to the table legs to keep them home. Always shouting at them, always slapping them, I was out of control, venting my anger on them. There were moments I wished they had never been born. As the days went slowly by there was no sign of Daid or the stranger.

Around the twentieth of each month most of the villagers received their dole and Family Allowances. If Trout Pond was frozen over, the plane dropped the mail near the Postmaster's house on Bradore Plains. When Manuel got his dole, he brought us potatoes and turnip, and Aunt Violet gave me another bun of bread as well as flour and a half a pack of yeast, enough to tide us over until Daid got back again. We both expected that he'd be home any day. His ritual was to arrive home one or two days before Christmas day, depending on the weather. I was thankful for the survival rations from Manuel and Aunt Violet, but it was never enough. I knew we couldn't survive another winter like the last. Uncle Willie and his sons were taking grub from their own tables to give to us. January seemed so far away, so long before the snowbirds came again. I could no longer pretend that Daid would stay home and help me raise the youngsters. Nor could I pretend that he would come back with enough grub for us to get through the long months ahead. This winter would be no different than the last. He'd arrive back from the country with some venison and once it was hung in the storehouse he'd be gone again. He would leave one quarter or shoulder and the rest he would give away. I knew the fate of the youngsters rested in my two empty hands. My fears, coupled with my rage, heightened to enormous proportions as each day came and went with no signs of Daid or the stranger returning.

DECEMBER 24, 1962

Christmas Eve finally arrived. Like the year before, I stand near the window, (the same broken window pane from the year beforewith cardboard stuck in the frame to keep out the rain and snow) staring down to the landwash for signs of Daid in the storehouse. I knew that if he were coming home this would be the day. I couldn't ever remember him not coming home for Christmas. Some part of me knew that if he didn't return this Christmas Eve, it meant that he had met with ill fate on the other side of the mountains somewhere. In my heart, I willed him to come home. As frustrated as I was, and as often as I said I wished he was dead, I didn't want my father to be gone forever.

Even though I had lost all hope of him staying at home and helping me take care of the youngsters, I wanted him to come back.

I couldn't stop dwelling on Grandpa and my mother. Thoughts about them occupied my every waking moment until I couldn't function anymore. My rage grew and grew until I could think of nothing else. I had to let Daid know it was not okay for Grandpa to stay with us, and that it was his responsibility to stay home with us. I kept thinking that perhaps some of us belonged to Grandpa and perhaps that was why Daid left us alone most of the time. And I wondered why did my father allow his father to come to our house to stay if he knew what went on between my mother and him. On this Christmas Eve, I knew that I had come to a point in my life when I needed to make a stand. There was no turning back. I didn't care whether he killed me or not. Before the day was done he would know all that was inside of me. The rage inside of me could not be silent any longer.

I sent all the youngsters down to Aunt Violet's place where I knew they'd be safe. I took my parka down off the hook and put it on. I put warm vamps in my rubber boots and put my mitts in my pocket. I had to be ready for whatever fate was to come to me.

Like a caged animal I paced back and forth from the stove to the window, waiting for signs of him down on the shoreline near the storehouse. It was early afternoon when he arrived. I see him standing near the heavy laden komatik, unharnessing the dogs. As I watched him from the window my heart felt no joy as it had the year before while I waited for him to come up to the shack.

I was ready and waiting, determined to be gone to god knows where because I sure didn't. I hadn't given a second thought to where I would go if he kicked me out.

Finally, he's standing in the doorway. And like the savage my mother always said I was, I began to shout at him before his foot even landed on the porch floor, not holding back one single thought as it entered my mind. All my frustrations, all my pent-up anger, all my fears boiled over my lips in uncontrollable rage.

I was dancing around the porch floor like someone gone mad. I let him know how sick and tired I was of trying to keep us all from starving to death and of trying to scrounge up enough wood to keep the fire burning. I said from then on he'd goddamn well better mind the youngsters himself because I was going and I wouldn't be back. And I said if he brought Grandpa to this house anymore I would kill him.

I was only partway through with telling him what was really on my mind when he yanked me by my parka hood, and with his boot, he drove me headlong into the snowbank. He drove me from the door like a dog, telling me to never come back home again because he didn't want another slut in the house like my mother. I danced and screamed with refueled rage as he slammed the door shut in my face. *I m not my mudder.*

Gawddamn youse. I m not my mudder.

The savage in him was greater than the savage in me. I had suspected he would drive me from the door, but I wasn't expecting him to brand me like the kinfolk branded my mother. The pain in my chest was far greater than the pain in my back from the kick he gave me. The fate of the youngsters was the last thing on my mind when I ran away that day. I ran and ran, vowing never to return.

I didn't stop running until I reached the bay. And as the last rays of the sun went down behind Jack's Cove, I stood on the bank staring down into the frozen cellar hole where I stand now, tears streaming down my face, willing God to take me from this Earth.

I had no idea why I came back to this place at all. No one lived in the bay any more; they had all moved to Bradore Plains. Perhaps I went to our old house expecting to see my mother. I longed to see my mother; I needed so much to hear my mother's voice. I wished with all my heart that I were dead on that desperate Christmas Eve.

One thing I knew for certain was that if Mum had lived, there would be more unwanted youngsters for me to mind. We were bastards, branded from birth, rats, forgotten, brought into the world by a lonely desperate woman caught up in the web of empty tomorrows, seeking love from all the wrong sources and being used and humiliated. At age fifteen, I had come full circle with my existence, and hers. I lamented her passing, I lamented our births and all I wanted to do was crawl in that hole in the ground and die. Anything was better than accepting the fact that because of my dead mother's infidelities, and with full understanding and knowledge of the reason why my father had abandoned us so often, I knew there was little hope the youngsters would survive without me. Yet I vowed never to go back and become a punching bag like her and be branded like her. I would never go back to be branded like her.

I can't say how long I was in the cellar hole. All I know is that the stars were out, the wind was up, the bay ice was cracking with the shifting tide, and my dog, Blackhead, was whimpering and licking my face. Familiar sights and sounds were all around me: the muffled roar of Norse Brook Falls, and the Northern Lights dancing in the cold night sky above the rim of Queen's Hill. It was as though I had gone to some faraway place and now I was back. I buried my face in Blackie's fur and wept and wept.

Some guiding power greater than me gave me the will to crawl out of the hole and go back in the direction of Lance Kinard, back to them. Perhaps it was my mother's spirit. I wasn't sure what I would do when I reached the shack. Whatever the reasoning, whatever spirit guided me, I walked back to where I wasn't wanted, barely able to stand on my frozen feet. Some hours later, I found myself near the broken window staring into the darkness to see if Brian was there with them. I had expected Daid to be long gone. Brian was standing near the stove, adding more wood to the fire. Some of the others were huddled around the stove. I could see Raymond sitting on a chair next to the fire. Daid was somewhere in the darkness nearby; I could hear him shouting at Brian to go up to bed. Brian was sassing him. I knew soon Daid would take off his belt and beat him. Brian kept on angrily stoking the fire in the stove. I squatted down in the snow beneath the window. I didn't want Brian to know I was there. I didn't want Daid to know that I had come back. I didn't want Brian to be beaten with the belt.

The wind was higher now and the snow swirled around on the ground. The night got colder while I waited for them to go to bed. To keep from freezing to death, I crawled up under the house with Blackie and huddled down among the other dogs. I intended to stay there until daybreak and then I would walk to Long Point to see if I could stay with Uncle John and his family. I knew I could never go back inside the house as long as he was there. I convinced myself that as long as I stayed away he would have to mind the youngsters himself.

Finally, when they had all settled down and I could hear Daid snoring, I crawled out from underneath the floorboards on my elbows. The dogs paid no mind to me; they were all curled up with their heads buried in their tails. I could hardly stand on my feet I was that numb from the cold. Common sense told me I had to get warm. I knew I couldn't go down to Uncle Willie's place. I knew both him and Aunt Violet would tell me to go on home and mind the youngsters. What choice did I have but creep back inside the house and take shelter? I would walk to Long Point in the morning when the stars were still in the sky.

As I crept painfully towards the porch door, I noticed a light in our summer house down on the shore. I had forgotten that Daid had given the house to Manuel, perhaps in lieu of money he owed him. I didn't realize Manuel was living there until I saw the light. I understood the house would be dismantled in the spring and the lumber used in the new house on the hill. It really didn't matter to me. All I knew is that the light was beckoning me. As I walked unsteadily toward the shore, I suddenly felt like I was going home. I knew I would find shelter there.

When I finally reached the summer house, I thudded upon the door with my frozen mitts. It seemed forever before Manuel came. He stood there with one hand on the latch and the lamp in his other hand. He jumped back in fright when he saw me standing there and quickly ushered me inside. He added wood to the dying fire and pried the mitts from my hands and the rubbers from my feet as I sobbed and sobbed. While he rubbed the life back into my hands and put my feet into the oven to get them warm, I told him about the fight I had with Daid. I told him what my father had said about my mother and me. I said all I ever wanted was for my father to stay home and help me raise the youngsters. All I ever wanted was for Daid to bring home the grub so I could keep us alive.

Pacing the floor, he kept repeating, *Poor Aunt May. Poor Aunt May. Youse gotta go back to mind dem youngsters, my maid. Youse gotta go back fer dere sakes and ers. Youse gotta go back.*

How could I make Manuel understand that I couldn't go back.

My cousin brought me to Long Point to stay with my Uncle John and his family. There I stayed until the next storm was over. When Uncle Willie found out that Manuel had taken me to Uncle John's place, he came to get me. He urged me to go back home to be with the youngsters. He was afraid that Daid would leave them all alone in the house without any fire in the stove. After Uncle Willie left, I thought long and hard and I knew in my heart that I had no choice but to go back. Even if I didn't go back to the shack, at least I could keep an eye on them while I stayed in the cottage on the shore.

On Old Christmas Day, there was a square dance in Long Point. After dark, I left Uncle John's place and walked up to the schoolhouse. There were many teams of dogs curled up on the snow banks beside the school. I waited outside until the dance was over. When Manuel came out I asked him to take me back home. I didn't tell him that I had no intention of going back to the house if Daid was still there.

When we arrived back at Lance Kinard and saw Daid's dog team near the house, I kept on going to the summer place on the shore. Nothing Manuel could say would make me change my mind. Somewhere inside my foolish mind I truly believed that I had just as much right to stay in the house as he did. And I really didn't care what gossip would be circulated around the village. I needed shelter and this house belonged to my mother still. This is where I belonged.

The next day, Brian, Raymond, Clyde and Geraldine came down to the shore. Brian informed me that Daid was still at home. Every day, after dark, I'd creep up to the house and peer in the window to see if Daid was still there. Most of the time Brian would be stoking the fire, and cursing on the fire just like I had done while they huddled around the stove trying to keep warm. Satisfied that they were all there I'd go back to the cottage on the shoreline.

Days passed, perhaps a week, before the next major storm stuck. It struck with such ferocity that whiteouts blanketed the land for three days. There was no way of knowing if the youngsters were safely inside the house upon the hill. On the morning the storm was over and the wind died down, I saw no smoke coming from the stovepipe. I didn't see any dogs running around the snow banks in search of food. I urged Manuel to go and fetch Uncle Willie. I knew Uncle Willie would go up there to check on the youngsters even though Daid was there. Uncle Willie was sick with the flu, but he got out of bed and went to the shack to see for himself if the youngsters were all right.

A short while later, I could see Uncle Willie walking towards the house. I saw him enter the house. Seconds later he came out running, shouting at me to come quickly, shouting at Manuel to fetch his dogs and latch the coach box onto the komatik. My heart was pounding in my ears as I ran. I knew something terrible had happened if he was asking Manuel to latch the coach box to the komatik. I didn't know what to expect. I ran with all my might up over the ridge towards the house. The door was open when I reached it. Uncle Willie would tell me later that the porch door was open when he approached it. It was evident by the snow in the porch. The inside door was open also. There, in my mother's bed lay the two youngest ones, in an unconscious state. Two dogs were curled up beside them, one at the foot of the bed beside Riley's head, the other at the head of the bed beside the baby. They both lay there, sprawled on their backs, eyes closed, their stomachs swollen, not moving. For two whole days, while the storm raged outside, James and Riley were inside the house alone. There was no way of knowing if they were ill before the storm struck, before Daid left them, before Brian and the others left the house, but I can only surmise they were. If the door was open and they were able to go outside before the storm struck they might have followed the others to Uncle Willie's place. And they might have smothered in the storm. Perhaps they were too ill to follow the rest. But as fate would have it, instead they were in bed, with two dogs curled up beside them, asleep. I see the picture inside my mind still. It will never leave me.

Screaming hysterically, I grabbed the baby and shook him. He was as limp as a rag doll. His head lolled to the side as if he was dead. By then, Aunt Violet was standing there beside me, holding Riley in her arms and shaking him. Uncle Willie plucked Riley and James from us and ran to the coach box and covered them in many quilts. Within seconds he was mushing the dogs up over the hill towards the hospital in Long Point.

Until that moment, I didn't even think about the others. I didn't think about the others until Aunt Violet ordered me to run to Pern's place to find out if they were there. She told me Geraldine and Clyde were asleep in bed at her place. The storm had come on so suddenly that she kept them there with her.

I ran the half-mile to Pern's house and bolted through the doorway.

Brian, Raymond and Elliot were sitting at the breakfast table safe and sound. Like his mother, Pern had kept them there when the storm struck. I told Pern that Daid had left the youngsters in the house alone. I told him that I thought they were both dead. I ran back to Aunt Violet to tell her the others were okay. Aunt Violet was pacing the floor and wringing her hands; she was beside herself with worry. My mother would turn over in her grave, she said. My mother would never forgive me for leaving them to fend for themselves, she said. She didn't have to remind me, I already felt responsible. Because of my stubbornness in trying to force him to take care of the youngsters, I had failed to heed my mother's voice. At this precise moment it wasn't my father who had abandoned the youngsters, it was me. Mum had begged me to guard them with my life, and I had let them down. Now here I stood, feeling the impact of the terrible wrongs brought down upon them, and knowing I was nothing more than the Jesus hard head my mother always said I was. It didn't matter if she or Aunt Violet would forgive me. I would never forgive myself.

I was full of self-loathing as I left Aunt Violet's place and ran back to that cold, miserable shack. As I stand in the room Mum had never slept in ard looked down at the bed, at the indentations where their tiny heads had lain I hear once more her pleading voice. *Guard dem youngsters wit yer life, my maid, guard dem youngsters wit yer life.*

I see the rounded hollowed out spots where the dogs had curled up beside them. I see them sprawled there unconscious, half naked, partially covered by the piss-soaked quilts. I don't know why they hadn't frozen to death. Perhaps they might have if the dogs weren't curled up beside them. Why did he leave them in the house all by themselves? How could he be so cruel? Why hadn't Brian come down to the shore to get me? I should have come back. Oh God, what have I done?

I began to question if Daid was ever there. Perhaps on the nights I saw Brian stoking the fire he was never there. Perhaps I pretended all along that he was there. Perhaps I passed on the responsibility to Brian just like Daid had done to me. And Brian, like me, had left them alone to fend for themselves. If they die, I know it's all my fault. As I stand in the aftermath, in the unbearable silence, I hear no crying, no shouting, no laughter. I see only misery inside the shack. Ashes on the stove, around the stove, the lifter in the corner, odd mittens and vamps here and there, the kettle with no lid. The pantry bare, no sign of any grub at all. Two chairs without backs near the stove. Dirt and dogshit everywhere. The place looked abandoned, like no one had lived there for months. Death stands in the corner, her voice moans in the eaves, yet the deafening silence surrounds me. I turn and walk towards the door just as I did on the day my father brought her back from the hospital for the last time. In shame and regret, I walk away from that dismal shack.

Two whole days went by before Uncle Willie came back from the hospital. He came to find me down on the shore. James and Riley were out of danger, and would survive, he said. He'd met with Dr. Marcoux and Social Services, and said the police officer was coming back to take the others away. I kept reminding him over and over they couldn't give the youngsters away, that I would go back to mind the youngsters. All I needed was grub to feed us wit. I kept reminding him of the promise I had made to my mother. I said it didn't matter if my father wouldn't stay and mind the youngsters, that I would go back.

Uncle Willie and I paced the floor, and when I refused to listen to him anymore he took hold of me and sat me in the chair, his voice firm and loud, drowning me out.

Lissen ta me, my maid, he said. *Youse is not gawd. Dem youngsters will die like er if youse doan lissen ta me. See what appened, two of dem is almost dead now. Youse kint do dat all by yer owntself. Youse haves nar red copper to feed dem youngsters with. Yer fadder is not comin back. Youse kint do nuddin. Youse is only a snip of a girl still. Dere comin ta take youse too. Dats why youse got ta lissen ta me now.*

What fer? I can take care off my owntsel. Dere not takin me, dats fer gawddamn shur.

Dey can take youse. Youse is not old enuff to make yer own decisions. Youse kint stay wit Manuel either. He s gonna go ta jail fer keepin youse here. Does youse understand now wat I m tryin ta git thru to youse?

Wot do youse mean, Uncle Willie? Gawddamn, wot youse mean?

Youse habs t do wot I sez now. Lissen ta me now. When dey comes ta git youse, youse is goin to t hospital. Youse gotta demand dat Dr. Marcoux examine youse. Dats the only way to save Manuel from goin ta jail. Youse have no choice. Youse gotta do dat fer es sake. Yer gawdfadder tole dem youse was sleeping ere with Manuel. He said being yer gawdfadder he feared dat you might git in the family way.

Oh dat son of a bitch. Who doos e tink e is? E bedder not interfere wit my life, dat bastard. E s tryin to clear es name now, cause he knows I tole dat policeman what he done. If e didn t steal dat Family Allowance, we d been okay.

Doan madder wot he sez, youse have to talk to Dr. Marcoux. Youse gotta do it, youse unnerstan? If youse dint do nuddin with nobody den youse can prove dat. Dats why youse gotta git t doctor examin youse.

It suddenly all became very clear to me, what Uncle Willie was trying to tell me. I could prove my innocence, and everyone, including my father, would know that I wasn't like my mother.

Uncle Willie left shortly afterwards to go down on the Labrador to find my father. It was much, much later before he told me that he had found my father at the house of the woman my mother had so often accused him of having the affair with.

A short while after he left, I walked across Bradore Plains to my Godfather's place. He was shocked when I burst through the doorway. I shouted at him that if he ever interfered in my life again I would kill him. I told him that just because he had his way with my mother it didn't give him the right to interfere with me. His response was that I was going to get knocked up if I stayed there with Manuel.

Aw youse ever cared bout is ta clear yer name. Youse knows youse stole dat Family Allowance to pay wot dey owes youse. If youse cared bout we, youse wud have helped me when I begged fer the gawddamn grub my mudder sed youse wuz gonna give me when I needed some. Now, cuz of youse and im dey might die. Gawddamn youse, I say. Gawddamn im. I wish youse both wuz dead. Yer not my gawddamn fadder, youse gawddamn whoremonger!"

Raging out of control, I went back to the shack on the shore and told Manuel what I had done. Manuel sat on the day bed, rocking back and forth, crying and repeating over and over, *Poor Aunt May. Poor Aunt May.*

The next morning, I walked to Long Point and made a phone call to Father Burke. I had to get a message to my Aunt Dorothy in Harrington. My mother had made me promise that if anything should happen and they came to take the youngsters away Geraldine was to go to live with Aunt Dot. Andrew gave me two dollars to pay for the call. I had never used a telephone before; everything mechanical scared me half to death. When Mr. Cormier cranked the phone and got Father Burke on the line, he handed me the earpiece. I didn't know what to do with the thing so I put it to my mouth to speak. Mr. Cormier showed me how to use it, then found a box for me to stand on to speak in the mouthpiece. I begged Father Burke to get a message to my aunt. I told him what was happening. I told him about my mother's dying request. He promised he would contact my aunt.

That same evening I stood near the window in the shack on the shore waiting for the policemen to arrive. I knew they were coming that evening because my Godfather had shouted as I was leaving his door that they were coming to take me away.

I see the snowmobile lights at the lip of the hill. I watched two lights make their way down over the snow towards the house. I'm assuming one is my father. When I opened the door to let the policeman in, I see my Godfather standing next to him. Blinded by rage, I reacted the only way I knew how, with my fists. And then I tried to grab the gun out of the holster attached to the officers side. The police officer grabbed me and pinned my arms to my sides and forced me back inside. Godfather followed him in.

You brazen son of a bitch, I screamed at him. *I ll see youse in Hell befer youse tinks youse can decide wot I doos wit my life. I doan belong to youse, youse bastard, now git out befer I kills youse. Git out, youse son of a bitch. Get out,* I screamed. Godfather left.

After my outburst, and when I thought Godfather was out of my sight,

I went willingly with the officer up over the ridge to the snowmobile. All the others were inside, all of them except Parmenas and Ronald. When I saw my father sitting at the front of the machine, near the driver, crying his eyes out, once more I went into a blinding rage. I screamed and lunged towards him and threatened him the same way I had Godfather. The officer had a grip on me and held me back. He told my father to move to the back of the snowmobile. All I could think of was what a spineless coward my father was. The officer held me tightly while I kicked and screamed and sobbed. All the way to the hospital he kept my face buried in his jacket, perhaps so I wouldn't have to look at my father. I screamed out loud how better off we'd be if we were all dead like her. Then we wouldn't have to face the likes of that coward, the heartless father who would get rid of us like rats. While the officer held my face to his chest, I could smell his clean scent, and suddenly it dawned on me how filthy I am. I know that Dr. Marcoux will see how filthy I am if I have to remove my clothes, but Im determined to prove my innocence. I have no choice but to prove my innocence, not just for Manuel's sake, but for mine, so everyone will know that I am no whore.

By the time we reached the hospital, I'm raging so out of control that the officer led me from the snowmobile to the hospital, while the others stayed inside. He released his hold on me only when the doors shut tight behind us.

You promised, you promised to come back, I sobbed. He apologizes then.

Its too late now, I say. *I promised Mum dat none off dem will ever be given up for adoption. I won t let him give dem away like dogs. I ll kill him befer I let him do dat. I promised er, I promised.*

Nothing is your fault, he says, *nothing is your fault.*

Dr. Marcoux is sitting behind his desk as we enter his office. I'm screaming and wailing like a raging lunatic. I know I'm not sane at this moment. I doubt if I'll ever be again. Defiantly, I stand beside the desk, glaring at Dr. Marcoux. The officer goes around the desk to stand beside the doctor. I stand facing them both as a nun enters the room and stands beside me.

Uncle Willie sez I can prove I dint do nuddin with Manuel. He seys fer me to tell youse to examine me. I want youse ta examine me now, I screamed.

Dr. Marcoux tries to get me to sit. Ignoring him, I stand and shout at the top of my lungs, demanding that I be examined like Uncle Willie said.

I *have to question you*, he said.

Go ahead, I say. I m not livin wit im, I shout. I m livin in my mudder s house, gawddamn. Tis my mudder s house.

Okay, miss, where do you sleep?

On t daybed besides the stove.

Where does your cousin sleep?

In t room where he always sleeps.

Did you have intercourse with this man?

Wots dat mean?

He looks at the officer standing beside him. The officer shrugs. With his finger and thumb he forms a hole then puts his other forefinger through the opening. With one sweep of my arm, everything leaves his desk, Including the lamp.

Gawddamn youse, I shout. *I jest sed dat Unce Willie seys I can prove I didn t hab nuddin t do wit hinnybody. I m not my gawddamn mudder. Befer I let any dawg crawl on me I d kill the bastard. Youse hear. I d kill the bastard.*

Okay, okay.

He waves and the nun went scurrying from the office.

A short while later, she returns and Mother Superior is with her. The doctor motions for the nun to take me into the examining room. She hands me a white gown and tells me to remove my clothes. She leaves, closing the door.

I removed my parka, my boots, my dirt-caked vamps, my sweater, my dirty slacks and lastly my stained filthy bloomers. Piece by piece I dropped everything to the floor. As I stand there naked, staring down at that filthy heap, hearing nothing in the room but my own rasping breathing, reality comes to me like a punch in the stomach. I realize that I will always be my dead mother's daughter.

And the coward who didn't have the guts to stand up for me, that was supposed to be my father, he abandoned them and me like unwanted pups to be thrown over the stagehead. He couldn't wait to be rid of all of us. No one cared, not for me, nor for them, no one cared if we lived or died.

The harshest reality was that my mother was never coming back.

The youngsters would all be given away, just like she had prophesied. Only God knows where they'll end up. While I stand there in my nakedness, trying so desperately to prove my innocence so they wouldn't take Manuel to jail, I felt so defiled, so used. I was nothing more than a pawn in everyone's game.

There was no one there in that dark room, no windows, no wind, just the awful silence and my mother's voice coming through the high walls.

I hear her accusations. I know it's my fault Riley and James are lying half dead inside those hospital walls. Because of me, they might die. I might never see any of them again.

All the reasons why I'm standing there fighting for my dignity don't matter anymore, I knew they might die because of my stubborn ways. Because of my fear of what might happen to me, I had forgotten them. And what did it matter, no one would believe that it wasn't me who had left them. Everyone felt so sorry for my father, for having to raise them by himself, to provide for them while his deranged daughter left them all alone to fend for themselves. Poor Uncle Bob, they said, poor Aunt May.

Not one single soul said poor Clarissy. I was all to blame for everything that had befallen them. Perhaps it was my fault she had died. It was all up to me, she'd said, and I had failed her and them. What did it matter anymore whether or not I could prove I was a jesus virgin? I was going to be put away.

Daid was free at last. And as I stood there I had convinced myself that he was already on his way back to his new life down on the Labrador. He was going back to be with the woman he had left her and us for, while I stood alone to be judged for their sins, his and hers, to be held accountable for my brothers and my sister and my cousin.

Perhaps, to him, I was already dead like her. Why would he go back to Labrador if he cared at all for us? Damn him and his crocodile tears. Why hadn't they put the cuffs on him?

We're all bastard children of our dead mother. I wondered what would have happened if I had never been born. I wish I had never been born. I know I stand here humiliated and shamed because of her, because of him. I feel this anger down to the tips of my filthy toes. As I stand there in the quiet, inside those walls, so ashamed, so used, so unloved, so alone, I lose the will to go on.

⌂ EPILOGUE

So much happened in the days and months that followed. The nuns took me in their care and nursed me back to health. Without them I might not had made it. In the spring they urged me to go outside, to feel the sun upon my face, to become whole again. I doubted if I would ever become whole again.

Earlier, Dr. Marcoux came so quietly to the examining room that I didn't know he was there until he lifted my face and forced me to look up at him. He refused to perform the examination that I had demanded previously and explained to me why it was not necessary, but he said that I would have to stay at the hospital. He informed me that my cousin Manuel was already on his way to Sept-Iles, Quebec to jail. But he would see to it that he would be released the next day. *You ll be safe here*, he said.

Now, years later, I wonder if perhaps he thought my father and my Godfather would be safe from me. In my emotional state, there was no telling what I might have done. Perhaps I might have carried out the threat to avenge my mother's death.

Before he had finished speaking, Sister Bernard, the same nun that took care of me when I was attacked by the dogs, covered my nakedness with a hospital gown and led me from the examining room. She led me along the corridor and downstairs to a room without windows in the basement of the hospital. I learned later that's where they kept people who were low-minded or a threat to themselves or others.

Sister Bernard talked to me continuously, mostly in French, all the while she was filling the bathtub, the first porcelain tub I had ever seen. I stood there silently with no more will to speak. When the tub was filled, she removed my gown and helped me into the soothing water. She handed me a cake of Cashmere soap and a facecloth. Then she left the room and returned a short while later with a bottle of stuff that she put in my lice infested hair. Afterwards, she bundled my head in a towel. She took a facecloth and scrubbed my face, my back, and my arms.

The clean smell of the soap is in my nostrils still. I associated that smell with the feeling of being clean again. That heavenly smell. Any time

I've encountered that smell I recall when the sister scrubbed my filthy body with Cashmere soap. She dried me with large fluffy towels, then dressed me in a clean gown and helped me into bed. *You sleep, ma petite,* she urged, after giving me two pills to swallow.

When I awoke the next morning, Sister Bernard was there beside me. I don't know how long I stayed in the room without windows. I had no desire to face anyone ever again. Days and nights went by with only Sister Bernard and Sister Martha by my side. They were there when I went to sleep and when I awoke. Dr. Marcoux came to see me once to let me know that James and Riley were eating on their own. He encouraged me to go and see them. He felt that I needed to see them, but I had no desire to see them. I just wanted to be left alone. Geraldine had gone to live with my Aunt Dorothy in Harrington, he said. Dr. Marcoux had kept his promise.

Geddy was where my mother wanted her to be. She was safe now.

The two youngest ones recovered and were sent to foster homes on the Labrador. Alfred and Mally Belbin of Lanse au Loup took James and Wilfred and Margaret Davies of Point Amour took Riley. Elliot stayed with our cousin Pernell Etheridge of Bradore. Parmenas, at age eighteen, quit school in Lance au Clair and went back to the house in Bradore to take care of Clyde and Brian until foster homes were found. Within a few months, Brian went to live with Bob and Marian Trimn in English Point, Labrador, and Cyril and Cathy Joncas of Bradore took Clyde to live with them.

My mother made me promise on her last day upon this earth that I would not allow them to be given up for adoption. She made me promise to keep us all together. So hardened by my father's desertion of us, so filled with hate and rage towards those who tried to change things to suit their purpose, I couldn't beg or plead with anyone to help me to fulfill her dying wish. Instead, on the night I was taken to Notre Dame Hospital, I demanded and screamed and shouted at Dr. Marcoux to take heed of my mother's last words. *Gard dem youngsters wit yer life,* she'd sobbed. *Gard dem youngsters wit yer life.* I screamed at him that I would kill my father if he gave any one of them up for adoption. Dr. Marcoux promised me that none of them would be given up for adoption. Instead, they all went to foster homes and the families that took them were paid for their upbringing.

Weeks went by. During that time, Sister Saint Joseph made new clothes for me. The clothes I wore when I was brought to the hospital were burned in the incinerator. She made me blouses, nightgowns, and slacks I was given brassieres and underpants. One day, Dr. Marcoux came to tell me that I would be working on the babies' ward. I would be closer to Riley and James and I would be paid seventeen dollars a month. Later, I would give some of that money to Parmenas so he could buy grub for him and Brian and Clyde.

The first week in the babies' ward, I was doing okay. Then one night I found myself alone with all the newborns. They awoke and began crying all at the same time. Panic-stricken, I stood over one of the newborn babies and began to shout at it to stop crying because I wasn't God and I didn't have any milk to give them, even though at the time I was preparing the formula at the sink. The louder the babies cried, the louder I shouted, until Dr. Marcoux came hurrying in and removed me from the ward. The sisters ran to the aid of the wailing newborns. Dr. Marcoux took me to his office and talked to me for a long time and removed me from the babies' ward for good. Once more, Sister Bernard and Sister Martha accompanied me to my room.

Days went by before Dr. Marcoux came to get me again. He told me that I would be working on the second floor with my cousin Florence, delivering trays, changing beds, and cleaning wards. It was spring then and the bay ice had broken up. As summer approached, I had a visit from Father Burke, the Anglican priest without a church, who had services in the schoolhouses along the coast. He said Bishop Brown of the diocese of Quebec had arranged to send me to a boarding school in the Eastern Townships of Quebec. All I had ever wanted was to go to school. I couldn't wait to be gone away from everything, the coast and all the pain still within me.

I wasn't allowed to leave the hospital until my broken mind had mended. I worked during the day and went to my room in the basement at night. In summer, I was allowed to go down on the Labrador to visit my little brothers. On Sundays, Alfreda and I would walk to Lanse au Loup, some twenty miles away. Sometimes, we got a lift from a passerby in a truck; most times we walked all the way there and back. Spending time with James, Riley and Brian helped me accept and understand why they were better off with the families that had taken them.

Father Burke had instructed me to listen to the five o'clock radio broadcast from Greenly Island every evening. Chesley Thomas was the lighthouse keeper on Greenly Island, a tiny island about a mile offshore from the hospital. Every evening, he would broadcast messages to people up and down the coast. Chesley would let me know when the plane would arrive at the airstrip to pick me up. I waited two months before I heard my name on the radio.

The first thing I did when I got the message was to send word to my brother Parmenas to get my birth certificate from my mother's trunk. I said I would be needing it where I was going. When my cousin Manuel heard that I was leaving, he arrived at the hospital, determined to see me before I went away. Almost six months had passed since I was taken from his place on the shore. I knew that all the tongues would be wagging once they saw his red truck outside on the gravel parking lot, in full view of the solarium where the patients sat to knit, gossip, and listen to Chesley Thomas's broadcast.

When Manuel arrived, I hid away on the third floor in the upper solarium so no one could see me or disturb me. I wanted to be as far away from him as possible. Only I knew what his intentions were. He wanted to marry me. When Dr. Marcoux found me hiding upstairs in the solarium, I told him why I didn't want to see Manuel. He said the choice was all mine and that he would send him away, and he did.

All afternoon, that banged up rusty piece of scrap metal sat there in plain view from the solarium windows. Manuel finally left, and I went back on the floor to help my cousin Florence deliver the supper trays. Everyone was whispering when I entered the solarium. Some were snickering; some just kept on knitting with downcast eyes. A young girl from up the coast apiece was there waiting to have her baby. She was sixteen or younger. When I set her tray down in front of her she brazenly laughed in my face. *Yer b y frind came ta see ya t day*, she snickered. Everyone laughed.

I don't remember dropping the tray on the floor. I heard someone screaming as my hands went around her throat. I see her bulging eyes, her rotting teeth, her rounded belly, large and full, jerking up and down as she tried to tear my hands away, as she tried to breathe. All I wanted to do right then was squeeze the life right out of her, and I might have if I hadn't seen the unborn baby beating itself against the protective walls of her belly.

Florence was trying to pry my hands loose. Someone slapped me before I let go, before I ran screaming from the room. Perhaps it was Dr. Marcoux who slapped me. Thank God that someone had sense enough to slap me. I heard Dr. Marcoux's voice loud and clear as I ran past him. His voice boomed down the hallway as I made my escape.

Later, when Sister Bernard found me, I was hiding in the bathroom stall, hiding in shame for what I had done to the unborn child. I kept sobbing over and over that I had killed the baby. She kept repeating that the baby was okay, that soon the baby would be born and they would both be okay. She said I needed to go with her to pray in the chapel on the upper floor, away from it all. She was the only person I trusted then, perhaps the only person I had ever trusted. When I finally let her inside the toilet stall, she folded me into her arms and led me upstairs to the chapel to pray. As she led me from the bathroom, the doctor and the other sisters were rushing past us with the screaming girl now in labour on a stretcher, heading towards the delivery room.

Inside the chapel, inside those peaceful walls, was a statue of Mary with outstretched hands. Jesus was on a cross nailed to the wall and a table in front was covered in a clean white cloth. Sister Bernard put prayer beads in my hands and asked me to repeat Hail Mary's with her. She kept telling me that it wasn't my fault, as I sobbed that I had killed the baby. Then she placed a bookmark in my hand, with a picture of God's hand holding a tiny bird. *You, ma petite, you,* she said, with tears streaming down her face. To this day, I still have the marker. In French it says, *You are my refuge and my strength.*

Much later, Sister Martha came to tell us that the baby was born and mother and child were doing fine.

Some time would pass before I was allowed back on the ward again. The nuns sent me to the basement, this time to remove the wax from the hall way floors so I could put it all behind me.

A few days later, I was working in the basement and when I looked up I saw my father coming down the corridor towards me. I spoke not one word, but stood rooted to the spot as he approached me. As he stood there in front of me he never asked how I was doing, he never acknowledged the daughter standing there. It was as if I had never existed. He was there to get a tooth pulled. Flo, who was cleaning the floors with me, pointed in the direction of the dentist's office and he walked away. I never spoke one single word, just watched him walk away. I didn't cry or shout or scream. I just watched him walk away. I can still see my father walking away.

When the girl I had attacked had gone home with her baby, I was sent back to work on the second floor. Later, I would learn that Dr. Marcoux was quite angry with everyone there on that day I went mad. He had told them that while I was in his care they were not to taunt me with their callous remarks.

I continued to work at the hospital while I waited for the plane that would fly me to my destination. On the day when I finally heard my name over the airwaves, I immediately sent for my father down on the Labrador.

Surprisingly, he came.

As I watched him walk again down that same long corridor, dressed in his finest clothes and seemingly without a care in the world, once more I saw him as the coward my mother always said he was. By the time we're face to face, I knew what I want to say.

I will never forgive you as long as I live. I say, I ll never forgive you for putting my mother in the ground, I say, as tears streamed down his face. *I ll never forgive you for leaving them youngsters alone to starve to death,* I say, as his shoulders sagged beneath the weight of his emotions. *I will hate you til the day I dies. I m goin away and I won t be back. Goddamn youse!* I say. His sobs filled the hallway yet he never spoke a single word. I turned and walked away.

⌂ **POSTSCRIPT**

On November 20, 1963, I left the coast and flew away from the soil of my birth to a brand new life. Upon my request to go back to school, Bishop Brown of the Anglican Diocese of Quebec made arrangements to send me to a boarding school in Coaticook, Quebec. Upon my arrival I entered into a new world.

Oh how I loved the deep mahogany wood, the spiral staircases, the rooms flooded with sunshine and electric light bulbs, the quiet chapel and the huge dining room that seated fifty girls or more, and the abundance of food the likes I had never seen before, in this mansion donated to orphaned girls. At Bishop Mountain Hall, I felt like a princess who had suddenly woke up from a very deep sleep.

On the day I arrived, the whole house was mourning the death of U.S. President John F. Kennedy, whom I knew nothing about. I didn't know the Prime Minister of Canada either, so isolated we were on the Quebec-Labrador coast that suddenly seemed a million miles away.

While the matrons and the older girls cried and talked about the president's assassination while sipping their evening tea and eating dainty cookies from a tray brought to them by the cook, I sat quietly, mesmerized as the death of this very important man unfolded in front of me on a black and white box they called television.

It's there my journey began

During the few years I stayed at Bishop Mountain Hall, I would learn many things. I would learn that no matter how terrible my life was and what brought me there, I knew there were others far worse off then me. From Bishop Mountain Hall I would go many places, down many roads, some of them heartbreaking, some of them joyful. I'm blessed with three beautiful children. Kimberly May, Jason Edgar and Jennifer Lynn. Kim has always been my rock of Gilbraltar, (my tower of strength) Jason, my ray of hope, and Jennifer, my ray of sunshine. They give me life.

Over the years, I would travel to the bottom of the globe and back. But no matter where I went I would always find myself returning to the place of my birth again and again, perhaps a hundred times or more over the years, and then I'd leave, always with the demons grabbing at my heels.

Many years would pass before I was able to put it all behind me and move forward with my life. I too was like a bird with broken wings, unable to function.

If I had waited for my father to come to me and tell me why he had deserted us, I would have waited a lifetime. In reality I had. I knew that he was never going to see or understand what he had done to her, to me, to them. I think in my father's mind he felt he wasn't responsible for his motherless children.

Social Services, and all those responsible, could have provided the money to hire someone to come into the house and help me raise the children. But until Uncle Willie brought the children to the hospital, until he threatened to hold someone accountable, and that included Dr. Marcoux, who was magistrate for the Lower North Shore, no one did anything. Seeing I was a minor, I was told I was not capable of raising the children, even thought I'd been doing it for years before my mother's death.

The solution seen fit by Social Services was to make the children wards of the state and pay foster families to take care of them. It wasn't until they were adults and on their own that I realized there was no longer any reason for me to go on fighting with the authorities or my father on their behalf.

Twenty years prior to my father's death, I made a decision to accept him back into my life without demanding answers from him. On the day we buried him, all save two of us were at his graveside.

Nearly half a century would pass before I finally came home for good. In the year 2000, the year we buried my father, I realized there was nothing stopping me from packing up and going home. My children were grown and on their own. My marriage had dissipated like footprints in the sand when the tide rolls on shore.

One morning, while I stood outside on the deck of my home in Antigonish, Nova Scotia, surrounded by towering pine, maple and apple trees, I saw a string of geese flying overhead and a longing to be home was so overwhelming that I heard a voice inside my head saying the words, *Go Home.*

I packed my car that very same day and drove to North Sydney where

I took the ferry across to Newfoundland. From Port aux Basques, it took me six hours to drive to St. Barbe where I boarded a second ferry and crossed the Strait of Belle Isle to Blanc Sablon.

When I saw the treeless rugged hill and lichen-covered rocks coming towards me, my heart filled with gladness. I drove to Bradore Bay, to the cove where our house no longer stood, and it was there I pitched my tent.

After a week of wrestling with my demons from the past in the fog, wind and rain, and with my brothers and sister thinking I had taken leave of my senses and not understanding my desire to be left alone, there on the same rugged shore that had brought me so much grief, I decided to build a place of my own. I've been settling here ever since.

ABOUT THE AUTHOR

Clarissa is now living in Bradore, near the Quebec/Labrador border, the place of her birth, enjoying the freedom of the great outdoors and walking the ancient trails her ancestors trod down through the years.

She does some writing for the *Northern Pen,* a newspaper on the Northern Peninsula, as she continues to write short stories and poetry and she's hoping to finish her next book before this year ends.

Clarissa started writing *Broken Wings* when she was in her early thirties but put it on the shelf to go into real estate. She became a licensed real estate broker and owned her own company for several years. While operating under the Century 21 heading, she earned countless awards for outstanding performance while dealing with the public. Yet, all of this, the prestige and the interaction with so many clients and wonderful friends who are still living in Nova Scotia, she left it all behind just so she could fulfill her lifelong dream to come back home.

And now, to make her life complete, she is blessed with having her youngest daughter, Jennifer, and her four-year-old granddaughter, Emma Lynn, relocate to the rugged land with her. "Life," she says, " is feeling her tiny fingers in mine, hearing her laughter as she splashes her rubber boots in the puddles just like her mother and I did before her."

Clarissa would like to thank her children, her family, and her friends for their encouragement down through the years in writing her story. She hopes her story will bring some comfort to others and encourage them to write their own stories and help preserve the memories of all those gone on before us, especially mothers and grandmothers who endured so much hardship in their time. Keeping their spirits alive is to arm the children of the future with knowledge of their past.